DATE			

PUBLIC ADMINISTRATION IN THE GLOBAL VILLAGE

PUBLIC ADMINISTRATION IN THE GLOBAL VILLAGE

Edited by
JEAN-CLAUDE GARCIA-ZAMOR
and
RENU KHATOR

PRAEGER

Westport, Connecticut
London

Library of Congress Cataloging-in-Publication Data

Public administration in the global village / edited by Jean-Claude
   Garcia-Zamor and Renu Khator.
      p.   cm.
   Includes bibliographical references and index.
   ISBN 0–275–94671–1 (alk. paper)
    1. Public administration.   2. Comparative government.   I. Garcia-
Zamor, Jean-Claude. II. Khator, Renu.
   JF1341.P83   1994
   350—dc20   93–23489

British Library Cataloguing in Publication Data is available.

Library of Congress Catalog Card Number: 93–23489
ISBN: 0–275–94671–1

First published in 1994

Praeger Publishers, 88 Post Road West, Westport, CT 06881
An imprint of Greenwood Publishing Group, Inc.

Printed in the United States of America

The paper used in this book complies with the
Permanent Paper Standard issued by the National
Information Standards Organization (Z39.48–1984).

10 9 8 7 6 5 4 3 2 1

To my children,
Jean-Claude Jr., Ruy, and Christabel,
with my grateful thanks
for their support and love

Jean-Claude Garcia-Zamor

To my daughters,
Pooja and Parul,
who give me a reason to
look beyond the present

Renu Khator

CONTENTS

ACKNOWLEDGMENTS

We owe a great deal to our friends, colleagues, and students for giving us what we have to offer in this volume. It is because of the challenges that we received, the directions that we followed, the ideas that we questioned, and the debates that we had that we are able to put together this collection.

We extend our special thanks to John Huffman, a graduate assistant at the University of South Florida, for his invaluable assistance in putting the pieces of this manuscript together.

Last, but not least, we wish to thank our families for putting up with us when we were too busy to acknowledge their support.

PUBLIC ADMINISTRATION IN THE GLOBAL VILLAGE

INTRODUCTION

RENU KHATOR *and* JEAN-CLAUDE GARCIA-ZAMOR

The emergence of a globally connected and interdependent world is beyond dispute. The fact that public administration as a discipline and public administrators as individual actors are parts of this global system is also beyond debate. What is needed, then, is the reflection and integration of this cognizance in the theory and practice of public administration. The call for integration is in fact a call for the rediscovery of comparative public administration on one hand and the reassertion of the international component of public administration on the other hand. Both dimensions—comparative and international—are the two sides of the same coin, for any effort to compare is irrelevant if we assume ourselves (Americans) to be uniquely different (whether superior or not) from other systems; similarly, any discussion on the global aspect of public administration is extraneous if we fail to accept the utility of learning from others' experiences. The literature in public administration assumes the relevance of global forces in individual areas (in the context of fiscal austerity and extended world markets); nevertheless, there is a definite dearth of paradigms that allow our thinking to become truly "global and comparative."

The chapters in this book, individually and collectively, stress the need for a new approach in public administration. The newness of this approach depends on the identification of what is lacking in the existing approach. Similarly, the relevance and credibility of this approach depend on the identification of the changes that have taken place since the acceptance of the existing approach.

Fred W. Riggs's chapter warns us of the blinding effects of the prevailing superficial distinction between politics and public administration. While the definitions offered in public administration textbooks willingly embrace the enveloping role of politics, the study of public administration is typically limited to the study of organizations, procedures, and individuals in a politically neutral environment. An undue care is usually taken to maintain the distinction between politics and public administration. Significant emphasis is placed on the depoliticized and neutralized nature of public administration. Currently, attempts are being made to blur the distinction between private and public administration. The present focus on privatization in the United States and Great Britain is an example of the clandestine attempt to take the "public" out of public administration by making it more like "business."

The dichotomy myth, as Riggs refers to it, has affected the field of comparative public administration from its inception. Early scholars, in their attempt to develop generalizable theories and models of public administration, had found that the scope and nature of public administration in various countries was not only different but that it corresponded very closely to its political surroundings (Diamant 1960; Dorsey 1962; Heady 1984). Consequently, some attempts were made to use the theories and models of comparative politics to capture the dynamic nature of public administration in non-Western and nondemocratic societies. However, comparative public administration as a field soon found itself caught in a serious quandary. While the scholars in this field were learning to view an administrative system as an inseparable part of the larger political system, the focus in the mainstream of public administration was necessarily on developing an exact science of administrative behavior and mechanisms irrespective of political surroundings. Needless to say, comparative public administration found itself engulfed in what some observers called an "identity crisis" (Henderson 1969; Jreisat 1975; Savage 1976; Sigelman 1976; Springer 1976).

A more profound effect of the perceived separation of politics and public administration appeared in the field of development administration. Development administration thrived in the 1960s and also in the early 1970s on the premises that development as a goal could be achieved through carefully crafted administrative strategies (Montgomery and Siffin 1966; Panandiker and Kshirsagar 1978; Swerdlow 1963). While in theory it was believed that the political setting was crucial in the administration of public choices (Irving Swerdlow, for instance, claimed in 1963 [xiv] that "poor countries have special characteristics that tend to create a different role for government"), in reality their insignificant, or often undesirable, role was assumed in development strategies. Logically, to recognize the relevance of development administration was to acknowledge the political setting of developing countries to be different from the political setting of developed countries. At the same time, to believe that administrative technologies could be transferred from Western polities to Eastern polities—the main thrust of development administration—was to ignore the fact that political processes in Western and Eastern countries were similar. This inherent paradox eventually led to the failure of development strategies in many countries. It also led some scholars to label the efforts in this field as the "four decades of disappointment" (Henderson and Dwivedi 1992).

Fred W. Riggs, in his chapter, rejects the dichotomy myth between politics and public administration. He further argues that the two in fact complement each other: although differences in political settings help us explain the variation found in the organization and functioning of public administrative systems, differences in public administrative systems also shed new light on the merits and demerits of political milieus. Riggs fortifies his evolving theory of presidentialist and parliamentary regimes. His argument that administrative practices in the United States are responsible for providing stability to the American political system is persuasive. According to him, the semipowered nature of the American public administrative system—which in itself is the result of a high level of professionalism—undermines the revolting tendencies of the civil services and allows the supremacy of political forces to continue. Although Riggs's theory is significant in linking politics with public administration, its most significant contribution is the message that comparative studies are mutually beneficial to developing and developed, to Western and Eastern, and to democratic and nondemocratic societies. It is only by examining other systems that we can fully comprehend the value of our own system. In the long run, Riggs's success in establishing a link between presidentialist regimes and public administrative systems may deliver a blow to the proponents of administrative technology transfer, for it will prove that the American administrative model is incompatible with the prevailing political context in most countries.

Gerald E. Caiden's chapter also points to the loss of "public" in public administration. He calls for making public administration distinctive; however, he clarifies this position by suggesting that distinctiveness cannot be achieved by shielding the field from other social science disciplines. Rather, Caiden argues that a broader approach that joins public administration with other disciplines is essential. Only after an open dialogue begins will we be able to develop a sense of our distinctiveness.

Another area in which the existing approach in public administration falls short of our expectations is the prevalence of "localism" in the field. Most of the chapters in this volume point to this glaring deficiency. Furthermore, textbooks in public administration are typically set in a local, as opposed to a global, context. Gerald E. Caiden, in his chapter, "Globalizing the Theory and Practice of Public Administration," calls the discipline idiosyncratic and concedes that parochialism still dominates the field. Among the leading factors behind this "pull of parochialism," as Caiden argues, are the centrality of the nation-state concept and the proactive stress in public administration. The centrality of nation-states confines the scope of civil servants to their individual national boundaries and does not allow them to accept "global" realities. Similarly, the proactive viewpoint forces public administrators to be constantly "on the go." Over the years, this proaction position has led to the uncontrolled expansion of administrative systems worldwide—an expansion that by now has transformed the image of administrative systems from heroic to parasitic entities.

The authors of this book challenge the parochialism prevailing in public administration. Riggs's article, for instance, questions the singular nature of American foreign policy in the wake of intense global interactions. He contends that global forces are penetrating individual agencies in the United States at every level and to such an extent that the idea of a singular foreign policy is misleading. The American administrative system is no longer covered under a single, national-interest blanket. Several points of interaction are emerging and individual agencies are finding themselves either defending their own interests against this global penetration or aggressively engaging themselves in pursuit of global integration. This again, according to Riggs, is the result of American professionalism, which inhibits coordination among professionals in civil services.

The fluid nature of administrative boundaries is also captured in Renu Khator's chapter on environmental management. In the field of environmental protection, transnational decisions are becoming increasingly common. Scientific agreements are often reached at the international level and forced down to national governments. Indeed, national governments are sovereign entities and reserve the right to decline any such influences. However, in reality, they are often bound by the pressures coming from their own scientists, who are part of the international scientific community. Environmental and environment-related agencies in the United States and in other countries are affected by the decisions taken at the global level. Khator's chapter on environmental policy, similar to Riggs's foreign policy scenario, questions the relevance of the localized version of public administration in theory and in practice. The existing approach to public administration does not take global vulnerability into account.

The powerful appeal of global movements and the subsequent feebleness of national governments are revealed by Ali Farazmand in his study of privatization and structural adjustments. The appeal of privatization has captivated even those countries who are neither equipped nor prepared to deal with it. Even where favorable conditions prevail, the effect of privatization has not been entirely desirable. In this context, there are enormous opportunities for countries to learn from one another. Farazmand is pessimistic about the utility of privatization as a tool to bring about social and political changes in poor countries. Western bias and parochialism inhibit the ability of international donor agencies to understand its implications and suitability for the Third World. Farazmand appeals for a move beyond American ethnocentrism.

Other than promoting the false ideals of a politically neutral environment and the parochial scope of public administration, the existing approach in public administration also lacks a comparative appeal. The utility of comparison is evident from a wide variety of case studies offered in this volume. Margaret F. Reid makes an attempt to provide a framework for comparison by conceptualizing change as a common denominator in developing and developed societies and by perceiving it on a continuum. However, the existing approach has failed to incorporate comparison as a tool to study public administration. Developing countries and their conditions are viewed as "foreign." Jean-Claude Garcia-Zamor's chapter provides an intriguing view of the New World Order from the eyes of the industrializing world.[1] He revisits the concept of development administration—an aspect of comparative public administration that has primarily focused on industrializing countries.[2] Even though development administration had the potential for comparative analyses, as the situation in several American municipalities and even states was not much different from the situation in industrializing countries, this potential was never fully exploited (Montgomery 1971). Garcia-Zamor claims that the countries of Latin America and Africa are too entangled in their domestic traps to be able to integrate favorably into the global village. They will indeed be affected by global forces, but it is doubtful whether they can in any way affect these forces.

The plight of the industrializing countries is evident from Ferrel Heady's case study of Colombia. Colombia, the fourth largest country in Latin America, is currently in the phase of restructuring its economy and polity. The worldwide privatization movement is also making its mark in Colombia. The forces of the global village are coercing the Colombian government to restructure its administrative system to correspond to the changing situation at home and abroad. However, as Heady points out, two adverse domestic forces are inhibiting the enforcement of the restructuring plan: insurgencies by radical guerrilla groups and the power of drug cartels. Neither of these forces, however, is really domestic, for the increasing global closeness fuels the fire of these malaises. Heady argues that "neither guerrilla insurgency nor illegal drug trafficking would have reached their current dimensions without motivation, support, and protection from outside." It is the close proximity of Colombia to the United States that allowed it to emerge as the main center for drug trafficking. Needless to say, the consumer demand for the product is most intense in the United States. Similarly, guerrilla insurgents get their energy from the leftist forces in Cuba, the former Soviet Union, and China. While the Colombian government has actively pursued the goal of curtailing the power of the guerrilla groups and the cartels, its evident limits are due to the transnationality of the issues. Colombia, despite all efforts of its government, has been reduced to what Heady calls a semisovereign state.

The existing approach in public administration, with its premises based on "American context," clearly fails to help either Colombia or the United States in grasping the problem. The Weberian assumptions of a rational, value-free, and hierarchical bureaucracy do not correspond with the situation in Colombia. The logic of development administration with foreign aid at its nucleus also fails to capture the vulnerability of the Colombian civil services to the unwanted forces of the global village. To say the least, Heady's case study depicts the lucid nature of the boundaries in the industrializing world—a fact that the comparative theories of public administration have so far failed to comprehend.

The case of Mozambique, as presented by Lawrence S. Graham in this volume, reasserts the need for a better understanding of the role of global forces in public administration. As in Colombia, the national and sovereign boundaries of Mozambique continue to be intruded into by external forces. Pressures to restructure and to decentralize are also evident in this African country. More than symbolic or ideological, these pressures are real, and they come in the form of donor support. As the result of foreign assistance, Graham argues, Mozambique has experienced not only economic but also political changes. International actors (United Nations Development Programme as well as Management Development Program officials) were involved in shaping the subnational distribution of power and in redefining the boundaries of local civil servants. Similar to the Colombian case, the case of Mozambique also reflects the conflict between the goals outlined in international mandates and the harsh realities found within a country.

The "comparative" argument is also stressed in Garcia-Zamor's article. He acknowledges the global appeal of structural adjustments; however, he also recognizes the futility of globally sought, rigid solutions to individual problems. The existence of generalizable characteristics (such as we observed in the cases of Colombia and Mozambique) should not undermine the uniqueness that each member of the global village possesses. In our attempt to find generalities, the call should be not for the homogenization of societies, but for their harmonization.

A NEW WORLD ORDER?

While the term "New World Order" is increasingly being used by scholars to describe the world since the end of the Cold War, there is hardly any agreement on what it actually entails. In this volume, Farazmand, Khator, and Garcia-Zamor tackle the definition and attributes of the New World Order. For them, the New World Order is more than the end of the Cold War. Instead, it is a reconfiguration of international power positions—power positions being determined by new forces and fresh interests. While the authors agree that the term is not an innovative one, they acknowledge that its attributes reflect something new. For Farazmand, the New World Order incorporates U.S. military might, the globalized economy, cultural penetration, the dominance of the global environment, the centrality of the marketplace, the emergence of the United Nations as a collective legitimizing instrument, and the absence of a single superpower. The outcome of these changes, according to Farazmand, is the development of a global administrative system with a global bureaucracy.

Khator views the properties of the New World Order in the light of increased concern for environmental values. For her, the New World Order means a greater interdependence among countries of the developed and the developing worlds and a more assertive role for environmental forces in international decisions. Khator identifies two significant changes under way: a continuous decline in the powers of national governments and a steady increase in the powers of the international community, on the one hand, and of nongovernmental actors, on the other. She claims that, as a result of these changes, a system of global federalism is emerging. Finally, Garcia-Zamor views the emergence of the New World Order in terms of the declining capacity of the poorer countries to seek financial assistance from the industrialized countries.

The implications of the New World Order for the discipline of public administration are analyzed by Riggs and Caiden in their chapters. Their analyses confirm the changed role of public administration and public administrators in the new era and call for an expanded, comprehensive, pluralistic, and "public" role for public administration in the future. Khator anticipates an inevitable, albeit gradual, shift in the perceived role of public administrators worldwide. The implications of the New World Order for developing countries and their public administrators are discussed in chapters by Farazmand and Garcia-Zamor. The new reconfiguration is likely to offer greater challenges for the less-developed world. Although they may have more opportunity as the new world begins to accept North-South (replacing the East-West) configurations, their ability to exploit these opportunities will be limited by their internal systems. The chapters by Ferrel Heady and Lawrence Graham afford us the opportunity to view the dynamics of these internal systems of these countries up close.

WHAT SHOULD BE NEW IN THE NEW APPROACH?

After distinguishing the properties of the new global landscape and after identifying the three major shortcomings in the existing approach to the study of public administration—perceived separation of public administration from politics, the localized scope of public administration, and the assumed noncomparability of administrative goals and practices—we can now focus on the prerequisites of the new approach. The following discussion provides a starting point in this direction.

Inclusive, Rather than Exclusive

The contributors of this book argue that the approach to the study of public administration must not be reductionist. The reductionist tendencies of the past have led to parochialism, ethnocentrism, and isolationism. Public administration in the past has been reduced to the actions related to the executive branch of the government or to the implementation aspect of public policy or to civilians within the public sector or even to development managers, in the case of the Third World. Public administration, as a field, must be afforded the largest possible latitude. This goal can be achieved when the context of public administration is expanded. A hypothesized model of public administration's context is depicted in Figure 1. Although the degree of influence may vary from country to country, some level of influence is expected to be exerted from all layers of systems. Public administrators must be sensitive to their vulnerability to global, international forces at the outset, and they must also be aware of their potential influence in the global context. The next layer of influence emerges from the social and cultural system. At the third level, the political system is perceived as being embedded within the larger global, social, and cultural system. Finally, the administrative system is viewed as being enveloped within the larger political system. Thus, public administration does not and cannot exist in a vacuum. Public administration and public administrators are affected and influenced by multiple forces in an extremely complex manner.

What does this mean for the subfield of international and comparative public administration? Ideally, as no public policy area and no public agency is free from the potential penetration of global forces, whether directly or indirectly, international and comparative aspects should become a natural and integral part of mainstream public administration. Even though scholars have been stressing this necessity from the very inception of public administration as a separate field (Dahl 1947; Dwivedi and Henderson 1990; Farazmand 1991; Heady 1991; Jun 1976; Riggs 1976), it still remains only a dream. Perhaps this dream has a more realistic chance of being materialized in the American literature now because of the direct, penetrating effects of global forces on the American economy itself and because of the recent realignments in international power positions. The United States, though still a major power, has lost its monopoly. It is interesting to note that most other countries pay far greater attention to the global context and external forces than do scholars and practitioners in America.

Comparative, Rather than Exceptional

With few exceptions, most comparative studies in public administration assume that more than one world exists. The idea of development administration evolved entirely on this premise. However, the acknowledgment of a single, global system has the potential of making comparative studies not only more natural but also more meaningful.

With reference to Figure 1, the nature and degree of penetration can offer us an alternative framework for comparison. It is possible to generalize, to identify, and then to classify administrative systems based upon their vulnerability to each of these layers and the level of penetration received from each. Because administrative systems must work within these contexts, we can assess their

Figure 1
A Hypothetical Model

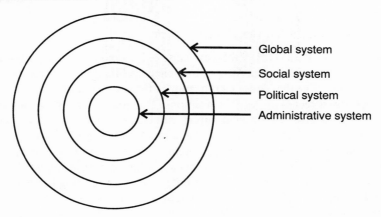

- Global system
- Social system
- Political system
- Administrative system

performance on the basis of the criteria evolving from them. This volume provides us with several country studies (Colombia, Mozambique, East Germany, and the United States) and several issue-area studies (foreign policy, environmental policy, privatization and structural adjustment, foreign assistance, and democratization). The country studies are particularly useful in developing and testing these criteria.

To begin with, we may ask: To what degree is a system capable of functioning in a global context? Colombia in Ferrel Heady's case study, for instance, does not convince us that it is able, as a country, to perform ably in this area. The failure of Colombia also reflects the boundaries of the American political and administrative systems that are affected directly and indirectly by Colombian drug cartels.

Second, to what extent is an administrative system able to correspond to the social and cultural norms of a society? Graham's case study of Mozambique and Reid's case study of American urban areas reveal the limitations that can arise in this context.

Third, to what extent is an administrative system congruous with its political setting? Here, Graham's case of Mozambique reveals useful insights. The German approach to total restructuring (discussed by Reid) also falters because of its incongruity with the political system.

But, like any other comparative framework, this framework needs conceptual groundwork. We must, for instance, ask: Why should we assume that the attainment of compatibility with its context is the ultimate goal of an administrative system? Is there a degree of penetration that is desirable, or should all forms of penetration be considered as unnecessary evils? What is the "right" balance of penetration? What if there is a conflict between the demands of the international context and that of the political system, as in Mozambique or in Riggs's example of Thailand? Is there a "right" yardstick to measure the performance of an administrative system under these conflicting pressures? Some of these questions can help form potentially rich hypotheses for future research.

Bilateralism, Rather than Unilateralism

In the New World Order, the new approach to public administration must necessarily assume that the flow of influences is bilateral. In other words, we must acknowledge that America is as much affected by external forces as other countries are affected by American actions. The drug cartels in Colombia are a stumbling block for Colombian public officials, but their presence is equally frustrating for American officials. The solution to the problem offers relief to both countries, and perhaps to other countries as well. Environmental problems and solutions, as discussed in Khator's chapter, have the same impact. Graham's case study also demonstrates that the process of restructuring in Mozambique has more than indigenous partners; international actors are actively involved in shaping the policies.

Furthermore, the donor-recipient equation, as described by Garcia-Zamor, shows the signs of bilateral dependencies. Because of the breakup of the Soviet bloc, the West is forced to reassess its assistance programs to incorporate the needs of the ex-Soviet countries. This need becomes even more acute when one considers the concentration of the nuclear arsenal in the Soviet-owned territory. What makes it difficult is the fact that the need for assistance arising from the countries of Asia, Africa, and Latin America is expected to remain the same, if not increase. In the future, the assistance programs in the West will necessarily take the changing global parameters into account.

To conclude, there is a need to globalize the theory and practice of public administration. As the contributors to this volume point out, the context of public administration has gone through profound changes. Although there is no need to reminisce about the meaning of public administration, it is critical, now more than ever, that the connotation behind its "public" part be reasserted. Similarly, there is no need to reinvent the wheel of holistic and comparative methodology; these methods should simply be put to use in all subfields of public administration. There is no reason to discard what we have collected; this collective knowledge should simply be absorbed and reflected at all levels of study and training in public administration. Only then will we be able to comprehend the meaning of public administration, and only then will we be producing an adequately trained class of public administrators.

ORGANIZATION OF THE BOOK AND INDIVIDUAL THEMES

The next eight chapters in this book are divided into two parts. Part I focuses on the concepts and theories of public administration in general. In its first chapter, Fred W. Riggs argues that a comparative and global study of public administration will show that the American bureaucracy (including its military officers) is politically weaker than that of any other industrialized democracy or of any Third World polity. Among the various historical and structural reasons for the relative weakness of U.S. bureaucracy mentioned by Riggs, one that has important international consequences involves the exceptionally strong presence of professionals in the ranks of American career civil servants. Not only are the reasons for the professionalization of the American bureaucracy exceptional in world history, but the consequences are important for overseas administration. Because of the high degree of autonomy enjoyed by American governmental agencies as a result of their professionalization, each of them to some degree becomes actively involved in international programs. Consequently, Riggs notes that one cannot speak of American foreign policy in the singular. Instead, there are a large number of foreign policies. He further contends that the more clearly Americans appreciate these global realities and both the problems and the opportunities they create, the greater will be their chances of achieving peace and progress in the context of the global village.

Gerald E. Caiden, in Chapter 2, decries the parochialism that dominates the practice of public administration in the United States. The same parochialism also affects the study or science of public administration. Caiden notes that parochialism will retain its dominant influence as long as the nation-state is the major actor in public administration. He feels that the emerging New World Order demands a public administration that is distinctive, all-encompassing, and more genuinely global.

Ali Farazmand argues in his chapter that the New World Order has both positive and negative consequences, perhaps more negative than positive. So far, the two superpowers have checked each other's behavior; but as there is no such counterbalancing force now, the entire global arena is left open for probable abuse. In the context of the emphasis on democratization in the New World Order, Farazmand contends that the global slogan of democratization is both misleading and dangerous. Misleading, because it is equated with market supremacy while market and democratic ideals clash on many grounds and contradict on both individual and societal levels. Dangerous, because it is being applied unevenly and inconsistently. More often than not, socialist and independent states are the targets of "democratization"; dictatorship in friendly states with market capitalism is usually overlooked, justified, protected, and even promoted. Farazmand is also critical of the newly found acceptance of structural adjustments in developing countries. He believes that the need to conform to the norms, rules, and values of the new global order is producing fundamental changes in these countries—changes that are not compatible with the needs of local people. In addition, the administrative system produced by the forces of the New World Order has fundamental structural features, including a tendency to centralize the flow of information and technological know-how; a vertical and horizontal integration of the organizational and administrative structure, with the top of the hierarchy in the United States; and perpetual dependency on Western concepts and ideas. Farazmand fears that a new concept of "colonization" may be in the making.

The last chapter in Part I, by Renu Khator, analyzes the causes and consequences of the New World Order through environmental lenses. It is her contention that the environmental crisis has undermined the power base of national governments by allowing some of their sovereignty to be shifted to the international level on one hand and to the grass-roots level on the other. Khator argues that two swings—upward from national governments to international organizations and downward from national governments to grass-roots nongovernmental organizations—are the keys to understanding the changes that confront public administrators in the 1990s. Khator speculates that the New World Order with its focus on interdependence and geophysical interests will expect public administrators to function in the complex web of global federalism by accepting vertically sensitive, horizontally open, and diagonally responsive relationships.

Part II offers several case studies from developing and developed countries. Its first chapter, by Jean-Claude Garcia-Zamor, begins with a brief historical overview of "development administration." Garcia-Zamor discusses the New World Order and donor responses in light of global changes. He also questions some of the structural adjustment programs of the World Bank and the International Monetary Fund. The chapter favorably reviews the new Human Development Index of the United Nations Development Programme (UNDP). This index, according to Garcia-Zamor, reveals that even countries with a low per-capita gross national product (GNP) may rank high on human development while countries with high per-capita GNP may still have low rankings on human development. The chapter concludes by suggesting four new approaches to guide the work of development administration practitioners: population control, indigenous democratization, regional alliances, and reversal of the brain drain flow.

Ferrel Heady, in Chapter 6, focuses on Colombia and discusses the dilemmas of development administration in the global village. He finds that Colombian achievements in development administration have so far been disappointing, primarily because of the prevalence of violence associated with guerilla groups and illegal drug syndicates. As a consequence, the state in Colombia is only semisovereign, restricted in its capabilities by threats from these domestic competitors for power and their allies in the global village, of which Colombia is inescapably a part. Heady believes that the resulting dilemma of how to reconcile potential opportunities with limiting realities presents tremendous problems for Colombian political and administrative leaders and that their prospects for success are uncertain.

Lawrence S. Graham discusses development administration in the context of Mozambique. He notes that an important issue facing public administration today concerns restructuring governments in developing countries in such a way that they can respond more effectively to internal and external market forces. The structural adjustments entailed in such endeavors are especially acute in countries emerging from an experiment with state socialism, where prior economic and political institutions were dismantled in favor of the Soviet and Eastern European models. However, the resources needed and available in the international community for such undertakings are limited, in that no single country has the capacity today to act unilaterally. As a consequence, much of the work being done today in development management involves negotiating and leveraging cooperative efforts within the donor community in conjunction with national governments in transition. Graham finds that old-style dependency relationships in Mozambique are disappearing and that in their place new interdependencies are appearing that are focusing attention at the regional level in such a way that previous national boundaries are being superseded as much from without as from within.

Margaret F. Reid in the final chapter draws attention to a significant aspect of change processes that both developed and developing countries must share. She labels it "an ethic-guiding change." Reid contends that in an era of massive transformation that affects all aspects of a society, the analysis of developmental change can no longer be confined to single organizations or to management practice. The framework advocated by Reid views development as a continuum of changes ranging from massive transformation (metamorphic change) to adjustments in authority or decisional patterns (isomorphic change). Change, Reid argues, must be viewed in three arenas: at the level of the institutional framework, in the transactional capacities, and in the rules of engagement that guide individual and collective choices. She presents two case studies of change in this proposed framework: One is a failed attempt of the former East German government to avert a radical reform of their political economy; the other is an American effort to recapture the sense of "community" through public-private partnerships.

NOTES

1. The term "industrializing" is used in place of "Third World," "developing," or "poor." Even though all of these terms have inherent contradictions, the term "industrializing" more fully distinguishes the countries of Latin America, Africa, Asia, and Eastern Europe from the industrialized countries of North America and Western Europe.

2. Fred Riggs made a distinction between the two aspects of development administration: the administration of development and the development of administration (1970). In both meanings, development administration had a comparative appeal. Nonetheless, studies in development administration in subsequent years restricted their scope to development in the Third World.

I

PUBLIC ADMINISTRATION
Theories and Concepts

1

GLOBAL FORCES AND THE DISCIPLINE OF PUBLIC ADMINISTRATION

FRED W. RIGGS

OUR GLOBAL VILLAGE

TV news brings daily images of violent and historic events around the world: Somalia, Bosnia, Nicaragua, Korea, Nigeria, South Africa, Lebanon, Israel and the Palestinians, Armenia and Azerbaijan, Sri Lanka, India, and Afghanistan— to say nothing of the United States, where Los Angeles, Miami, Detroit, Chicago, and Washington all have their own horror stories to tell. George Bush used to speak glowingly of a "New World Order," and Francis Fukuyama of the "end of history," but there is still plenty of excitement and terror to people our nightmares, even since the Cold War has ended. We have become part of a "capitalist world system" or a "global village," with all its horrendous problems and surprising opportunities: Whatever happens elsewhere becomes part of our experience, and whatever we experience becomes a global happening.

Nevertheless, we Americans still think parochially, as though the United States could drift along as a land of promise where the American Dream can be fulfilled independently of the rest of the world. We fantasize happenings abroad as essentially irrelevant to us. We have yet to internalize the fact that we are part of a highly interdependent world. Yet we can understand our own problems only in a global perspective; without knowing ourselves, we cannot really comprehend the rest of the world.

This is generally true for all the social sciences. However, here I shall focus only on how Americans specializing in Public Administration look at the world. Fortunately, the editors of this volume have given us an opportunity and a stimulus to reshape our reading of the American scene and to revise the way we see the rest of the world. Two closely linked phenomena—limited *bureau-cratic power* and the *role of professionals* in public office—have profound importance in the American system of public administration, and they shape the conduct of American programs and policies abroad. Their influence is uniquely American, a proposition that can be sustained only by making comparisons.

The enhanced understanding of our own system of government that such an analysis provides enables us to reconstruct the American approach to the study and teaching of Public Administration. Such an exercise will also improve our insight into administrative problems overseas, especially how American foreign policies are administered and why they cause so many unintended consequences. The rest of this chapter is divided into two parts: first, an inquiry into how a global perspective can help Americans improve their understanding of our own system of government, the role of our public officials, and our peculiar way of looking at public administration; second, a discussion of our world role, of how Americans carry out our foreign policies and affect the stability and development of other countries.

DOMESTIC PERCEPTIONS

Bureaucracy and Politics

Virtually all countries have bureaucracies that are more powerful than their American counterparts. In many countries, bureaucracies dominate the polity, as they have in some fifty-seven Third World polities: 40 percent of the 143 that I counted in 1985 (Riggs 1993a: 215). A major exception involves single-party dictatorships where, by contrast, bureaucrats are relatively powerless and can almost never stage a successful coup.[1] In all other countries, they are powerful enough to play a major political role and, in a serious crisis, to seize power. In the United States, by contrast, despite the inherent difficulty of managing a presidentialist constitutional system based on the separation of powers, our regime has survived for 200 years and our military officers have never seized power.

Important reasons for this record include the ways our Congress, executive, electoral, and party systems have been organized, but an additional reason lies in the political weakness of our government bureaucracy, that is, in all appointed officials, military and civil, long-term and transient. It is neither very powerful nor powerless; rather; it is semipowered.[2] Consequently, even when the government fails to solve a major crisis, the American bureaucracy, military and civil, is unable to stage a coup and seize power as its counterparts in many other countries have done.

To Americans, the possibility of a military coup seems remote indeed. I have not found any discussion of this possibility in the American literature of Public

Administration, Bureaucratic Politics, or Political Science. Two reasons account for this blind spot, the first conceptual and the second substantive.

A Terminological Question. A conceptual blinder arises from our practice of limiting the notion of *bureaucracy* to career civil servants and thinking of the armed forces as nonbureaucrats. This blind spot obscures the political role of whole bureaucracies. We typically view a coup d'état as the work of military officers whose arrogance and greed lead them to plot against legitimate governments—rather like seeing only an engine and not the vehicle to which it is attached. We have words like *automobile* and *train* to remind us of a whole that cannot move without an engine. Politically, however, we think of a bureaucracy as a motor car without a motor. Bureaucrats can and do seize power, but only when led by armed officers.[3]

However, the military officers who organize a coup could never govern effectively without the support of civil servants (technocrats), many of whom are coopted into the ruling circle. To think they could rule alone is like expecting an automobile engine to move without wheels or a body. As modern bureaucrats depend heavily on salaries for their livelihood, all of them are adversely affected by unresolved political crises, especially crises that hurt their income and security. Consequently, civil servants and military officers typically share the grievances that lead to military revolts and bureaucratic rule. The role of civil servants remains largely invisible, however, because they cannot play the leading role in a coup: To seize power by violence always requires the capacity to use arms and military force.

More significantly, we fail to see that the primary causes of a coup can be found in the inability of a government to govern effectively, that is, to make policies that respond adequately to crisis situations. Although the greed and ambition of military officers may be a factor and although possessing power is a requisite,[4] I believe the driving force in every coup is a regime's political failure. Such failures can be attributed not only to cultural and economic factors but also, I believe, to the way a political system is constituted. More specifically, any regime based on the American constitutional model is almost sure to experience coups, whereas less than half of the Third World countries that have adopted parliamentary systems of government have experienced coups.

The American Exception

Anyone who looks at the records of all the regimes that have adopted the American constitutional design will soon realize that they have all confronted the dangers of a coup d'état followed by bureaucratic domination. When we compare the types of Third World regimes in which coups have occurred, we discover a remarkable fact. In 1985, when I made such a survey, I found about thirty countries that could be classified as having presidentialist regimes modeled on that of the United States, wherein the separation of powers among three branches with independent authority prevailed. Of these regimes, 91 percent (thirty out of thirty-three) collapsed because of a coup d'état. By contrast, only 31 percent of the parliamentary regimes (thirteen out of forty-three) had experienced such breakdowns (Riggs 1993a: 215).[5] Moreover, all of the industrially advanced democracies whose constitutions were established after the American Revolution have opted for some kind of parliamentary system. Considered as a whole, the ability of such systems to remain viable greatly exceeds that of all the presidentialist regimes.[6]

Because American *comparativists*—specialists on "foreign countries"—typically ignore the United States while studying other polities, they have presupposed the essential viability of presidentialist regimes and tried to explain their collapse by geographical, historical, cultural, economic, or other factors, but not by reference to their constitutional design. Had they looked at the institutional framework of these countries, they would have discovered that every presidentialist regime is an endangered species, based on an outdated eighteenth-century design for democratic self-government. We should not expect any such regime to survive.

By far the most likely cause of a breakdown is the imbalance in these regimes between the power of the bureaucracies and that of the elected politicians. Because of the separation of powers, they are unable to confront crises and secure consensus on public policies that deal with them promptly and well enough. A much less likely cause of breakdown involves the seizure of power by an elected president, as happened in 1992 in Peru when President Fujimori, following a crisis in his relations with Congress, seized power and dissolved both the constitution and the legislature.[7]

The Proof. In this context, the United States is the deviant case, the true exception that proves a rule, that is, that tests its validity. A remarkable test of the rule that presidentialist regimes are doomed to breakdowns can be provided by explaining why the same fate has not happened in America.[8] Much of the explanation can be ascribed to features of this political system, which, despite its severe handicaps, has managed to work more successfully than any other presidentialist regime. An important part of the explanation, however, is based on the relative weakness of the U.S. bureaucracy, its semipowered status (Riggs 1994a).

To explain the semipowered status of the U.S. bureaucracy, five important causes should be considered. These include (1) federalism, which fragments the bureaucracy into many autonomous subsystems; (2) privatization, which greatly reduces the functions performed by government through contracting many of them to private organizations, both for-profit and not-for-profit; (3) the prevalence of transients in public service, a component that fills top-level positions of authority in the bureaucracy but is inherently incapable of mobilizing bureaucratic power; (4) the exceptional dispersal of power in the armed forces, both geographically and functionally; and (5) the extraordinary degree to which professionals hold positions in the career bureaucracy.

All of these factors are discussed in Riggs (1994a), including the causes of bureaucratic professionalization as an unintended result of the Pendleton Act of 1883 and the Morrill Land Grant Act of 1862. A summary of the argument can also be found in Riggs (1993c). The main focus of these earlier essays was on the domestic implications of a semipowered bureaucracy. Here, however, in order to help explain America's role in the emerging global village, I shall focus on certain consequences of bureaucratic professionalism in the U.S. bureaucracy that have profound international implications.

Our heavy reliance on professionalism has fundamental global consequences, both directly and indirectly. Directly, it undergirds the proliferation of external programs and projects sponsored by U.S. government agencies. Indirectly, because professionalism has curtailed the power position of the bureaucracy, driven the development of American Public Administration, and provided a continuing rationale for the myth of a dichotomy between politics and administration, it has critically affected the thinking of everyone involved in the administration of America's many foreign policies and programs. These consequences are examined below in the "International Implications" section. Before we can explain them, however, I need to clarify some of the domestic implications of bureaucratic professionalism that lead to these results.

Professionalism and Power. Proportionally, more professionals are bureaucrats in the United States than in almost any other country. The far-reaching significance of this difference can be understood only after we understand the contrasting roles played by mandarins and retainers in other contemporary bureaucracies.

In most parliamentary regimes, in contrast to American presidentialism, we find a centralized *mandarinate* that is capable of leading and coordinating a bureaucracy, managing the affairs of the state in a coherent way. The term *administrative state* refers quite appropriately to such regimes.[9] Their leading officers are experienced generalists (mandarins) with the capacity to coordinate public programs and policies. They are also politically powerful—so powerful, in fact, that no presidentialist regime (i.e., one based on the separation of powers) could maintain its authority over a mandarinate for any length of time. By contrast, the fused power characteristic of parliamentary regimes typically enables them to assert effective control over powerful mandarin bureaucracies and thereby to assure a sufficiently high level of administrative performance to blunt both revolutionary pressures and coup attempts.

In all presidentialist regimes that were established in the nineteenth century, except for the United States, *retainer* bureaucracies prevail. We can refer to any state with a predominantly retainer bureaucracy as a *cliental state*: This term should be clearly distinguished from "client state," that is, one that is dependent on another state. Patron/client relationships typify both the public and private spheres of life in a cliental state.[10]

At the administrative level, a mandarin bureaucracy is much more efficient than a retainer bureaucracy; it can implement public policies more effectively. A cliental state could scarcely maintain its authority over a mandarinate. During its formative years, however, a cliental state is normally able to sustain its control over a retainer bureaucracy. Nevertheless, with the passage of time, two complementary processes undermine such regimes. First, the inherent limitations of any retainer bureaucracy seriously impair its administrative capabilities, not only undermining public confidence in the regime but eroding the loyalty of bureaucrats, who begin to hate their political masters. Second, retainers are able to mobilize to seize power; indeed, their skills in informal organization were cultivated in order to safeguard their official posts and perquisites, especially by blocking the introduction of merit systems. This long-term experience provided a basis for organizing to seize power.

Most parliamentary regimes were able during the nineteenth century to curtail the power of retainers and to replace them with mandarins. However, the dispersed power structures prevalent in presidentialist regimes typically impeded any efforts to carry out such reforms. A vicious circle emerged: Recalcitrant retainers who lacked the qualifications and standards needed to administer well were, nevertheless, capable of seizing power. Whenever the performance of the state fails, they easily become disaffected and willing to support a military coup.

At the opposite extreme, any presidentialist regime with a mandarin bureaucracy would, I believe, be totally incapable of maintaining control over the bureaucracy and would quickly succumb to a coup: This was the story in such twentieth-century regimes as those of South Vietnam and South Korea where, under American military influence, presidentialist regimes were established after World War II. Because most of the states with presidentialist regimes were established in the nineteenth century, these cliental states had retainer bureaucracies, which they somehow managed to keep under control until well into the twentieth century.

Had the United States maintained the retainer bureaucracy that was launched in 1789, it would almost certainly have succumbed to coups, as have almost all other presidentialist regimes. However, had a mandarinate been established, as initially advocated by nineteenth-century reformers, bureaucratic domination would surely have evolved rather quickly. Avoiding both options, the United States created a new type of career bureaucracy oriented to *professionalism*. Professionals, as public officials in America, typically support norms and standards endorsed by the professional associations to which they belong. They often identify more with these external reference groups than they do with their hierarchic superiors.

The Network State. This contributes to a distinctively American *network state*, one composed of an infinitely complex maze of interest networks oriented to the overlapping concerns of corporations, nonprofit agencies, professional

associations, and government vehicles (including both congressional committees and bureaucratic agencies). Each of them maintains complex links to
central, state, and local governments; the legislative, executive, and judicial
branches of governance; and a host of autonomous boards, commissions, and
self-governing bodies.[11]

Today's American network state is exceptional, and it has evolved slowly. Its
bureaucracy has always been so weak that it could never organize a successful
military coup. Even when concentrated and focused leadership joined with
coherent government policies is lacking, professionals in the American bureaucracy are often able to carry out needed policies and programs within their
niches, especially when these policies are consistent with their professional
standards.

Moreover, the satisfactions experienced by professionals who are able to
achieve their personal goals mean that they do not want to seize power. The
most significant consequence of professionalism in the American bureaucracy,
therefore, involves its contribution to the survival of an inescapably fragile
constitutional system at the very moment when the increasing complexity of
our global village places ever more severe demands upon this system. Because
of its semipowered status, to which professionalism makes an important contribution, the American bureaucracy has been incapable of seizing power.

Had the United States maintained its original retainer system or switched to
a mandarinate, it would surely have experienced bureaucratic domination. By
creating a professionalized bureaucracy, the United States followed a middle
road that has enabled its presidentialist regime to survive. However, it pays a
high cost for this tenaciousness. As long as it retains its presidentialist design,
the United States will continue to experience gridlocks, but its constitutional
system will not collapse. A professionalized bureaucracy performs its administrative functions much more effectively than a retainer bureaucracy can,
without generating the power potential that both retainer and mandarin bureaucracies are capable of. Consequently, it reduces the pressures that lead to a coup
d'état while also limiting the capacity of public officials to seize power. A more
extended discussion of this point can be found in Riggs (1994a).

A secondary consequence of the professionalization of the U.S. bureaucracy
involves the development of Public Administration as a discipline or field of
study. Let us now take a look at this phenomenon, leading eventually to a
discussion of its implications in the conduct of foreign affairs in the "International Implications" section.

The Rise of American Public Administration

The stipulations of the Pendleton Act (see note 9) reinforced each other to
generate the forces that led, gradually, to the emergence of professionalism in
the American bureaucracy—and also to the field of Public Administration as

an unsuccessful candidate for professional status. After the act, the new land-
grant colleges hastened to equip their graduates for success in the new "practical" exams. On these foundations, a vast network of professional schools in
state universities evolved. Through professional associations linking these
schools with public officials and private practitioners, powerful networks were
established that have continually expanded their influence in government and
society.

However, Public Administration was not a recognized profession when the
Pendleton Act was passed, nor were "practical" exams created to test administrative capabilities until almost half a century had passed. Gradually, however,
the need for explicit training in Public Administration began to gain recognition,
some textbooks were written, and professional training in this area evolved.
Although many professionals in the bureaucracy recognized the need for
additional training and knowledge to help them administer more effectively, no
professional role as a general line administrator has been institutionalized in
the American bureaucracy. Exceptionally, army generals might qualify as such,
but their training stresses military functions. At best, some of the staff fields of
Public Administration have gained such recognition, that is, one can be a
professional in personnel, budgeting, accounting and auditing, planning, or
office management, but it is difficult to find positions earmarked for "professionals" in general Public Administration.

The new Public Administration training programs chose to focus on preparing civil servants for entry to the nonpartisan career services. Military officers
already had their own training programs, including West Point and the other
military academies and staff colleges. Partisan appointees were typically politi-
cos whose party services were being rewarded; professionally oriented training
programs could scarcely reach them. Given these constraints, Public Administration necessarily evolved as an activity designed primarily for future and
present nonpartisan career civil servants who already had professional training
in some other field. The peculiarly American approach to the study and theory
of Public Administration took shape under these constraints.

A notable aspect of Public Administration as a would-be professional field
in America is its disposition to avoid party politics. This attitude is rooted in
the Pendleton Act's stipulation that careerists should be nonpartisan, neither
supporting financially nor working in an electoral campaign. Of course, careerists were delighted with this rule, which overcame an onerous burden that
patronage appointees (both retainers and transients) had long carried. They were
happy to support, instead, the myth of a dichotomy between "politics" (i.e.,
partisanship) and administration.

However, nonpartisanship did not imply any commitment to Public Administration as a profession; most careerists were already committed to the established
professions that led to their appointments in the bureaucracy. Although the
dichotomy myth no doubt contributed to the success of the civil service reform

effort, it has become an incubus today. Its persistence, despite long-sustained efforts to combat it (Riggs 1993d), has shaped the subsequent development of Public Administration and Political Science as academic fields in America, producing misconceptions that blind us to the essential dynamics of our own system of governance and seriously hamper the administration of U.S. overseas programs.

Blinding Effects of the Dichotomy Myth. The study of government, as a unified focus of teaching and research, became subdivided into two contrasting and sometimes antagonistic fields: Public Administration programs eschewed "politics," turning to business management and all the social sciences except politics for inspiration, while political scientists systematically downplayed Public Administration as either a field unworthy of serious study or even an essentially "nonpolitical" activity (Waldo 1968).

As long as serious inquiry into the phenomenon of bureaucratic power can be avoided, public administrationists are protected from threatening scrutiny by officials and bureaucrats who imagine that they are well shielded from scholarly inquiry. American political scientists, who might have been expected to look critically at the power position of career officials, relied on the dichotomy myth to rationalize their disregard for the subject. Moreover, the semipowered status of the American bureaucracy seemed to justify their disregard for its political significance. Finally, our penchant for specialization led us to focus on the components of governmental systems and thus to explain away the neglect of bureaucracy by political scientists who were only too glad to assign this thorny subject to specialists in Public Administration.

Although the dichotomy myth still prevails in America, there are exceptions that deserve attention. For example, Nachmias and Rosenbloom (1978: 10) remark that "all developed nations are thoroughly dependent upon a body of highly specialized and hierarchically organized administrators . . . bureaucrats have sometimes been considered a (new) ruling class." Heady (1991: 6) has explained that "comparative public administration is linked closely to the study of comparative politics, and must start from the base provided by recent and current developments in the comparative study of whole political systems." Scholars like these may eventually help both public administrationists and political scientists in America see how bureaucracy inescapably links politics and administration. They may come to understand that systems of government are organic wholes whose interdependent parts cannot be understood in isolation from each other.

Meanwhile, unfortunately, the bifurcation in our understanding of government has seriously impaired the capacity of Americans to understand the nature of government outside the United States. Because the dichotomy myth gained part of its plausibility from the semipowered status of American bureaucracy, the myth became a blinder leading Americans working overseas to imagine that public administration everywhere could be influenced and understood in a nonpolitical way. Projects to train bureaucrats or to reorganize government services came to be viewed as innocent of significant political consequences. Because bureaucracies that are administratively ineffective may nevertheless be politically powerful, such projects often, I believe, have had the unintended result of augmenting bureau power and contributing to the incidence of coups and bureaucratic domination, clearly an important consequence that I will explore in more detail in the latter portion of this chapter. But first, we need to reflect further on the global pervasiveness of bureaucratic power.

The Ubiquity of Bureaucratic Power. A clear understanding of governments outside the United States requires Americans, I believe, to erase the dichotomy myth from their minds. Perhaps when they understand how the uniquely semipowered American bureaucracy reinforced this myth and how it has shaped the development of Public Administration as a would-be profession in the United States, they will more willingly reject it. When they see that bureaucracies are powerful everywhere, except in single-party regimes and in the United States, they will see that administration and politics are truly inseparable throughout the world, that projects to influence administrative performance always have far-reaching political consequences, and that political institutions and processes deeply affect the management of public affairs.

Such an understanding may also help them recognize the sources of resistance to reforms that appear eminently reasonable and practical from an American point of view. Ruffing-Hilliard (1991) has given us a pathetic picture of the largely unsuccessful efforts of public administration consultants sponsored by the United States and the United Nations to promote career system reforms in various Latin American countries. They were so blinded by the dichotomy myth, I believe, that they could not see how essentially political their efforts were nor understand the motives of those who successfully resisted their proposals.

By rejecting the myth, moreover, we will more easily understand the uniqueness of the historical forces that (1) drove the reform projects of the Jacksonian era, when rotation-in-office curtailed the growth of retainer power, and (2) the equally exceptional movement to counteract the flagrant abuses in public office, exacerbated by the Jacksonian reforms, that led to the Pendleton Act. We will also see that the uniquely American bureaucratic system in which specialists (especially professionals) dominate the public services had profoundly political causes and consequences that cannot be replicated in any other country.

Where retainers are powerful (see note 10), as they typically are throughout Latin America, it is naive to expect them to surrender their power and privileges in response to the recommendations of foreign consultants. Moreover, in the presidentialist cliental regimes that prevail in the Americas, governmental authority is so fragmented by the separation of powers that effective control over retainer bureaucracies is problematic. Projects to achieve fundamental administrative reforms face gigantic political obstacles. Deep historical forces that occurred uniquely in the United States were responsible for its exceptional bureaucratic transformations, which led to a network state. Such forces have not been replicated elsewhere in the world.

By contrast, parliamentary governments succeeded, especially in Europe during the nineteenth century, in overcoming retainer power and establishing career bureaucracies, leading to the formation of mandarin-based administrative states. A variety of factors affected the success of these reforms, but above all the concentrated power available to governments in any parliamentary regime permitted them to formulate and implement policies more successfully than any presidentialist regime could hope for (Riggs 1994a). Effective control over mandarin bureaucracies also explains the relatively high levels of administrative performance and regime maintenance found in these parliamentary states. An understanding of the interdependence of politics and administration helps us explain how the inherently weaker presidentialist regime in America was able to improve administration by creating a professionalized bureaucracy that would be semipowered and hence no threat to the regime.

INTERNATIONAL IMPLICATIONS

Hubris

When most Americans talk about the role of the United States in the world, they often refer to its status as a superpower or as an exemplar of democracy, attitudes reflecting a hubris born of insularity and ethnocentrism. In the context of a global village, both terms are arrogant and misleading. The United States cannot and ought not try to "throw its weight around" as though it had any right to dominate other states or provide a model for them to emulate. This critical point is so obvious that I shall not comment on it further, except to remark that the exceptional wealth and power of the United States mislead many non-Americans, making them gullible enough to accept these pretensions.

A naive willingness to copy American practices and accept American advice is especially dangerous when the American presidentialist regime is equated with democracy. Precisely because the American political system, including its bureaucratic components, is so different from what is normal in other countries, both the American example and the advice given by Americans often produce results that are both unintended and disastrous. Americans working abroad or with foreign students and visitors to the United States need to become aware of this danger and to cultivate humility in order to avoid a misleading hubris that easily deceives everyone involved.

I shall focus here on two aspects of the American bureaucracy that are typically irrelevant to the needs of other countries and, when emulated, produce unintended and often harmful effects. They also profoundly affect the conduct of American foreign relations, often producing surprising and dysfunctional results. These aspects are (1) the exceptionally influential role of professionals in the American bureaucracy and (2) the semipowered position of the bureaucracy in American governance.[12]

Consequences of Bureaucratic Professionalism

The exceptionally autonomous position of American government agencies, as explained in the preceding "Domestic Perceptions" section, results from the high degree of professionalization of career officials, their responsiveness to congressional committees rather than to the fused power of a parliamentary cabinet, and the decisive influence of judicial decisions. As a result, each agency has the power, to some degree at least, to become actively involved in international programs. We cannot, therefore, speak of American foreign policy in the singular; instead, we have a large number of foreign policies.

Not only do bureaucratic fractionalization and professionalization hamper the coordination of government programs internally but also, internationally, each agency tends to operate autonomously, frequently in opposition to the activities of other U.S. government agencies. Nominally, the State Department, as represented by an ambassador in each country, is responsible for the coordination of all American governmental activities in that country. However, this is only a myth that scarcely reflects the reality.

An Anomaly in Thailand. Many years ago, when I was conducting field research in Thailand, I became aware of some consequences of this phenomenon without really understanding its causes. As a research focus designed to help me understand the dynamics of the Thai bureaucratic system, I focused my attention on the production, processing, and distribution of rice, an activity basic to the local economy and one that led to a wide variety of government programs. Among them, an important component stemmed from U.S. foreign aid projects, including one intended to help increase rice yields through the experimental development of new varieties and their widespread dissemination among farmers.

A highly qualified American professional, an expert on plant breeding and extension services, became my guide. One day, I was startled to learn that he had given up his work with the Rice Department and would instead help a different agency promote the development of wheat and corn. He explained that crop diversification would be good for Thailand and that too much emphasis on rice could lead to all the evils of monoculture, a major problem in many Third World countries.

When I probed a bit, however, I discovered that American rice producers, working through the Department of Agriculture in Washington, had been able to persuade our aid program to stop helping foreign rivals compete with American exports. As Thailand was already a major rice exporter, orders went out from Washington for our experts to help them develop new crops that could not compete with American products. Subsequently, I was pleased to discover that my friend had managed to accommodate his professional norms to his bureaucratic obligations by secretly continuing to work with his colleagues in the Thai Rice Department.

However, somewhat earlier, while this expert was still overtly promoting increased rice production in Thailand, he had rejected a proposal that would have helped diversify crop production, in response to an initiative from the Irrigation Department. Although both the Rice and the Irrigation Departments were in the Ministry of Agriculture, their own interagency rivalries may have been responsible, but the American expert could surely have been more receptive to this proposal. It asked for additional research on a shorter growing season for rice that would permit other crops to be grown in rotation with rice during the dry season. A large dam under construction was expected to create opportunities for year-round cultivation, but it could not supply enough water for paddy rice farming. Because the U.S. aid program refused to support the Irrigation Department's proposal, the Thai government turned to alternate sources of external assistance and found help from the U.N. Food and Agriculture Organization (UN-FAO). Ultimately, Thai farmers were to choose between rice varieties promoted by two rival government agencies.

At the time I viewed this conflict as a reflection, primarily, of interdepartmental struggles in Thailand, but now I see that the local turf war was reinforced by the professionalism of American advisers. They wanted to use their existing expertise to enhance rice output without confronting the new problems that would result both from developing varieties with a shorter growing season and from introducing new crops during the dry season.

Foreign Policy Pluralism. An illuminating panel on the overseas operations of several U.S. government agencies was presented at a recent conference of the American Society for Public Administration. The papers demonstrated that, in addition to the State and Defense Departments and U.S. foreign aid and information programs, many other U.S. government agencies were actively involved in foreign affairs. The subject was viewed as a challenge to public administration because it raised difficult problems of coordination, both in Washington and in the host countries. We may also explain the phenomenon as a result, in foreign affairs, of American bureaucratic professionalism.

Because of the formal responsibility of American ambassadors to coordinate all U.S. government programs in the countries where they are posted, I proposed that we ask the State Department to conduct a global inventory or census. It would have the limited purpose of describing all the overseas activities of U.S. government agencies. To start the inquiry, every bureau in Washington could be asked by the Executive Office of the President to supply a list of countries in which it had operations, with a local address for each agency's representatives. A database produced from the responses could easily generate a country-by-country inventory that would enable each ambassador to send a questionnaire to all U.S. offices within his or her jurisdiction. As far as I know, there has never been a follow-up to this suggestion; and we still have only anecdotes, like my Thai story, to illustrate what is, undoubtedly, a ubiquitous phenomenon.

Global Implications. Learning the facts, of course, does not provide an explanation. I believe the extent to which America's role in the world is played by a host of federal government agencies reflects both the power of professionalism in the U.S. bureaucracy and a cost of presidentialism. Specialists in every bureau readily believe that their services and the problems they understand have global implications. They want to contribute to the solution of these problems, but they may think that changes in the policies and programs of other countries might also help them deal with domestic problems and, no doubt, enhance the importance and funding of their own budgets. Although they might be able to achieve their goals by influencing and working through the U.S. Agency for International Development (AID) or the State Department, direct overseas involvement provides an alternative that many professionals in government prefer. They trust their own judgment in preference to that of the nonprofessionals working in our foreign relations agencies.

Actually, the international activities of professionals in U.S. federal agencies are only a "tip of the iceberg." Virtually every state and city government in the United States also has its own foreign policies and projects. Moreover, government agencies at all these levels are both influenced and supported in their global activities by ubiquitous multinational corporations, religious and ethnic communities, professional associations, trade unions, and other private organizations in America, virtually all of which have interests and concerns outside the United States. My experience in state universities tells me that, even at this lowly level, so many international activities are under way that effective internal coordination within just one university is almost impossible.

Multinational corporations have already been studied intensively, and there is a substantial literature about their direct impact in many countries. Much of this analysis is pejorative and highly critical of the adverse impact of these companies on development and social justice in the countries where they operate. I cannot evaluate this literature here, but it is certainly important. American corporations working abroad often seek and obtain help from a variety of U.S. government agencies, although, I suspect, they are likely to protest that they don't get nearly enough support from these sources.

Much less is known about the many international professional associations with which American counterpart bodies are affiliated. They provide a network of channels through which American professionals become acquainted with their counterparts in other countries and share with them their expert knowledge and normative standards. Because American professionals in the bureaucracy are free to belong to these associations, they also have the opportunity to work indirectly abroad through personal contacts and mechanisms that operate outside the formal structures of government. The Union of International Associations, headquartered in Brussels, maintains a database of information about more than 8,000 international organizations (UIA Yearbook) and publishes an encyclopedia identifying the problems with which they deal (UIA Encyclopedia 1986). This vast and increasingly complex jungle of professional networks permits American professionals working abroad to establish contacts with others who share their concerns and both to learn from and to influence them.

Certification vs. Standards. At this point, readers may well protest that the American bureaucracy may not differ much from its counterparts in other countries. If professionals serve all governments, as they no doubt do, are their functions in the U.S. government truly distinctive? To answer this question, we need to distinguish among professional standards, certification, and competence. The word *professional* can mean each or all of these things and we need to be clear about what we have in mind.

James Q. Wilson has described (1989) how professionals in the American government strive to live up to *standards* set by their professional associations. These associations are typically nongovernmental and usually include more members in private practice than in public agencies. Professional schools are also well represented in them and heavily influence their standards. In the United States these associations are very powerful, and they clearly influence the conduct of all their members, including government officials.

Helping shape government policy is an important goal of professional associations, which often sponsor political action committees (PACs) to support the campaigns of key members of Congress and to lobby the relevant committees to promote their standards and values. Professionals in the bureaucracy participate in this work as association members. All these activities reflect the power of technical standards and ethical norms, producing what could more precisely be called *missioned professionals*. In addition to their official responsibilities, they become missionaries dedicated to the promotion of their profession's standards. Their sense of mission, moreover, often provokes arguments between them and their bureaucratic colleagues.

In most governments we find many *certified functionaries* or *professionalists* who have, indeed, received advanced training and degrees in professional schools but lack the sense of commitment to extrabureaucratic standards felt by missioned professionals. This lack may be due to structural reasons, when bureaucratic discipline and controls are strong enough to override whatever obligations an official may feel toward externally established standards. Reliance on certified functionaries enables a government to recruit officials who are qualified to perform specialized tasks without taking the risk that their sense of mission will undermine compliance with the policies and priorities set by the government.

In authoritarian regimes and bureaucratic polities, governments may go beyond reliance on hierarchic authority to monitor and control the conduct of certified functionaries (professionalists). They may, for example, actually subsidize and organize professional associations so that they can impose their own standards on them. In the Thai case, for example, I discovered years ago that most physicians hold government appointments and that the Thai Medical Association accepted norms and standards set by the government through its Ministry of Health. Under such conditions, no real conflicts between medical and government standards are likely to arise.

A government that does not dominate its professional societies can nevertheless control the conduct of certified functionaries if it has a powerful enough top echelon of experienced and competent generalist officials, that is, of mandarins or professionists. Such people can be thought of as professionals in public administration, even though they never studied Public Administration. Instead, mandarins are typically recruited as youths by means of general examinations in law or various academic disciplines. To call them professionals emphasizes their long-term career commitment and experience as administrators, that is, their *competence*. However, they lack the sense of mission we normally associate with professional status.

In most parliamentary systems some kind of mandarin system is the norm (see note 9). Their loyalty to the state takes top priority, overriding any standards or values formulated by extragovernmental associations. They are free, therefore, to enforce government policy without ambivalence. If we refer to them as mandarins or professionists, we shall avoid unnecessary confusion. They are professionally competent without adhering to extrabureaucratic professional standards.[13]

No doubt, mandarins need the help of certified professionals who have acquired the specialized expertise they lack because of their generalist training and experience. However, they have learned by experience how to control the conduct of certified functionaries under their authority, which enables them to coordinate government activities and develop a unified foreign policy. They do not need to dominate the professional associations as authoritarian and bureaucratic regimes do. Moreover, the competence that enables mandarins to control the professionalists under their authority also makes them capable of mobilizing so much power that they can organize themselves to seize power. They become dependable administrators, therefore, only when the political system is really able to control them. Such political control is possible in parliamentary regimes but not, I believe, in presidentialist systems.

The Sense of Mission. The American presidentialist regime, exceptionally, has been able to maintain control over its bureaucracy only because it has not evolved a mandarin class. Rather, it has relied on transient "in-and-outers" to staff its top administrative positions. These bureaucrats have neither the motives for nor the possibility of organizing enough power to displace the institutions of representative government. The persistent reliance of American governments on rotation to staff top posts, ever since the Jacksonian revolution of 1829, has contributed greatly to the survival of our precarious presidentialist system of government.

Rotationism has been supplemented by a growing dependence on missioned professionals to staff career posts throughout the American bureaucracy. Two major benefits and one huge cost have resulted. First, the competence needed for effective public administration has been secured, thereby reducing the motives for both revolutionary protests and coups. Moreover, the dispersed loyalties of careerists—and especially of the bureaucratic professionals—have further diminished the capacity of American officials to organize themselves to exercise power, leading to the semipowered bureaucracy described previously. Both of these benefits have helped the American presidentialist regime survive.

Other presidentialist regimes have recruited many certified functionaries (professionalists) whose lack of a sense of mission permits them to join fellow bureaucrats in order to enhance their power position. The heavy dependence on retainers in these countries has enabled mobilized bureaucrats to seize power during severe crises motivated, in part at least, by the relative inability of retainers to administer effectively. Even those with professional degrees lack a sense of mission that would bar them from collaborating in struggles to enhance bureaucratic power.

As to the cost, the lack of a top echelon of mandarins means that missioned professionals are free to implement their professional loyalties even when these conflict with their official obligations to their hierarchic superiors. Their responsiveness to congressional committees and interest groups also produces monumental obstacles to effective coordination. The international significance of the resulting dispersal of power becomes apparent when we see how American missioned professionals are able to promote, on a global basis, the standards that they value so much.

Americans are often surprised and disappointed when they find that the mandarins (professionists) with whom they work in other countries give so much weight to the policies and standards set by their governments. They are also puzzled by the conduct of professionalists (certified functionaries) in bureaucratic polities who, although they have also been trained in professional schools, do not share their own sense of mission. They are unaware that, because American administrative superiors are in-and-outers (or professionals) and the separation of powers prevails, public administration in the United States cannot be well coordinated and that the latitude given to missioned professionals to follow their own norms is truly exceptional.

Interest Networks

The exceptional influence of missioned professionals in the American bureaucracy should help us understand why the United States is not an *administrative state* in the usual meaning of this term. Such a state typically exists when its bureaucratic elites are mandarins. As explained previously, in the "Certification vs. Standards" section, as long as they remain under effective political control, mandarins are able to coordinate and direct the professionalists (certi-fied functionaries) under their authority.

By contrast, the United States is a network state (see the "Professionalism and Power" section). It is governed by a congeries of overlapping *interest networks* (iron triangles, issue networks, and golden grids),[14] each of which links public and private interests in complex and overlapping patterns that defy simple description but somehow enable most important public policies to be carried out in a reasonably effective though disconnected way.

To most Americans, these networks are as natural and invisible as water must be to a fish. When they find themselves working abroad, they cannot understand why people in other countries behave so differently. To most Europeans, the notion of a *state* is very real, and enforceable obligations to the administrative state are a compelling fact of life, especially for mandarins. For American officials, by contrast, the notion of the state seems abstract and confusing; they appreciate the contrast between government and society, but they cannot empathize with a concept that links both of these ideas in a comprehensive and ordered pattern. In the context of a network state, the notion of a state looks like an illusory reification.

The way a network state operates overseas can be illustrated by a study I made years ago in Taiwan (Riggs 1973). The U.S. foreign aid program had employed a private consulting firm to advise the Chinese authorities on the problems they faced while trying to release a hundred thousand or so "combat ineffective" soldiers who had moved with them from the mainland and could not return to their home villages. The authorities wanted to discharge them, but they were too old, sick, and uneducated to care for themselves. Unable to return to their families, they would easily be victimized, becoming a cause of violence and social disorder.

The consulting firm sent a team composed mainly of missioned professionals recruited from the U.S. Veterans Administration. Their standards for handling veterans differed radically from the pragmatic goals of the Chinese regime, and many conflicts and misunderstandings arose. Among the Americans, protracted controversy also arose with the local AID staff, whose liaison officer had quite different ideas about what should be done, based on a set of developmental priorities. He could not accept the preferences of either the Chinese authorities or the agency's American consultants.

At the time, I blamed the American officials for their apparent insensitivity to the constraints under which the Taiwan regime operated in the late 1950s. Now I can see that the problem was much deeper: The American professionals, both the foreign aid officer and the consultants, had internalized competing standards that were inapplicable in a situation where the local officials faced a highly politicized and bureaucratized environment. The norms set by the visiting consultants could not be implemented, but they were eventually ex-ploited by the Chinese to serve regime goals quite different from those that both groups of Americans had supported.

The confusing outcome in the case of the Chinese veterans was almost inescapable because the Americans abroad could interpret the local situation only in terms of the network state with which they were familiar. As individuals and professionals, Americans are used to an extremely complex maze of relatively open relationships in which negotiation and bargained agreements permit a wide range of apparently incompatible public and private activities to coexist. Working in diverse government agencies and private organizations overseas, they find themselves trapped in unfamiliar situations that baffle and often humiliate them. These include the mandarinate contexts of well-established administrative states based on parliamentary democracy. What Americans find in bureaucratic polities is even more of a puzzle to them.

Prismatic Contradictions. In bureaucratic polities, that is, in the Third World countries where public officials, headed by military officers, dominate the government—*prismatic* situations prevail. Typically, standards imposed by the outside world are given lip service while the expedient interests of dominant bureaucrats prevail (Riggs 1964). In such contexts, American agencies and officials find that formally accepted agreements often lead to unintended and unacceptable results.

In order to understand what they find in such situations, Americans need to gain a deeper understanding of why missioned professionals can exercise so much influence in our own network state. They will gain such an understanding only after they learn to use the comparative analysis of other countries—especially those that have accepted constitutional forms of government based on the American presidentialist design—to create the theoretical framework needed to interpret and explain the exceptional dynamics of government in the United States. Such a vision will also enable us to see how the strength of missioned professionalism in the American bureaucracy hampers the effective administration of American foreign relations. Then we will grasp the implications of what is happening outside the United States, in the global village, and we will then, I believe, also be able to relate more helpfully to the world's problems.

No doubt the foregoing explanation involves some oversimplification. Genuine differences of interest seriously affect all relationships between the United States and other countries. In particular, many Third World countries have been unfairly treated and exploited by more powerful countries, and the fabled prosperity of America reflects the inequalities of center/periphery relationships that have enabled the rich to become richer at the expense of the poor, who became poorer.

To the degree that this is true—and I think this interpretation is sometimes exaggerated—it is also true that the American government and many private organizations want to compensate for past injustices by helping less-fortunate countries in various ways. In an increasingly interdependent global village, such efforts need to be more effective. We should not allow the international inequities and misunderstandings that already exist to be compounded by our own inability to understand the dynamics of America's truly exceptional network state and the role played in it by a bureaucracy in which missioned professionals play an extraordinarily important role.

Global Effects of a Semipowered Bureaucracy

The global consequences of professionalization in American public administration and our network state need to be understood in the context of the semipowered status of our bureaucracy (see previous "Bureaucracy and Politics" section). Some consequences have already been discussed, notably, the fact that American bureaucrats are far less able to coordinate their energies in order to seize power than are the members of any other bureaucracy, except those under the domination of single-party authoritarianism (Riggs 1993c).

Indirectly, the semipowered status of the American bureaucracy has reinforced the myth of a dichotomy between politics and administration. No doubt this myth facilitated the efforts of the reformers who were able, finally, to launch specialized career services in the American bureaucracy in accordance with provisions of the Pendleton Act of 1883. Although the myth has been denounced by many of the leading students of Public Administration, its popularization still offers a dysfunctional rationale for the work of American public administration advisers overseas. Moreover, it blinds us to the underlying dynamics of polities in which administratively ineffective but powerful bureaucracies become politically dominant.

Two consequences reinforce each other. On the American side, technical advisers in Public Administration argue that they can help a government enhance its capacity to administer development programs by implementing a variety of projects that are "nonpolitical" in character and involve trying to upgrade the capabilities of public officials, both military officers and civil servants. On the host-country side, this argument is welcomed because it reassures insecure bureaucratic elites that their own status and power will not be jeopardized by the American programs; instead, they expect that their capacity to maintain a dominant position at home will be enhanced, as will their ability to gain international credibility. Consequently, there is a convergence of perceptions between American advisers and host governments that has led in many countries to the proliferation of projects, in both public agencies and universities, designed to promote the study and practice of American-style public administration.

Paradoxical Consequences. In order to understand the paradoxical results of these efforts, we need to remember that almost all the new states, when they gained their independence, inherited potentially powerful bureaucratic institutions created by the imperial power. However, they did not inherit political systems capable of dominating these bureaucracies. Predictably, therefore, many new states could not sustain effective control over the bureaucracies they had inherited.

At first, as expatriate top officials withdrew and were replaced by inexperienced local personnel, through the process of bureaucratic indigenization, the bureaucracies of the new states were so frail and ineffectual that they could not seize power. Gradually, however, as they gained strength and experience (helped in many cases by foreign advisers), the bureaucracies reached a stage in which, if the new regime stumbled and failed to cope effectively with severe problems, frustrated bureaucrats—under the leadership of military officers who monopolized the necessary means of violence—were able to seize power, suspend whatever constitution existed, and depose all elected politicians.

Ironically, U.S. technical assistance programs designed to be "nonpolitical" and to promote developmental capabilities in both the civil and military services contributed to outcomes that exactly reversed their nominal goals. Because virtually all bureaucracies (except, of course, that of the United States) are inherently powerful, projects designed to enhance their capabilities have made them even more powerful and have thereby contributed to the flood of coups d'état through which governments dominated by appointed officials (military and civil) have emerged.

Whenever bureaucrats dominate a country, however, their administrative performance declines as their power position increases. In any republic, only officials who are controlled through politically responsive (elected) institutions can be counted on to administer effectively; monarchies are sometimes also able to rule efficiently, but few of them remain. By strengthening bureaucracies without at the same time helping to empower a country's democratic political institutions, U.S. foreign aid has unintentionally achieved adverse political results.

Instead of enhancing a country's capacity to manage public programs more efficiently—the intended result of development administration projects—bureaucrats who seize power through a coup d'état are able to exercise their authority without restraint: They are therefore free to abuse their power with impunity. If they choose to be corrupt, lazy, or abusive, no one can discipline them. Thus, paradoxically, programs designed to improve administrative performance by nonpolitical means have perversely undermined public administration by contributing politically to the breakdown of fragile constitutional regimes.

Of course, we should not exaggerate the impact of Public Administration programs set up to help civil servants. Military aid programs probably have had an even greater impact. Moreover, all U.S. government programs in Third World countries, including those sponsored by many different agencies, not just technical assistance projects, for reasons explained previously, are administered on a "government-to-government" basis. This means that bureaucratic counterparts work with each other. Inadvertently, without intending to do so, bureaucratic structures in recipient countries are strengthened while the political institutions that might control them languish and, quite often, collapse.

Extrabureaucratic Power. The most important force for better public administration in any country exists outside its bureaucracy. When democratic political institutions are able to control public officials, these officials find that they are rewarded for doing a good job. Consequently, they embrace new managerial techniques that help them serve the public better. An important feedback process ensures that the better the administrative performance of a bureaucracy, the more satisfied the public and the officials themselves will be. Consequently, the risks of rebellion and of coups will also be reduced. Perversely, without a context of democratic political control, bureaucrats also welcome new managerial techniques, but they are able to abuse them in order to enhance their own power and wealth while tyrannizing a subdued population.

Many Americans, including political scientists and lawyers, as well as specialists in Public Administration, view the American constitutional system as a model or exemplar that ought to be emulated by other countries. Consequently, even when the United States sponsors programs designed to strengthen democratic political institutions, they inadvertently reinforce the perils just noted by promoting presidentialist structures that institutionalize the separation of powers, thereby generating cross-pressures that severely hamper the capacity of any such regime to control its bureaucracy.

By contrast, the fused structure of power in parliamentary (cabinet) government enables these regimes to maintain control over their bureaucracies more easily than can any presidentialist regime. Consequently, to the degree that U.S. policy seeks to promote presidentialism overseas, it courts disaster. The adverse results of U.S. influence in establishing presidentialist regimes in South Vietnam and South Korea are notorious. By contrast, when both West Germany and Japan, despite American military occupation, established parliamentary governments, they were able to lift their countries out of the depths of postwar depression and chaos to become the leading industrialized democracies they are today.

If current U.S. policy were to lead to the institutionalization of presidentialism in the Russian Federation—or in any other ex-Soviet or Eastern European republic—the outcome will, in each case, surely be a catastrophic breakdown. The evidence for this position can be found in the much higher survival rate of the new states with parliamentary constitutions, as compared with the dismal record of all presidentialist regimes—except, as explained previously, for the United States (Riggs 1993a). Our inability to understand these fateful realities hinges, I believe, on the pervasive influence of missioned professionals in the American bureaucracy, its semipowered nonpartisan status in our constitutional system, and the associated dichotomy myth that leads us to think of public administration as a nonpolitical process.

Solving the Mystery: American Public Administration in a Global Village

The emergence of a global village helps us solve the mystery posed by American Public Administration. At the domestic level, it unmasks the way we see ourselves. Instead of viewing bureaucracy as a nonpolitical force that can and should perform only administrative functions, we need to understand that in all countries bureaucrats are *political actors*, in both a positive and a negative sense. Positively, they intervene to help shape public policies and thereby to influence every country's political system. Negatively, although good public administration strengthens any regime, poor public administration undermines its viability; thus, even ostensibly nonpolitical actions by a bureaucracy have significant political consequences.

For historical reasons, the American national bureaucracy is only semipowered. This makes the American illusion of a dichotomy between politics and administration seem plausible whereas, by contrast, the uniformly powerful role played by public officials (military and civil) in all countries not dominated by a single authoritarian party makes this dichotomy patently ludicrous. American theories of Public Administration have been heavily influenced by the dichotomy myth, and admittedly it played an important role in the development of professionalized career civil services in our presidentialist regime. All other presidentialist regimes, however, because of the separation of powers, are handicapped both in making public policies and in managing their more powerful bureaucracies.

Bureaucratic Power. The powerful bureaucracies found in all presidentialist regimes except that of the United States have, typically, been able to seize power, under military leadership, whenever the constitutional authorities were unable to govern effectively during a major crisis. The semipowered status of the U.S. bureaucracy made such a seizure of power impossible. Consequently, American political scientists, unaware of the experience of other presidentialist regimes, came to view our constitutional system as essentially viable. Meanwhile, specialists in comparative politics tried to explain its universal collapse elsewhere by local conditions; they have not considered the possibility that all such systems are vulnerable to catastrophic breakdowns and that only the U.S. exception needs to be explained.

One of the contributing factors to the political weakness of the American bureaucracy was the role specialization that evolved as a result of the stipulations of the Pendleton Act of 1883 and the availability of agricultural and mechanical land-grant colleges. This specialization, in turn, permitted the emergence of innumerable missioned professionals in the civil services and the development of highly autonomous government agencies, reinforced by their responsiveness to congressional committees and private interest groups, leading to the formation of a *network state*. The rise of American Public Administration, based on the dichotomy myth, can be explained in this context. Thus the survival of presidentialism and the peculiar status and nonpolitical orientation of public administration in America are both attributable to the peculiar features of its semipowered bureaucratic system.

Unintended Outcomes. Mysterious consequences for the administration of America's international relations can now be explained. *Missioned profession-*

alism and the dispersal of power in American government are reflected in the proliferation of autonomous foreign projects within the domains of a host of separate government agencies. These activities have further empowered the bureaucracies of many Third World countries, contributing to the destabilization of embryonic democracies.

A significant, though not a major, contributor to these developments has been the deliberate effort to promote enhanced public administration as a nonpolitical activity, under the heading of *development administration*. Perversely, to the degree that newly empowered indigenous bureaucracies in precarious regimes have seized power, these efforts have had unintended and adverse political consequences without improving the administrative capabilities of host countries. Only by gaining a better understanding of our own domestic governmental system, in the perspective provided by the emergent global village, can we solve the mystery of American public administration. Finding this solution will, I believe, help us relate to the rest of the world in a way that should enhance the valued goals of all peoples and contribute to the peace and prosperity that everyone seeks.

NOTES

1. Single-party dictatorships, whether of the right or left, monopolize power by suppressing civil liberties and opposition parties. This gives the ruling party the ability not only to control the courts and the elected assembly (e.g., a *Soviet*) but also to dominate the bureaucracy. In Communist regimes, for example, in the celebrated contest between *red* (Communist Party enthusiast) and *expert* (someone with technical expertise), the red always rules. The linkage between bureaucratic power and administrative performance is highlighted in this situation: Powerless bureaucrats are unable to administer effectively because their expertise is invalidated. When they cannot use their experience, training, and special competence to implement public policies in the face of contradictory party mandates, they necessarily fail and become personally demoralized. They cling to office because of the security it offers when no viable alternatives are available and also because they can use corrupt means to enrich themselves.

No doubt many such officials, accepting the inexorable, join the "enemy" and become party activists and commissars, helping foist the current line on other officeholders. As such regimes decay, the boundary between party officials and public servants gradually dissolves, obscuring the distinctions drawn in this note. Nevertheless, the chaos that can follow the collapse of a ruling party demonstrates that a powerless bureaucracy by itself is unable to carry out the minimal functions of governance, leading to anarchy. Somalia today provides a good example. Earlier in this century, the collapse of the Manchus in China (1911) was followed by a long period of anarchy; that country's celebrated mandarinate had become so demoralized and powerless by the end of the dynasty that it could no longer govern the country in the absence of a strong ruler. When the Kuomintang and subsequently the Communist Party established themselves in China, they gradually reconstituted a weak state bureaucracy under single-party domination.

2. *Power* is a variable with at least two significant levels in addition to the polar contraries *powerful* and *powerless*. At one extreme, bureaucracies can be *dominant*, as in bureaucratic dictatorships, typically following a coup d'état, where military officers and civil servants constitute

a ruling elite. At the opposite extreme, bureaucracies are *powerless*, as in single-party dictatorships; see note 1. In between, the most prevalent situation is that of a powerful bureaucracy, namely, one that can sway public policy by influencing but not controlling the decisions of elected politicians who constitute a governing elite. In virtually all democracies, regardless of constitutional format, bureaucracies are powerful. A bureaucracy whose power position lies between "powerful" and "powerless" may be called semipowered, and the United States offers the leading example. For a detailed discussion of this exceptional situation see Riggs (1994a).

When discussing bureaucratic power we should distinguish between systemic and individual levels of power. We are all familiar with the notion that industrial workers who lack power individually can wield substantial power by unionization. Conversely, powerful individuals often lack collective power: This is the situation in the American bureaucracy. Bureaucratic professionals often carry great weight when making decisions that affect their official responsibilities, but as professionals they are reluctant to unite with fellow professionals in diverse subject fields to protect their interests as public employees.

Many academics have personal experience of the controversies provoked in some universities by a drive to unionize faculty members. They view efforts to enhance faculty power as a selfish violation of their professional obligations. Thus a professor whose power is decisive for students under his or her authority may be politically impotent when dealing with the university administration. A parallel situation exists, at the macro level, in the U.S. bureaucracy.

3. The first meaning of *bureaucracy*, as this word is defined in *Webster's Third New International Dictionary*, is the set of all the appointed officials of a government. Other meanings include subsets of bureaucrats or modes of administration better designated by such words as *bureaupathology* and *bureaurationality*. American Public Administration has restricted its understanding of the word to include only one subset of appointed officials, namely, those who are neither military personnel nor political appointees. In other words, by bureaucrat they normally mean only career civil servants.

The narrowing of the concept occurred for historical reasons that are explained in this chapter. Its effect, however, has been to intensify the parochialism of American thinking about public administration and politics. Valid comparisons between countries having quite different ways of organizing their bureaucracies can be made only by means of the first concept given in the dictionary, that is, all public officials, including civil and military personnel, careerists, and political appointees. When comparisons are usefully made among the career civil servants of different countries, it is better to use this phrase rather than to corrupt the meaning of bureaucracy by misusing it to mean only this subset of bureaucrats.

4. One way to make sure a regime cannot be overthrown by a coup is to eliminate its armed forces, a decision that has helped Costa Rica sustain its presidentialist regime since 1948.

5. Predictably, because of the weakness of their bureaucracies, only 17 percent of the single-party regimes (six out of thirty-five) had experienced coups, according to my findings in 1985 (Riggs 1993a: 215). *Monarchical regimes*, that is, monarchies in which the king ruled as the head of the government, not just as head of state, were less likely than parliamentary systems to experience a coup (25% or eight out of thirty-two), but they collapsed more often for other reasons, such as foreign intervention, revolutions, evolution into parliamentary limited monarchies, or palace revolutions. Five successful revolts were organized by highly placed civilian politicians. As these politicians were also appointed officials, one might classify their revolts as a special type of coup, in which case we would find that thirteen of the thirty-two monarchical regimes, or 40 percent, were victims of a coup.

6. Although turbulence and civil wars have frequently occurred in Europe, their parliamentary regimes have rarely been overthrown by a coup. A notable exception is Greece, where the coup of 1967 can be blamed, in part at least, on the ambitious connivance of King Constantine. Earlier examples can be found in Eastern Europe, for example, the military dictatorship of

Marshal Pilsudski in Poland (from 1926) and of Admiral Horthy in Hungary (from 1919). A so-called coup terminated the French Second Republic in 1851 and led to the Second Empire the following year. However, Louis Napoleon, who organized this "coup," had been elected president in 1848, under a presidentialist constitution; his seizure of power, therefore, resembled those of Presidents Marcos and Fujimori. The rise of Nazi and Fascist totalitarianism represented the seizure of power by a militant political party, replicating the scenario whereby the Communist Party came to power in Russia. Although military coups have occurred in about a third of the parliamentary regimes of the Third World, the phenomenon is far less prevalent than it has been in the presidentialist countries, where 90 percent of all such regimes have experienced coups.

7. Although most presidentialist regimes collapse because of a military coup, they are also vulnerable to presidential autocracy. Frequently enough, elected presidents, facing gridlock with their legislatures, are able with military support to abrogate the legislature and annul the constitution. Both types of breakdown can occur in the same country: Argentina, Brazil, and Peru are examples. In the Philippines, President Ferdinand Marcos seized power in 1972 and ruled autocratically, discharging the congress and imposing a pseudoparliamentary system of government, until presidentialism was restored under President Corazon Aquino in 1986. Six unsuccessful coups were attempted during her administration, evidence of the relative weakness of the American-style bureaucracy that had been established during the U.S. domination of that country. As for Peru, President Keinya Fujimori's autocratic rule continues, and it is too early to predict how it will end.

8. Every regime has faced severe crises, and the United States is no exception: The Civil War, the Great Depression, and two world wars are leading examples. During such crises, American presidents have no doubt used their executive powers unconstitutionally, but they have never suspended the Constitution nor discharged the Congress. In every coup, both of these events occur.

The reasons why the American constitutional system, exceptionally, has been able to survive for more than two centuries are discussed in Riggs (1988 and 1993b). These essays discuss factors affecting the design of the presidency, the Congress, and the cabinet, plus their interactions, the role of the party and electoral systems, and the attitudes of American voters (and nonvoters). A full understanding of the arguments offered here requires some acquaintance with the arguments presented in these articles. However, it is impossible to recapitulate them here.

9. The Chinese term *mandarin* has been generalized to refer to any bureaucrat who, recruited by a general examination to serve in an elite cadre of officials, after years of rotation in office, both geographically and functionally, serves as a top-level coordinator and adviser of government. Historically, the mandarin system was borrowed from China by the British East India Company to enable it to retain control over its far-flung empire. During the 1850s, the English administrative class was established on the same model. Details can be found in Teng (1943) and Chapman (1970).

The mandarin system is found today in many parliamentary regimes (Dogan 1975). Governments served by a mandarin bureaucracy are exemplars for the concept of an *administrative state*. The substance of this concept is actualized by the relatively coordinated power of a cohesive top echelon of generalists and the idealized notion of a state to which they profess loyalty.

Although the mandarin model served as a frame of reference for the congressional debates that led to the Pendleton Act in 1883, the law itself departed radically from the British model in fundamental respects, as explained in Van Riper (1958: 96–112). The basic differences involved the use of practical exams; the apportionment of appointments among all the states in proportion to population; recruitment to positions according to qualifications, at any age; and the nonpartisanship of careerists. An explanation of the consequences of these rules and how they contributed to the rise of professionalism in the American bureaucracy will be found in Riggs (1994a).

10. Although *retainer* was traditionally used to mean a family servant, it has also been employed to mean "civil service retainers," and I shall use it only in this sense, to identify patronage (political) appointees who retain their posts indefinitely. The concept must be distinguished clearly from merit-based *careerists*, whose tenure in office is assured by a legally binding contract with the state. Historically, a king's retainers became officials, and the word was long used to refer to them. Although the word has fallen out of use in democratic regimes, I see no reason not to use it to refer to patronage appointees who retain their offices on a long-term basis.

We not only lack an established term for the concept of bureaucratic retainers, but also have no name for a state in which most bureaucrats are retainers. Because patron/client relations in private as well as public life are decisively important in these countries, it seems appropriate to refer to them as clientel states. Although this term focuses attention on the state, all social relationships in such a state also tend to be dominated by clientelism.

11. Like all other presidentialist regimes in the Americas, the United States initially established a retainer bureaucracy, producing a cliental state. However, its members were too few and inexperienced to organize themselves effectively before their power potential was destroyed in 1829 by President Jackson who introduced the rotation principle. The guiding principle of the Jacksonian revolution was that of a civic state, that is, one in which every citizen is, in principle, qualified to carry out administrative responsibilities (White 1954; Crenson 1975). The historical exemplar of a civic state was the classical Athenian democracy. America still retains this principle in the jury trial procedures whereby citizens are recruited, more or less at random, to make life-and-death decisions. The same principle also applies in some local governments, where ultimate political authority lies in town meetings open to all citizens and where, by means of a long ballot, many local officials are elected to perform purely administrative tasks.

Ever since President Jackson, in the spirit of a civic state, introduced the rotation principle, all top officials in the U.S. bureaucracy have been transients (the "in-and-outers" or "spoilsmen") whose short terms in office deprive them of both the motive and the opportunity to organize to seize power. When career officials were appointed, after 1883, their specializations and, eventually, professionalization rendered them also incapable of organizing a successful coup. Gradually, the cliental state of the nineteenth century has been transformed into the network state of the twentieth. The structure of power in such a state is so fragmented and dispersed that, although the regime may limp clumsily from crisis to crisis, it resists disruption by any group, including the bureaucracy, that might want to seize power and impose order.

12. A third important difference also needs attention: the socioethnic representativeness of the American bureaucracy by contrast with what is typical in other countries. However, space forbids discussion of this difference here, and the subject is reserved for treatment elsewhere.

13. Because of the unavoidable confusion associated with our use of the term *professional*, it may be helpful to define more formally the following different though overlapping concepts.

1. *Professionalist*, or *certified functionary*: One who holds a professional degree but feels no obligation to uphold standards set by an independent professional association or is unable to implement them even when they exist.

2. *Professionist*, or *mandarin*: A competent and experienced generalist administrator in a high-level post who lacks professional certification and is not committed to standards set outside the government by a professional association.

3. *Professional*, or *missioned professional*: A certified and competent person with a
   sense of mission or commitment to standards and goals developed outside the
   bureaucracy by a professional association.

The sense of mission is crucial: True professionals in this sense feel an obligation to promote
the ethical norms and approved practices of their profession; they exhibit a kind of missionary
zeal in their pursuit of these objectives. Americans ordinarily think about missioned professionals when they use the word *professional*. However, the word is also used loosely to identify all
three concepts defined here. Wherever ambiguity seems likely, we can avoid it by using
missioned professional instead of *professional*.

Only by keeping these distinctions in mind can we understand why missioned professionalism in the U.S. bureaucracy is such an important and distinctive force, both domestically and
internationally. Although graduates of professional schools (certified functionaries or professionalists) and experienced mandarins (professionists) are numerous in many bureaucracies,
they do not create the problems of internal coordination and foreign policy activism that are
generated by a high level of missioned professionalism in government.

14. The concepts of an *iron triangle* (or subgovernment) and an *issue network* are familiar
in the American literature of Public Administration (McCurdy 1977: 108–114; Riggs 1994a:
note 46; Rourke 1991). The notion of a *golden grid* should be added: it refers to a network
created by in-and-outers as consultants and lobbyists and also as employees of private firms,
nonprofit organizations, and universities. The pejorative term "beltway bandit" unfairly belittles
many of the "amphibians" (Campbell 1986: 200) who rotate in and out of government and the
private sector, creating powerful alliances that differ significantly from, while supplementing,
the more familiar and larger networks mentioned previously. Ultimately, they merge in the
infinite complexity of interest networks, the definitive characteristic of a network state.

2

GLOBALIZING THE THEORY AND PRACTICE OF PUBLIC ADMINISTRATION

GERALD E. CAIDEN

That the emerging world order embraces the concepts of Spaceship Earth and global village reflects the dawning reality that all creatures share a common fate. Until the nuclear threat disabused people about fifty years ago, they still clung to the comforting thought that somehow, somewhere, they could isolate themselves from everybody else and go their own way unmindful of others. That prospect has now almost entirely disappeared. Modern technology has virtually unified the world. Almost nobody can escape the risk of being photographed from spacecraft they cannot see, recorded by equipment they cannot hear, detected by heat sensors they cannot feel, infected by noxious gasses they cannot smell, or poisoned by chemicals they cannot taste. Almost everyone is affected by changes in the global environment, shifts in world economic patterns, movements in international alignments, and movements in popular culture (particularly in personal appearance, clothes, and music). Events across the globe are watched as they unfold even ahead of local knowledge, while fans know more about their foreign idols than about their domestic leaders. The wide differences among peoples that once distinguished international gatherings are being narrowed fast; they have to work hard to preserve their uniqueness.

Yet parochialism still dominates public administration. The vast majority of public officials will never experience anything other than the national administrative systems in which they work and then probably only a handful of different organization cultures within that narrow confine. Relatively few will get to experience any other national administration from within or join any international organization that will force them to confront administrative styles different from that to which they have been accustomed. Even though the number who travel and mix with foreign counterparts grows, it still remains relatively low: It contains the selected few. Most public administration practitioners never suffer culture shock, never have to adjust to something quite alien to their upbringing, never have to socialize with counterparts who think and act differently, and never have to develop accommodating skills to shift between different administrative cultures unless they make a deliberate effort to shift careers or to move around the organizational landscape during their career.

The same parochialism still afflicts too much of the study or science of public administration. Much of what purports to be universalistic is actually highly culture bound and idiosyncratic. Probably Americans are the worst offenders. Too many, ignorant of the world outside the United States, merely generalize about American public administration, not recognizing that American ideas and practices are idiosyncratic and the exception rather than the rule. They seem to want everyone in the world to be like them simply by Americanizing their public administration ideas and practices. The British and French are possibly less blinkered, but many of them are also so convinced by the obvious (to them) superiority of their national administrative systems that they too fail to recognize how culture bound and idiosyncratic are their ideas and practices and how intimately they are related to their specific circumstances, institutions, and values. They too are guilty of false universality, hoping to convert everyone else to their ways of thinking.

But everybody has the tendency to do the same thing. It is not just patriotism, although many are justifiably proud of their country's administrative legacy. More likely, it is difficult to step outside one's own socialization and to view one's national heritage disinterestedly. Once trapped, one cannot easily escape. Yet some people manage. Employees of international organizations, such as the United Nations family of organizations, do try to take a global view and do endeavor to standardize concepts and procedures around the world. They seek in their awkward ways to internationalize or globalize public administration, as do leading professional associations such as the International Institute of Administrative Sciences and to a lesser extent the American Society for Public Administration and the European Institute of Public Administration. At their meetings and through their publications, they play down the parochial factor. Nonetheless, parochialism has such a powerful hold over public administration that it will take much effort to break it.

THE PULL OF PAROCHIALISM

Parochialism will retain its dominant influence as long as the nation-state is the major actor in public administration. Its grip may be weakened by the imposition of supranational entities from above and the enlargement of local autonomy from below and possibly by the reassessment of its role in contemporary society. But these developments are unlikely to supersede the country approach and concentration on national administrative cultures. After all, the nation-state is real, powerful, and bent on active intervention to improve on the status quo. As such, it requires a large administrative apparatus, both public and private, to enforce its policies, laws, and decisions. This combination of activism and bureaucracy makes the administrative state the natural focus of public administration, not the purely instrumental features of national government (or governance when inclusive of nongovernmental bodies) or the management of public organizations. Ever since the activist secular nation-state emerged gradually on the world scene during the second half of the eighteenth century, public administration has concerned itself largely with the state in action.

Several novel features of this new administrative state together distinguished it from previous forms of government and public management. First, although it might still retain some religious symbols, it was secular, that is, separated entirely from religious doctrines and institutions. Second, its spiritual side was wedded to advancing the public interest, the national interest, and the collective benefit of all its residents. Third, its physical side was held to be collectively owned, as distinct from the personal property of public officeholders held publicly accountable for their administration of it. Fourth, public office was held to be a sacred public trust to be exercised in a publicly responsible manner. Fifth, officeholders were expected to dignify the state, not disgrace it. Sixth, a social contract was implied between officeholders and non-officeholders, which could be nullified by tyrannical, cruel, and unjust actions. Seventh, all without exception were subject to the rule of law and constitutionalism and liable for prosecution for alleged misuse of public authority. Eighth, officeholders were expected to prepare themselves properly, to act professionally, and to enhance the craft of statesmanship or government. Thus administration *of* the public was transformed into administration *for* the public, requiring more than bureaucratic skills or knowledge of the cameral sciences considered useful at the time of transition.

The need to develop a more exact science of public administration became more obvious when over the course of the next 100 years, the new administrative states raised fully equipped, professionally led armies; enlarged huge overseas empires; introduced new forms of taxation; enumerated the population and national assets; financed canal, rail, and highway systems; fostered scientific research and technological development; cared for the poor; provided public schools; experimented with urban policing; reformed laws governing land, property, and investment; enlarged public health and medical services; and encouraged public utilities, museums, galleries, and recreational facilities. By the turn of the twentieth century, several of these activities had become so large and specialized that they required public service professionals and an intellectual concentration of their own. They were hived off almost completely into separate disciplines, such as diplomacy and international relations, criminal justice, military sciences, urban planning, public education, public health, social work, and nursing. Although they all managed to globalize their disciplines, public administration, now resembling more a piece of Gruyere cheese, that is, full of holes, did not. It remained parochial, largely fixed on the idiosyncratic ideas and practices of national administrative systems.

What each state did varied from nation to nation according to its internal dynamics and its external opportunities. Russia and the United States occupied whole continents. Great Britain and France, together with their neighbors, occupied large chunks of other continents. Germany and Italy unified and consolidated. The Scandinavian countries and Switzerland further democratized. Similarly, what instruments they used varied from place to place. The United States and Great Britain stressed free trade, private enterprise, and competition. France and other European countries preferred public law and regulation. The Scandinavians and Germany fostered government intervention and public initiatives. What administrative behavior patterns they exhibited also reflected different national traits. The Russians resorted to harsh authoritarian measures. The central Europeans were inclined to bureaucratic officiousness. The British and Americans were more prone to amateurism and sloppiness. The Scandinavians were more egalitarian and civil, professional and correct compared with the southern Europeans, who were more lax, arbitrary, and slow. These national or allegedly national characteristics could be compared and contrasted, for there were striking resemblances and differences that visitors were quick to notice and discuss among themselves. What was equally significant was that these contrasting styles were exported and imposed on subject peoples around the globe, best illustrated in Africa where the differences between Anglophile and Francophile countries is still marked today.

Well into the twentieth century, the study of public administration largely consisted of learning as much as one could of one's national administrative system and culture and perhaps a smattering of those of the leading nation-states for contrast. Not all of these were fully fledged administrative states yet, and when the list of other countries was expanded one found some very strange creatures. Indeed, classifying countries according to political regime, extent of state intervention, and dominant elite was quite hazardous. It became even more difficult when many colonies became independent states after World War II. One could find theocracies; embryonic administrative states; quasi-administrative states, military-dominant, bureaucratic-dominant, and totalitarian administrative states; and mixtures between. But it did seem in the 1960s that all were set on becoming fully fledged administrative states employing public intervention as their chosen or principal instrument for national development, aided and abetted in this by international agencies.

By now the United States had discovered the rest of the world. Of course, American scholars had known it was there all the time, and despite the country's official policy of isolationalism they had visited other countries where they had compared and contrasted their national administrative system and culture with those elsewhere. A few practitioners had done the same and familiarized themselves with foreign administrative ideas and practices. Some had even become colonial administrators endeavoring to reshape American colonies into mini-Americas capable of taking charge of their own affairs. World War II had ended that naive period of American public administration. Thereafter, Americans had been called upon to confront authoritarian regimes, to rehabilitate and democratize defeated enemies, to staff international organizations, and to aid in the process of worldwide decolonization. Because of wartime destruction and preoccupation with domestic affairs elsewhere, they virtually had the field to themselves. Among them were rampant American cultural imperialists who sought to Americanize the rest of the world or at least those parts independent of the Soviet sphere of influence. Also among them were genuine internationalists and globalists who found a temporary home in the Comparative Administration Group (CAG) of the American Society for Public Administration (ASPA), which linked up with like-minded public administrators in the International Institute of Administrative Sciences and the United Nations Organization to overcome the pull of parochialism.

By the time CAG merged into ASPA's Section for International and Comparative Administration in the mid-1970s, parochialism had barely been dented. Public administration bordered on a country parody, combining several distinctive national traditions and contributions. First, there were the French with their emphasis on state intervention, public (Napoleonic) law and regulation, military organization, and the execution of public policy. Second came the British, who stressed the exercise of public power, governance, public institutions, professionalism, competence, and integrity. Germany stood for Weberian style bureaucracy, administrative science, organizational design and leadership, performance, and effectiveness. The United States (and to a lesser extent Canada) emphasized constitutionalism, human rights, public policy choices, public management, economy and efficiency, due process, and public participation. The Scandinavian contribution included democratization of state administration, ethics, welfare state, humanitarianism, public enterprise, and affordability. Australasia was credited for equity and decency. The Soviet Union had added national planning, state-owned enterprise, collectivization, productivity, and accessibility. Other countries' contributions were barely acknowledged. They were expected to look up to the models exemplified by those fifteen or so world leaders.

Thereafter, CAG's case against parochialism gained momentum. The vaunted models began to unravel. Instead of producing expected results, they fell short or actually failed to produce at all. Many Third World countries that put their faith in the administrative state failed to progress and in some tragic cases declined. Even the wealthiest countries found that many public services were too expensive even for them, and productivity or rather the lack of improvement in performance hardly merited the investment. Too little attention had been paid to the dysfunctions of bureaucracy and the reduction of effectiveness with increased economies of size. The long run of successes of the administrative state had beguiled governments into believing that it could succeed at anything, which they were discovering was not the case. Not only was the administrative state doing things it could not do at all or did worse than nonpublic delivery, but in many functions where it was performing well it was getting out of hand. It was time to step back and consider comparative performance. But parochialism did not allow this. In any event few realistic measures for comparative analysis were adequate for evaluating delivery systems between countries and sectors within countries.

The stumbling of the administrative state was at first hidden by the world boom of the 1960s, which automatically provided sufficient resources for government to conduct business as usual and cover administrative deficiencies. But when boom turned to bust in the 1970s, the situation could no longer be disguised. The administrative state could no longer be guaranteed the resources it needed to continue functioning in its accustomed ways. Hard choices would have to be made as to what to sacrifice unless the world economy recovered; given questions about sustainable development, recovery was unlikely to happen quickly, as turned out to be the case. Meantime, the administrative state was caught off guard by street violence; international terrorism; OPEC-induced energy shortages; illegal markets and underground economies; dramatic shifts in world investment, trade, technology, and commerce; deforestation, over-fishing, and global warming; new killer diseases; and other global problems whose solutions were obstructed by national administrative frameworks.

Impatience with the administrative state mounted. Ideologically, it was no longer seen as a hero but as a villain, not as the solution but as part of the problem. More and more people viewed it more as a stumbling block to national and international development than as an aid. It had grown too big. It had undertaken activities that it could not manage. It had promoted parasitism at the cost of enterprise. It suffered from too many bureaupathologies to be sufficiently economic, productive, efficient, and effective. It would have to be reduced and tamed, thereby releasing scarce resources for private initiatives. It would have to turn over some of its activities to private delivery. It would have to be revitalized and become more businesslike. But how? In this quest for more effective governance, parochialism was irrelevant. Comparative analysis was imperative. More important was the realization that all these problems were universal and had common global roots. Public administration had to shed its parochialism.

Nobody needed any further convincing after the sudden and unexpected collapse of the Communist bloc. Totalitarianism had failed miserably. A heavy-handed administrative state had made too many irrevocable bad decisions with disastrous consequences. Bureaucratic centralism had worked too cumbrously and too slowly. The system had been eaten away by corruption. Disincentives had replaced incentives to work, save, and invest. The quality of public goods and services was generally poor and productivity was too low, given the sacrifices made. Communism had to be dismantled and replaced. But with what? How? Clearly, by a more liberal society with a much-diminished administrative state. But once country after country began to abandon communism and weaken totalitarianism, suppressed political forces reemerged that threatened to split states apart, as they did in the case of the Soviet Union and Yugoslavia, which broke up into several smaller states. How far would destabilization spread? Was any large, diverse state safe? Clearly, public administration needs something much different than the traditional national administrative culture approach to deal with the emerging reconstructed world political and economic order.

MAKING PUBLIC ADMINISTRATION DISTINCTIVE

The most pressing issue is the separate identity of something calling itself public administration. Only in the United States has public administration firmly established itself as a distinct discipline or separate field of study, and even there it is beset still by self-doubts as to whether it deserves independence. Elsewhere, public administration is part of another discipline such as law, government, political science, or administrative science, where it is considered a specialization. Public administration has yet to decide whether it is a supradiscipline, a discipline, or a subdiscipline and whether its practitioners belong to a master profession that includes all public employees or constitute a profession of government that would line up alongside other recognized professions or belong to several public service professions. It does not know whether it is any of these or just a special focus of interest, concentrating on governance, government, public policy and management, public sector, public bureaucracy, public goods and services delivery, and public and administrative law or on just some of these or all of these and more. It cannot decide where in this universe of the administrative state it should confine itself, letting go of all or most of the holes that have been carved out by other special interests like the military, police, diplomatic corps, social work, librarianship, and nursing, which all claim, unlike public administration, to have a distinct universalistic theoretical base, commonly shared practitioner concerns, and similar technology. Divided on all these issues, it cannot fend off powerful rivals that nibble at its edges and every so often lay claim to sizable parts of its domain or internal aspirants who wish to break away on their own with their own particular pieces like public policy or international organization or parastatal entities (quasi-autonomous nongovernmental organizations or QANGO). Various permutations and combinations of these divisions can be found throughout the world and can be illustrated by the motley titles of American graduate schools belonging to the National Association of Schools of Public Affairs and Administration.

What is distinctive about public administration is that it is *public* and that at heart it contains the essence of the administrative state. To understand its distinctiveness means joining forces with other disciplines that also contain a significant dose of publicness and also have a large interest in the state as the institutionalization of collective decision-making and action. The social sciences and public professions between them define the nature of the collective being and what constitutes its publicness. Then each uses its own special lens to study what it believes to be its own particular concerns, which invariably overlap because they are parts of an indivisible object.

Public administration employs not the legal or economic or political or social lens but the *administrative* lens, concentrating on what does or does not work in the collective interest, what is or is not useful for the common welfare, what is or is not economic, productive, efficient, effective, valuable, decent, humane, honest, fair, accessible, convenient, sensible, and right, and what is or is not publicly accountable and subject to institutional fail-safe devices against contempt of public trust. Although public administration shares much with other social sciences, it does have this distinctive intellectual and practical territory to itself. Moreover, that territory lends itself to universalistic thinking and practice just as other distinctive territories, a universalism that is not confined in space or time.

Unfortunately, preoccupation with parochialism has prevented public administration from developing universalistic frameworks and general theories. Much is still missing that would provide public administration with such a distinctive body of theory. Among key components that still need common agreement and upon which common agreement is within reach are the following elements:

- a theory of collective intervention
- a theory of the public interest
- a theory of public trust, responsibility, and accountability
- a theory of public law
- a theory of collective regulation
- a theory of public policy
- a theory of public goods and services (ownership)
- a theory of public initiatives and enterprise
- a theory of public investment and employment
- a theory of public rights and obligations (citizenship)
- a theory of public bureaucracy

- a theory of parastatals (QANGOs)
- a theory of public planning and utilization of resources
- a theory of collective security, safety, and survival
- a theory of social welfare and equity
- a theory of public value
- a theory of public accessibility
- a theory of public service
- a theory of public conduct
- a theory of administrative due process
- a theory of public maladministration
- a theory of privacy and collective limitations
- a theory of public control and participation
- a theory of public management
- a theory of public evaluation
- a theory of public finance (budgeting, accounting, auditing, debt, taxation)
- a theory of human resources management
- a theory of the good society.

Many of these universalistic theories of public administration are almost complete and meet with worldwide approval at least in lip service. Others are highly disputed as being too culture bound or parochial as formulated and not universally valid. Some are still on the drafting board in sketchy outlines only. All are capable when properly developed of providing public administration with a strong intellectual foundation stripped of parochialism. They all apply to public administration wherever found and practiced irrespective of locale, from the smallest hamlet to the largest international (and perhaps one day interplanetary) organization. Where they fit constitutes the distinctive area occupied and rightly governed by public administration.

IMPROVING PUBLIC ADMINISTRATION PERFORMANCE

What distinguishes public administration from other disciplines and what makes it so controversial is that it also has a mission to improve the performance of its practitioners. It feels obliged to advance the state of the art. This is not just in response to criticism of public maladministration, although that is reason enough. There has been a moralistic streak to excel among its progressive practitioners, who have experienced much internal conservatism, indifference, and hostility. The drive to reform and revitalize poorly performing public organizations has largely come from within. The general public and career politicians have only fitfully concerned themselves with administrative matters, having more important things on their minds and being unlearned in the whys and wherefores of public administration, which they have left largely to the professionals to settle among themselves. On the whole, the professionals have responded well within their narrow technical confines, but they have not been able to do much beyond them or have disagreed. Busy people, they have rarely had the opportunity of stepping back and looking critically on their handiwork or the means to make more than incremental changes. Unless some public scandal has forced action, they tend to let things drift and proceed as usual. After all,

> Public policy makers and managers work in complex political and bureau-
> cratic environments, responding to a multiplicity of competing goals,
> suffering from "information overload," and never armed with sufficient
> staff, time or financial resources to meet all the demands placed on them.
> Responsibility and authority are fragmented among multiple public agen-
> cies, among different levels of government, and between the public and
> private sectors. Services are fragmented among programs with overlap-
> ping but different goals. Even within a single agency or program, there is
> disagreement over what would constitute "high performance": disagree-
> ment over goals, over priorities, disagreement over the most important
> measures of performance. Policy makers and managers lack information
> on current performance and lack information on how to achieve higher
> performance. Given the constraints, uncertainties, and disincentives they
> face, policy makers and managers tend to place relatively low priority on
> improving the performance of the agencies and programs for which they
> are responsible. (Wholey and Newcomer 1989: 1)

Consequently, despite the advocacy of reform and overhaul, not much happens in practice; when it does, compromise prevails and things tend to drift back to where they used to be. In the absence of other incentives to improve, self-mo-tivation may be inadequate to raise public administration performance.

Again, this practical issue is universal. There is too much public maladmin-istration everywhere. There is room for improvement, in some public agencies much room for improvement, again irrespective of locale. Just as one finds well-administered public agencies in the unlikeliest places, so too one finds poorly administered agencies in the most highly respected systems. The crite-rion of performance is deliberately chosen in preference to more technical measures because it is more inclusive and it is conditional on the circumstances. Performance is also related to public expectations; although an agency might be doing well by its own professional standards, it still may not be doing well enough from the public's perspective. Its poor public image may be due to factors beyond its control, which also have to be taken into account.

When all the factors necessary to improve public administration performance are included, a practical as well as a theoretical framework is given for a universalistic public administration. The variety of these factors shows how much public administration is integrated into contemporary global society. Even if the more limited definition of administrative reform suggested by the United Nations, "the deliberate use of authority and influence to apply new measures to an administrative system so as to change its goals, structures and procedures with a view to improving it for development purposes" (United Nations 1983: 1), were employed, one would still be forced to consider the ends sought, not just the means, which takes us far afield of traditional public administration.

To minimalize its core boundaries, public administration could keep to the territory traditionally contained within the folklore of administrative reform, which has been universally accepted since the 1960s. It contains the following major areas for constant revision and overhaul:

- scope and activities for public intervention and determination
- nature of public power and authority
- national agenda setting and national planning
- public information and public relations
- machinery of government and organizational design
- rule of law and administrative discretion
- public policy-making
- public entitlements
- public program execution and delivery
- public physical planning and public works design
- public finance
- public infrastructure and public sector employment
- public regulation
- public property
- public capital formation
- general administrative services
- publicly sponsored enterprises and parastatals (QANGOs)
- public management practices
- public ethics and official conduct
- public participation and citizenship

- public control and accountability
- public administration research, education, and training.

An urgent item is restoring the image and status of public sector employment, which has taken a heavy beating in the last decade and is still being undermined worldwide by the policy of the International Monetary Fund. Another priority is the need to overhaul military administration, which everywhere absorbs inordinate public resources for questionable returns. Finally, corruption also detracts universally from performance, and around the globe internationally organized crime seeks to penetrate the public sector and expand its share of available public spoils.

What is important to stress is that these areas are all common to public administration and that comparative experience is useful in improving the performance of public agencies, irrespective of their context and peculiarities. Much can be learned from studying the mistakes of others as well as their successes. There is no need to keep reinventing the wheel. Reliable and accessible studies accumulate. Regular meetings of those undertaking administrative reform take place annually around the globe. Administrative reformers seem to enjoy exchanging war stories and sharing their lessons. A body of universally valid information on practical concerns exists, the stuff on which good universalistic theory can evolve. More importantly, it is the stuff out of which good universalistic practices can also spread.

ASSESSING PUBLIC ADMINISTRATION ACHIEVEMENTS

Improving the performance of public administration requires a base line, a time scale, and suitable performance indicators for each and every public agency, activity, function, and administrative system. In the absence of market-imposed discipline, such improvement is out of the question. Although much progress has been made over the past few decades, attaining acceptable indicators of adequate performance is still in its infancy. Virtually nothing has been done at the international level where, in the absence of concrete measures and critical self-assessments, international agencies reassure the world that they are doing their best in the circumstances and indulge in much self-justifying and in self-congratulatory public relations. They are much better at measuring or attempting to evaluate member-country efforts on a comparative basis, which provides approximate ideas about country achievements. Some national governments are beginning likewise to assess the performance of subunits within their administrative systems, although they have yet to get much beyond the drafting board.

The problems involved in reaching and applying appropriate guidelines and measures are among the most intricate and taxing in the social sciences.

Progress would be slow in any event, given all the goodwill in the world and serious resolve to do a good job. But so far the goodwill has been slow in coming and serious resolve even more sluggish. Possibly the International Monetary Fund has had the most success, but it started out with the advantage of international consensus among most world economists about the ingredients of economic indicators and considerable investments in statistical services around the globe. Closely related organizations like the International Labor Organization and the World Bank have also benefited. The World Health Organization has done well out of the banks of medical records and statistics that most governments have kept for several decades. But strangely, one of the oldest international organizations, the International Postal Union, has not shown the same enthusiasm for assessing comparative country performance in delivering the mail. Thus, while the international community eagerly awaits the assessments by Amnesty International and the U.S. Department of State of the world situation as regards human rights in general and the status of political prisoners in particular and the reports of the United Nations on world social development indicators and of the World Bank on world economic development indicators to see how individual countries are faring, it has very little reliable information on comparative administrative performance.

The closest attempt to fill some of the void was made nearly two decades ago by Robert Fried in *Performance in American Bureaucracy* (1976), whose introductory framework provided a basis for comparing state performance. He suggested three major summary criteria: (1) effectiveness—how well a system achieves its goals, (2) responsiveness—congruence between the system's goals and those desired by the public, and (3) liberalism—amount of respect shown by the system for human rights, by which he defined performance as "effectiveness in securing collective goals by due process." Is public administration making things better or worse, for whom, by what standards, and why? What are its consequences for the quality of life of every individual, group, and community it is supposed to serve? (Fried 1976: 20). Extrapolating from his analysis, indicators of public administration performance would include:

- assessment of public leadership
- assessment of diplomatic efforts in warding off foreign exploitation and internal ability to protect sovereignty
- assessment of internal security, stability, law-abidingness, criminality, and violence
- assessment of economic well-being and economic performance
- assessment of the quality of life and social well-being
- assessment of political performance, constitutionalism, political representativeness, human rights, freedom, and civic culture

- assessment of credit-worthiness of the state, its financial management performance, and value from public investment
- assessment of equal opportunity in public employment, competence of public employees, and fair labor practices
- assessment of administrative due process
- assessment of official corruption and public restitution
- assessment of public accountability
- assessment of official–public relations
- assessment of functional productivity and enterprise

Each of these would no doubt merit several subcategories. Probably, right now, somewhere around the world, hordes of administrative assessors are filling them in. At their head are the value-for-money auditors who seek the best possible use of public funds. Although they do not demand perfection of public administrators, they do expect them to meet reasonable expectations and to ensure value for money. They go well beyond financial audits to challenge government policy, administrative assessments, and managerial qualities. They shift direction from the adequacy of administrative processes to the overall impact of government performance.

If this trend continues, value-for-money indicators will eventually link up with several other indicators that are being developed:

- net national product indicators
- national security indicators
- public sector economic indicators
- social justice indicators
- health and welfare indicators
- crime and safety indicators
- education and research indicators
- environmental indicators
- international treasures indicators (Caiden 1991c: 302)

Soon, the myth that government is different (from business) and that its outputs cannot be measured will be dispelled. Once the indicators are employed, they should have a momentum of their own, propelling administrative reform and improved performance as they are important tools for goal setting, strategic planning, monitoring, and feedback. They should point to the possible elimination of unnecessary government intervention, the reduction of costs, and an increase in public sector productivity and government performance. Again, their adoption will speed the globalization of public administration theory and practice because if they work in any part of the world, they should work elsewhere and their use somewhere should stimulate their employment everywhere. Failure to adopt them after their demonstrable utility would be professionally indicting.

CONCLUSION

The emerging New World Order demands a public administration that is far less parochial and more genuinely globalized or internationalized. Many human problems cannot be tackled on a country-by-country basis; they are global in scope. Feasible solutions can be found only on a global basis through an enlarged international policy-making network relying on expanded international organization and much-improved nation-state administrative systems. Parochial solutions will not work, but only exacerbate the problems. Public administrators need to jettison much of their parochialism and their parochial thinking. They need to globalize their theory and practice. A start could be made by reorganizing what they already know into different global frameworks rather than searching for new knowledge within existing parochial frameworks. Three illustrations of the kinds of new thinking required have been suggested, one dealing with the essence of *public* administration, another with improving administrative performance, and a third outlining indicators of administrative performance. Together, they indicate that instead of searching the heavens for new ideas to perfect public administration on this planet, one should rearrange what is already known to reduce public maladministration globally.

3

THE NEW WORLD ORDER AND GLOBAL PUBLIC ADMINISTRATION
A Critical Essay

ALI FARAZMAND

The history of world civilization has always been characterized by revolutionary upheavals and changes in human organization of governance and in political, social, and economic structures of societies. Both quantitative and qualitative changes have contributed to the evolutionary process of human societies and to their social systems. The qualitative, transformational changes from slavery and feudalism to capitalism have been a remarkable human progress. If we accept the Marxist view of historical evolution, the next transformational qualitative change would have to be to socialism and communism. But the fall of the Soviet Union and most other socialist systems has led to a widespread belief in the death of socialism and communism. Whether this is a foregone conclusion or an illusion is not the concern of this essay. Nonetheless, it is a relevant point, for the changes of the twentieth century have been of a different nature with far different significance and with fundamental implications for public administration theory and practice.

The rise and fall of empires from ancient times, the rise of the nation-states, and the revolutions in science and technology have brought significant qualitative changes to human civilization. But the twentieth century has been a turning point in human history. Fundamental political, social, economic, cultural, and scientific changes in this century have been remarkable. The bourgeois transformation of feudal and absolute systems of empires, the reign of mercantilism-colonialism and its transformation to modern capitalism and imperialism, and the following revolutionary changes leading to decolonialization and the emergence of new nation-states are among the most outstanding transformational, qualitative changes that occurred during this century. Perhaps one of the most outstanding changes of this century was the emergence of the new sociopolitical system of world socialism as a result of the Russian Revolution of 1917.

The rise of world socialism led by the Soviet Union altered the nature of ideological, political, social, cultural, and military relations at global level for the next seventy years, until 1992. The global division into capitalist and socialist camps was not an illusion; it was a profound division with profound implications for politics, economics, and public administration. More than anything else, perhaps, it had tremendous implications for the Third World countries struggling for the numerous advantages the advanced industrialized nations of the West have taken for granted for a long time. The polarization of the world into two global camps was further reinforced after World War II; the victorious Allies, including the Soviet Union—with a human loss of twenty million of its population—defeated Nazi Germany and Japan, two warring nations claiming global superiority. Had they succeeded in defeating the Allies, what would have been the fate of the nations and their peoples today? But that is not the issue here. The relevant issue is that Hitler and Mussolini also claimed a new "world order." Hitler's vision was perhaps a global system of government under Germany; he definitely had a global design in mind.

In short, the Cold War era was a major change with great implications for humanity and the nations. The socialist system promoted a greater need for trained and professional public administrators to manage a huge, monopolized economy. The capitalist nations of the West invested tremendous amounts of resources every year in infrastructural programs and in economic projects domestically and internationally to outcompete the socialist system, which was always struggling to compete with the West but, less exploitative by nature, had little success in competing with the capitalist system.

Both systems devoted monumental amounts of resources and energy to military competition, and both engaged in a constant war of attrition through their client states or peoples. The Cold War was fought in many grounds, but it was also always fought as a "hot war" in developing countries. In the capitalist nations the governments were forced to take a more active role in resource allocation, in redistribution of wealth, in managing the disenchanted citizens, and in controlling the "explosive mix" of their populations. They spent more and more on "welfare" measures in order to prevent potential revolutions, to level off income distributions, and to save and enhance their systems. They faced many crises and responded to these crises in many ways.

The rise of the welfare state or administrative state has been a direct result of the inevitable responses the modern capitalist system has had to introduce. There has been an increasing expansion of the administrative state and a greater demand for professionalization of public administration in the capitalist nations, both developed and developing, ever since the turn of this century. An immediate implication of this global trend has been a greater demand for a theory of public administration as a self-conscious enterprise as well as for a continuous expansion of public administration. But the trend tended to take a different global swing in the 1980s, when neoconservative politicians and their economic allies were able to take leadership seats in Washington and London.

Privatization and the turning back of many state functions to the private sector were the ideological answer to the many deep problems of the economic crisis that the capitalist systems have been facing since the 1970s. The market was considered the only answer to economic and social problems. That ideological current for a decade had fundamental impacts on all aspects of politics and administration not only in the United States and Great Britain but also almost everywhere else on the globe. Such a trend is still in full motion, although it has somewhat slowed down recently. Change, therefore, has been a key denominator of twentieth-century history, as it has always been.

Unfortunately, not all these changes have been positive. The ability to destroy the environment and all humanity is a consequence that is also associated with the twentieth century. This is not the place to analyze the nature and significance of "change" in human history. However, it is important to note that change has been the norm of history, politically and socioeconomically. If change has been the norm, so has been continuity in the social system structure and process of societies. Hence, it seems that both change and continuity work together in a dialectical way, both reinforcing each other and bringing qualitative transformation to human society.

The significant revolutionary upheavals and changes that have taken place in governments and in their economic and political systems since the 1970s have had profound structural consequences economically, politically, and administratively for peoples in various societies. However, fundamental inconsistencies characterize these changes and the forces or ideologies—external or internal—that are behind them. Just as the formerly divided world had major implications for public administration, so the fall of the Soviet Union and socialist power and the new global era have important but contradictory implications for public administration and public management.

The only superpower leading and dominating the world is the United States, with its allies sharing the same ideology and goals. Almost the entire world, developing and developed, is forced to adjust to the new global conditions and reconfigurations dominated by the United States and other major Western nations. Undoubtedly, there are many positive and negative aspects of this new changing world order dominated by the United States. Social scientists have been less critical about the usage of this term. Some public administrationists have enthusiastically analyzed the emerging global order with implications for public administration. The concept of "globalism," not even mentioned in most textbooks of the field, has suddenly become a frequently cited term in public administration publications. Globalism and global interdependence are frequent subjects and topics of conferences and publications. Some theorists have even attempted to develop a universal, global theory of public administration (Caiden 1991b), and others have envisioned a new world of public administration in a "global village" (Garcia-Zamor 1992; Khator 1992a).

This chapter attempts to analyze some of the key changing patterns of public administration and politics under the New World Order, or "disorder," as some critics (Sedghi 1992) have argued, and also to suggest an emerging global public administration. The focus is on the following five topics: (1) the nature of the New World Order and what it would mean for different countries; (2) the global slogan of democratization and its theoretical and practical paradoxes or inconsistencies around the world; (3) marketization and globalized privatization; (4) the issue of structural adjustments in political, economic, and administrative systems in various countries with uneven consequences in prospect for an emerging "global public administration model"; and (5) the challenges and opportunities that these changes and newly global public administration will likely create for public management education and practice around the globe. The chapter's conclusion pulls together the overall discussions.

THE NATURE OF THE NEW WORLD ORDER

The concept of a New World Order is a rhetorical device that is not new. In fact, it is as old as the notion of empire building in ancient times. When Cyrus the Great conquered virtually the entire known world and expanded his "World-State" Persian Achaemenid Empire, his vision was to create a synthesis of civilization and to unite all peoples of the world under the universal Persian rule with a global world order characterized by peace, stability, economic prosperity, and religious and cultural tolerance. For two centuries that world order was maintained by both military might and Persian gold: Whenever the military force was not applicable, the gold did the job; and in most cases both the military and the gold functioned together (Frye 1963, 1975; Farazmand 1991a). Similarly, Alexander the Great also established a New World Order. The Romans and the following mighty empires had the same concept in mind. The concept was also very fashionable after World War I and World War II. The world order of the twentieth century was until recently a shared one, dominated by the two superpowers of the United States and the USSR.

This world order was dual in nature, characterized by superpower competition, rivalry, suspicion, hostility, and wasteful consumption of human, natural, material, and technological resources in all spheres of life. Ideology played a key role in the two world systems. Consequently, players in the international arena—politicians, administrators, theorists, and the like—knew what the dividing lines were. The rules of the game were spelled out under this dual world order system, and events seemed predictable to a great extent. In an excellent book, *Turbulence in World Politics*, James Rosenau (1990) gave a clear picture of the New World Order to emerge from this new world system characterized by constant change and challenges. To Rosenau, the new world system would enjoy more stability and peace than ever before. He predicted that ideology would decay, governments would narrow in competence, people would demand more and that "an emergent global culture" would be characterized by global interdependence (Rosenau 1990: 419). Somewhat similar arguments were made earlier in a collection of essays edited by Keohane and Nye (1977) in their book, *Power and Interdependence*.

With the emergence of Gorbachev as the reformist leader of the Soviet Union calling for restructuring, openness, a new way of global thinking, peace for all, superpower cooperation, and an end to the Cold War era, the concept of a New World Order emerged again. In fact, Gorbachev used the term in his speech addressed to the U.N. General Assembly in December 1988, at which then U.S. President Reagan and Vice President Bush were present (Sedghi 1992). After the Helsinki summit with Gorbachev in September 1990, Bush increasingly used the term. It should make no difference who borrowed the term from whom. What is important is its meaning and implications.

The New World Order denotes a system of collective world security where states and peoples can live in peace with each other, ideologies aside, and "observe each other's borders and maintain collective security interests" (Sedghi 1992: 62). Policing others will not be required by powerful states; rather, a combination of several states will maintain stability in unstable areas. The Persian Gulf War was arguably fought in the service of the New World Order. In fact, during that international crisis, Bush announced that the war was to "stand up for what is right and condemn what is wrong" (Trudeau 1992: 21).

Two schools of thought seem to have dominated the literature on world order and global power relationships: the "declinist" and the "anti-declinist." Analyzing the "longevity" of the U.S. ability to maintain the "number one" position in world affairs, the declinists, represented by Paul Kennedy (1989), make analogies with previous Great Powers and point to the risks they ran: Their imperial stretch went too far, and their deaths eventually did come. According to Kennedy, America will inevitably decline because of the imperative economic development at home, the imbalance in international military commitments, and the changing nature of the global power players. Rejecting this view, the anti-declinists, represented by Rostow (1988) and Brzezinski (1986), argue that the United States is more powerful than any other country in the world and will continue to occupy the leading position in international affairs.

Regardless of which school of thought is accepted, the fundamental underpinnings of this New World Order include the following: U.S. military might and its capability to destroy the world, an unprecedented phenomenon in world history; the globalized economic nature of the United States, with its performance crisis at home and its corporate opportunities and dominance abroad; her cultural penetration and dominance of the global environment; her self-declared guardianship of the marketplace and its ideology; her political ability to maneuver globally on economic and military grounds; her ability to manipulate the United Nations as a collective instrumentality for action legitimation; the young age of the nation and its people; the lack of another superpower as competition; and the economic system of capitalism with its global penetration and dominance.

The United States has achieved outstanding economic and military might in a relatively short period of time, and the nation still is full of youthful energy. Defending U.S. interests globally is the central aspect of the New World Order (Hamilton 1989). Under the New World Order the United Nations and its vast number of affiliated organizations will likely play a more active role in various international affairs, primarily under the U.S. hegemonic banner. It will serve as a conduit for legitimating international actions or inactions. "National sovereignty" may be overridden by international community actions, and a "world government" with a "global management" will likely emerge (Wilson 1994).

Whatever the argument, the United States will no doubt continue to play the leadership role in the New World Order based on such underpinnings. But what will this mean for other developed and developing nations? It is beyond the scope of this chapter to analyze this question fully, but suffice it to say that the implications are far greater for developing nations than for the advanced ones. Unlike the past, the new era will likely be characterized by North–South conflicts and struggles. The New World Order will have major consequences for developing nations and their public administration. It will have a complex web of dominant structures that will encompass the developing nations' economic, political, social, cultural, security, and military systems. There will be few, if any, nations capable of escaping such a penetrating and dominating structure. Exceptions will likely exist, however.

Governments in the developing world will likely adopt similar policies toward their domestic and international affairs. Washington will be the city that most roads will lead to. The developed countries of the world will probably resemble the United States to some extent, but internal competition and rivalry are also likely to drive advanced nations like Germany, France, and Japan in the race for global market supremacy. However, the military and science and technology and their selective application will likely keep the United States in the leading position for decades to come as long as it is willing to press for global submission, defend the capitalists and large landowners around the world, protect global trade routes, police the world, and provide an "insurance policy" for the free world (Klare 1988, 1990).

Under the dual world order, the two superpowers and their allies provided support and protection to developing nations struggling for independence from the colonial rule or experiencing internal revolutions. The superpowers counterbalanced each other in the international community of nations. As under the New World Order there will be no such counterbalancing, the New World Order will have uneven consequences for developing versus developed nations, the former being subjected to pressures from every direction. As will be seen later, this fact has major implications, positive and negative, for developing nations and for some developed countries.

DEMOCRATIZATION

A key aspect of the New World Order is claimed to be democracy and democratization. Democracy and democratization as political processes are valued as basic foundations for human freedom and free society. It is argued that the socialist systems of the Soviet Union and Eastern Europe, as well as others in Africa and Asia, have not been democratic. Their totalitarian system has been centralized and controlled by a planned, command economy inhibiting individual freedom and incentives for growth. The only way to be free, then, is to get rid of this system and to join the free capitalist world in which the marketplace provides all opportunities for individual growth and economic development. Politically, individuals are free to choose their preferences, which is done through voting. Voting is therefore considered an exercise of individual freedom, a necessary condition for good citizenship.

The concept of democracy, however, is not clearly defined. There are confusions over the fundamentals of its meaning. Various theories attempt to explain it from various perspectives. The Marxists present several forms of democracy, including feudal democracy; capitalist or bourgeois democracy, in which the upper-class minority rules the middle class and the working class; socialist democracy, in which the majority of the working class and the middle class rule the minority through the state ownership of almost all properties; and communist democracy, a classless society, in which there is no class-based ruler (Lenin 1971).

The pluralistic explanation of democracy rests primarily not on class-based society, but on the function of different groups, all striving for collective decisions through participation, compromises, and majority rule. Citizens get organized into interest groups in order to influence or to change the decision structures in pursuit of maximizing their interests. Participation through voting is an essential aspect of the democratic process leading to the election of representative officials and separation of powers regulated by constitutional laws. Money, however, is a key requirement for success in pluralism, for those with more resources are better organized and are better equipped to influence the public policy process and policy outcomes (Jones 1984; Parenti 1988; Zeigler 1964). While conservatives favor a limited role of government in society and economy, liberals realize a more active governmental role. Both viewpoints stress the central role of elections for regime legitimation and agree on having private enterprise or the market as the economic basis in society (Dahl 1971; DiPalma 1990; Huntington 1991; Luebert 1991).

Diamond, Linz, and Lipset (1990: 6) define democracy to "signify a political system, separate and apart from the economic and social system to which it is joined." The proponents of the market-based elite theory of democracy (Dye and Zeigler 1990) and the critical theorists (Parenti 1988) argue for a democracy based on broad representation, but the latter is critical of the pluralistic system in which democracy works for the "few," those who have the "sword and the dollar" (Parenti 1989).

Whatever the ideological underpinning, the term *democracy* is appealing to peoples around the world. A key problem, therefore, is the confusion over its meaning. As Waldo notes, the definitional problem is "severe." "Democracy of course means 'rule by the people.' But what does that mean?" asks Waldo (1990: 202). Obviously, the confusion arises when key questions are raised over who the people are, what the rule is to look like, who makes the rule, and what limitations exist to control the rulers. The problem seems to be solved by the strictly political meaning of democracy as a commonly accepted Western concept to denote "secret or at least uncoerced voting, broad suffrage, free expression, free association (including the right to form political parties), representation, legislative bodies, [and] a considerable respect for and guarantees of rights" (Waldo 1990: 202–204). Waldo soundly defines democracy as "a striving toward equality and freedom."

However, an immediate problem may arise from this sound definition: How long should a people or nation strive toward equality and freedom? Who should determine that period? Dictators around the world, from Somoza of Nicaragua to the shah of Iran, from General Pinochet of Chile to Marcos of the Philippines, and others elsewhere frequently argued that their peoples were not ready for democracy and freedom and that freedom is dangerous and that there should be a long waiting term! Are elections sufficient to ensure representation? Who usually is able to run and get elected to public office in a market-based society? Above all, can a democratic society or people or its government promote or support authoritarian regimes or help overthrow democratically elected representative governments abroad because they are not friendly to other democratic governments, say, the United States? Put differently, can the United States as a democratic form of government remain democratic when it continues to support nondemocratic, repressive regimes around the world? Is there a contradiction or inconsistency here? These are some of the key questions critics raise.

As the leader of the free world, the United States has claimed to promote democracy and democratization abroad. "Exporting democracy" has been an international role the United States has played for decades, with some qualifying positive results (Lowenthal 1991). But the record does not seem to be very encouraging. In fact, great democracies of the West including the United States have a strong record of supporting "some of the most repressive and exploitative dictatorships" around the globe (Kitschell 1992). Many revolutions of the twentieth century occurred as a result of such support of those repressive regimes by the

United States and other Western nations (Farazmand 1991b; Schutz and Slater 1990). Whether fighting communism in the Cold War era is a justifiable reason, as many argue, or simply serving the American national and business interests, as others have argued, is not the point here. The point is that there is an inconsistency in the way that the great democratic powers of the free world carry out the democratization slogan. Cases like Iran, Chile, Turkey, Egypt, Zaire, Argentina, Nicaragua, and the Philippines, to name a few, are good examples.

The slogan of democratization has been emphasized as a necessary condition for normalizing relations with governments that are not so friendly and with some with socialist orientations, such as Nicaragua under the Sandinistas, Angola, Vietnam, North Korea, and Cuba. During the gigantic wave of major changes taking place in the Soviet Union and the Eastern European nations, the United States and other major Western powers seem to have encouraged and supported democratization through political elections and representations. While democratization of the socialist "totalitarian" systems has been emphasized, repressive regimes around the world have continued to receive the full political, military, and economic support of the United States. Hence, there is a big inconsistency in raising the slogan of democratization in the free world.

It may be argued that the major source of this inconsistency would have to rest on the problem of equating democracy with market. Therefore, the global slogan of democratization is misleading and may have dangerous consequences. It is misleading because it is equated with market supremacy while market and democratic ideals have many reasons to clash and contradict on both individual and societal levels. As Heilbroner (1990: 105) notes, "It is of course, foolish to suggest that capitalism is the *sine qua non* of democracy, or to claim that democracy, with its commitment to political equality, does not conflict in many ways with the inequalities built into capitalism." But this equating concept has been repeatedly used by both politicians and social scientists, including public administrationists. Marketization of the socialist world is considered democratization, even without elections. And the nondemocratic regimes of Africa, Asia, the Middle East, and Latin America with market-based economic systems are considered already democratic and therefore part of the free world. No free political parties, no free associations, no free labor unions, no freedom of expression, and no representative governments exist in most of these nations; their elections, if any, are usually farcical and meaningless and are "demonstration elections" (Hermand and Broadhead 1984). Nicaragua under Somoza had an election a few months before the popular revolution toppled the regime. Similar phenomena were observed in Iran under the shah and in the Middle East (Bill 1984; Binder 1962; Farazmand 1989a).

Democratization as a slogan is also dangerous because it has been applied unevenly and inconsistently. While socialist and independent states are targeted for democratization, dictatorship in friendly states with market capitalism is often overlooked, to say the least, and justified, promoted, and protected for national and business/corporate interests[1] (Gibbs 1991; Hamilton 1989). The democratization slogan is further dangerous because it tends to raise expectations for freedom and democracy among peoples who may choose alternative democratic governments not too friendly to the West. An example is the Kurdish and Shia peoples in Iraq, who were highly encouraged by the U.S. slogan of democratization during and after the Persian Gulf War but were allowed to be slaughtered by Saddam Hussein's repressive regime.

The neoconservative democratic theory of the last two decades seems to have dominated the entire world. Based on the neoclassical conservative "public choice" theory, methodological individualism and the decentralization of organizational and administrative arrangements for service delivery are the central characteristics of the market-based democratic model. The individual is seen as a self-interested, self-utility maximizer in the marketplace, searching freely with adequate information for political, economic, and administrative choices that maximize his or her interests. Therefore, the free, self-maximizing individual engages in collective actions that would benefit his or her self-interests both domestically and internationally.

Highly promoted under the Reagan administration in the United States and abroad in the 1980s and still dominating the world, this conservative theory has had profound implications for public administration and politics around the globe; it is a market theory of democracy, organization, and public administration. It has called for shrinking government, limiting its intervention in society and economy, market supremacy, and consumer sovereignty (Buchanan and Tullock 1962; Downs 1957; Ostrom 1973). Despite its intellectual and theoretical utilities, the market-based public choice democratic theory has serious flaws and is criticized on many grounds (DeGregori 1974; Golembiewski 1977; Farazmand 1994b).

The market-based conservative economic theory of democracy has been internationalized since the 1980s and has been an integral part of the New World Order, as explained below. Equating democracy with market alone, therefore, has been a major pattern pervading public administration and will likely continue, despite the election of Democrats to office in the United States. Unfortunately, students and scholars of public administration have used the concept of democratization and marketization uncritically, which has set a distorted trend of explaining public administration in democracy.

MARKETIZATION AND PRIVATIZATION

Marketization and privatization are two key elements or requirements that have been emphasized by the United States and other Western nations. Both concepts have been elevated to an ideological level, particularly during the 1980s, in the United States and Britain. Conservative governments under Reagan and Thatcher pursued a rigorous policy of privatization in America and

England, with serious consequences for public administration and for developing nations. Although privatization of public, government-owned enterprises has been pursued nonstop everywhere, it is more intense in the former socialist nations in Eastern Europe and in the nations of Asia and Africa. Marketization and the privatization of public sector functions have been major preconditions for democratic development and requirements for foreign aid to these and other nations. The newly independent nations of the former USSR and the Eastern European socialist countries have adopted the market system. The American and Western European experts have been consulting them on how fast to implement it. The countries resisting full-fledged marketization have not received important support—financial or political—from the capitalist powers. Investment in these nations has been withheld by multinational corporations. Under pressure many formerly socialist nations of Eastern Europe have already marketized their economies.

At the same time, the privatization of state-owned enterprises is also being pursued in capitalist nations, developed and developing, East and West. Research on privatization is growing every day and has already produced a significant body of literature, but the results are mixed. Privatization is not a new concept; in fact, most nations have experienced it over time. What is significant about it today is that it has become almost a theology in politics and administration. It has been considered a solution to most problems supposedly created by big government and by the welfare state. It is beyond the scope of this essay to analyze the theoretical, practical, and ideological aspects of this concept. What follows is a brief discussion of privatization and its forms and its implications for global public administration.

Elsewhere (Farazmand 1989b), I have argued that two of the central characteristics of the American political system are its "consistent inconsistency" and its "reactive nature." For almost a century, the two ideological, political, and economic orientations of conservatism and liberalism represented by the Republican and Democratic parties have dominated the policy process and outcomes in the United States, creating a framework or mainstream arena for acceptable and unacceptable policy choices. The inconsistency has consistently appeared in society when one political party in power tried to undo what the other party administration had introduced and implemented. For example, the Berger Court tried to undo what the Warren Court had accomplished. Similarly, the Reagan administration tried, and succeeded to some extent, in undoing what had been accomplished by the Roosevelt administration during the New Deal era. The damages of the 1980s to the economy and society are now being repaired by the new administration. These inconsistencies have consistently produced damaging effects to the society, economy, and peoples. Certainly, they have had major implications for public administration.

The "reactive nature" of the government and political system may be explained by its tendency to act after damages have been inflicted and problems or crises have occurred. The history of the United States and many other capitalist nations is characterized by periodic crises in economic and political systems. The state and its public administration have also faced significant crises of legitimacy as a result of these (Arrow 1963; Farazmand 1989b; Habermass 1975; Macpherson 1987; O'Conner 1973; Offe 1985). The state must respond in a reactive way to the crises and problems that it faces. For several decades, the administrative state was allowed to grow. The 1980s was the turning point, and the 1990s are the years to repair the damages to the infrastructure and other aspects of society. This damage was done mainly by equating the concept of conservative democracy with marketization and privatization. But the monumental literature on market failure seems to have been overlooked or ignored, and the government has been advised to turn its functions over to the private sector for efficiency and economy. However, the purpose of democratic governments is not to produce efficiency, although it is a desirable objective. Rather, they must provide economic, social, and political justice for all citizens and to preclude the exercise of tyranny and arbitrary power (Rosenbloom 1989: 19).

Marketization and privatization, although valued for many purposes, are not the answers to the problems and crises faced by modern governments. The rising expectations of peoples around the globe, the environmental crises, the population explosion, the demand for better services, the technological revolutions, and many other issues have pressed nations and governments to find solutions. Privatization has been an ideological answer that the corporate sector and the conservative theorists of the West have tried to push on a global scale. The result has been a movement that has invaded almost all countries of the globe.

However, privatization can be misleading because state-owned functions and enterprises—generally established and operated for broad social, political, and economic purposes—may not be transferred to private individuals and businesses. Often, these enterprises end up in the hands of large, often multinational corporations, which are hardly private. As Dahl (1970: 102) notes, "Surely it is a delusion to consider it [the corporation] a private enterprise."

Privatization as an economic and political strategy has had mixed results in advanced democratic countries where more stringent laws and regulations exist. Its implementation in developing countries may have serious ramifications, where there is no self-regulating, strong market system and no strong representative governments capable of keeping corporations accountable. Full-fledged privatization, in which state enterprises and governmental functions are turned over to the marketplace, and semiprivatization, in which major functions of government are contracted out to the private sector providers, have both advantages and disadvantages. Admittedly, there are certain functions that the market could perform more efficiently, which has been recognized by almost all governments for millennia.

But privatization of the functions essential to society and people may be dangerous. In areas where there is an incentive for the market to perform, there could be, as has always been the case, enormous social costs that the market produces—costs that ultimately the government and its people must pay. Some costs are so heavy that they may never be compensated. Technological externalities and environmental pollution are but two examples (Ascher 1987; Cook 1988; Cowan 1990; Farazmand 1994e; Letwin 1988; Savas 1982; Vernon 1988). Privatization also also incurs significant costs on the part of governments in the form of monitoring the expanded functions of the marketplace and controlling abuse and fraud. Examples of market failure, fraud, and abuse of public funds are not few. Privatization of these functions in advanced capitalist nations like the United States where the market is well developed, albeit not necessarily free (Galbraith 1974), has had major problems and therefore is not being recommended by the critics (Goodsell 1990). Needless to say, it will produce far greater problems for governments of the Third World societies, where the market is neither well developed nor adequately regulated.

It is worth noting that the concept of privatization, as promoted by its proponents in the United States and Europe, does not include the nonsocialist, cooperative systems organized and operated on the principles of capitalism. In fact, such a system, even if it is efficient and productive, has been denounced by U.S. foreign service advisers and American agricultural experts. For example, a U.S. Presidential Agricultural Task Force to Peru in 1981 argued that cooperative enterprise "decimated the basic structure of Peruvian agriculture," while, according to a U.N. Food and Agriculture Organization (UN-FAO) study, the country's "yields for sugar and rice (majorities of which [were] produced on the cooperatives) [were] among the highest in the world some ten years after the reform" (McClintock 1987: 88). The underlying purpose of the privatization movement, the critics argue, is the transfer of the huge sector of the public enterprises, particularly the profitable ones, to large corporate private enterprises with direct ties to multinational corporations (Parenti 1978, 1988).

As mentioned earlier, privatization and marketization have been used by the major international donors to pressure the recipients of foreign aid. For example, the International Monetary Fund (IMF), the World Bank, and the United States, Germany, and other Western nations have made it clear that receiving foreign aid is contingent upon nations' efforts to privatize government enterprises and marketize their state-controlled economies[2] (Garcia-Zamor 1992; Hayter 1971). Consequently, many developing nations, highly dependent on international aid, have been forced to implement the measures of privatization and structural adjustments. Such structural adjustments, however, are reported to be global in nature. Privatization and structural adjustments have had significant implications and consequences for developing countries and for public administration theory and practice; there is an emerging global public administration with a fundamental shift of service focus toward private business interests rather than the general public interest.

STRUCTURAL ADJUSTMENTS AND GLOBAL PUBLIC ADMINISTRATION

The changes in the 1980s and the New World Order have led almost all nations, particularly developing countries, to reform and readjust to the new global conditions. The structural adjustments in developing countries to conform to the norms, rules, and values of the new global order have led to fundamental revisions in the public and private sectors' relationships, in the role of government in society and the economy, and in the extent to which the market can stretch its sphere of political and economic influence. The key terms under the new conditions are readjustment, reform, redefining, reconsideration, redevelopment, reintegration, reevaluation, and reinvention (Farazmand 1994d). These structural adjustments or readjustments have, and will likely continue to have, major impacts on public administration in the United States and abroad.

The following section suggests some structural changes leading to the emergence of a global public administration.

Readjustment in Public and Private Sector Relationships

The global movements of marketization and privatization have significantly altered the scope and boundaries of public sector functions and activities in both developed and developing countries. Almost all nations around the world have undergone a significant process of redefining and restructuring their public and private sector relations in favor of the private market sector. The underlying rationale behind this conservative movement has been to attain greater efficiency in managing governmental functions and to improve economic productivity and performance. Privatization and contracting out, as discussed above, have been used as means of achieving greater efficiency and economy by governments.

Privatization has also affected the third, nonprofit sector as well as the cooperative sectors around the globe. Many governments in developing countries with successful and productive cooperative enterprise systems have been forced to cut financial and technical support to these enterprises and to abandon and sell them to large landowners and agribusinesses. The major international influential force behind this boundary readjustment has been the United States since the 1980s. This redefinition of the boundaries and scope of public administration and business enterprises has led to massive layoffs and displacements in many countries around the globe. Ironically, at the same time the private corporate sector has enjoyed all types of tax breaks and financial supports from these governments. Often, the corporate enterprises have even been bailed out by their governments.

The structural boundary readjustment toward marketization has had and will continue to have significant implications for public administration. Although the size of the workforce may have decreased, the governmental responsibilities and public administration functions have not. Unless governments vacate the field of given public policy areas totally, in favor of a complete privatization scheme of production and service provision, "then the responsibilities of public organizations do not disappear" (Wise 1994).

Organizational Reconfiguration and Redesign

The sectoral boundary restructuring has led to organizational reconfigurations and restructuring in order to meet the demands of the new era. The traditional organizational designs have been questioned for their inflexibility, while new alternative design structures have been proposed, adopted, and implemented in many countries, including the United States and Europe. A number of organizational design problems emerge as a result of these reconfigurations. These may include the key issues of organizational complexity, centralization and decentralization, the changing role of environment and its effects on organizational adaptiveness and flexibility, the tasks of coordinating multiorganizational efforts in service delivery, the problem of overlapping organizations, the problem of achieving accountability in both public and private sectors, the problem of national resource allocation, the task of coordinating and balancing public and private sectors, the problem of private sector regulation and enforcement of those regulations, and a host of other issues.

These and many other organizational design issues will likely present major problems in the reconfiguration of public organizations of governments around the globe. Already many old organizations have been dismantled in many former socialist nations without a clear idea of what to do with the functions that they had performed. Also, public organizations have been abolished because of popular sentiments against the bureaucracies of the old regimes. It is much easier to abolish an institution than to build one, and replacing the old bureaucracy has not been an easy challenge for the new regime leaders, revolutionary or otherwise (Carino 1991; Farazmand 1989a, 1991b; Lenin 1971).

The new organizational reconfiguration around the globe will likely reflect the requirements for flexibility of decentralization and fragmentation, on the one hand, and adequate coordination and control through centralization of authority and power, on the other. The managerial, political, economic, and organizational dimensions of the new design configurations will have to be adaptive to the changing local and global environmental determinants. Developing countries have a formidable challenge to deal with, for it is the international capital and public administration experts of the leading global powers that will determine the key factors of the organizational reconfiguration structure. The economic and political dependence of many Third World countries on the West leaves them with little room to maneuver in the new global era.

Changes in the organizational structure and behavior will be directed more toward serving the private market sector than toward serving the general public. Decentralization will likely lead to chaos, while centralization will appeal as an imperative instrument of political and security control.

Consequently, more bureaucratization will likely characterize the organizational structure of developing countries. Their administrators and the bureaucratic cultures will have to internalize the exogenous, imported values and norms of administration and culture. Conversely, they will have to externalize their indigenous cultural and institutional values of their administrative systems. One manifestation of this externalization tendency is, and will be, the internalization of Western organizational values of rationality, impersonalization, formalization, and other bureaucratic values associated with the Weberian ideal-type bureaucracy. Such a system of organization has by nature proven to be alienating and at odds with the native cultures of the non-Western world. A result of this organizational and value transformation will likely broaden the gulf that already exists between the corrupt bureaucratic culture on the one hand and the popular, mass culture on the other. Eventually, this will have serious political consequences for political authorities and regimes around the globe.

Administrative Reform

Administrative reform has been a common feature of most governments around the world. It is beyond the scope and purpose of this essay to discuss the extensive literature on this important subject. Suffice it to say that, generally, governments reform their administrative system in order to obtain or broaden their legitimacy, improve their administrative performance, become more responsive and accountable to citizens, increase managerial efficiency, make the system more flexible, satisfy international donors' requirements, satisfy opposition groups' demands, restructure the governmental system, and often just for the sake of reform itself.

Unless seriously taken and genuinely followed and implemented, administrative reforms are nothing but ideas on paper. Comparative research shows that administrative reforms have often failed, although for varying reasons (Caiden 1991a, 1991b; Farazmand 1989a, 1994d; Peters 1994).

The administrative reforms that have taken place or will take place around the globe have mainly corresponded with the objectives of marketization, privatization, and democratization. These reforms include centralization and decentralization of local administrative systems, changes in the personnel and budgeting systems, changes in the civil service systems, changes in administrative regulations and deregulation, and changes in a host of other sectoral administrations, namely, the rural, urban, commercial, industrial, and service areas of a country (Subramaniam 1990; Dillman 1994; United Nations-DESD 1992; William 1993).

The new administrative reforms in the developing and some of the developed nations appear to develop a fundamental structural integration linked to the leading Western nations, particularly the United States and Western European countries. This structural integration refers to the vertical and horizontal restructuring, bringing the administrative systems of other nations in line with the American and Western structures. Patterns of communication, decision-making, data analysis, strategic coordination, strategic planning, and other strategic managerial functions will likely be developed and integrated into a new hierarchical form along with a *heterarchical* structure denoting the multiple centers of command, decision coordination, and control[3] (Daft 1992; Farazmand 1994b; Hedlund 1986). These multiple centers of the heterarchy will likely be located in key nations around the globe, but they will be linked together and controlled by the hierarchical command system located in the United States. Such a hierarchical-heterarchical structure of the new globally integrated administrative system will be facilitated by the advancement in new computer technologies in the United States and other leading capitalist nations.

The new global structure of the administrative system will increasingly socialize the bureaucrats of the international community into a global village-like culture in which values and norms of administrative behavior will originate from different sources, but eventually they will mainly be of the American ethnocentric nature. Of course, they may be influenced by other cultural perspectives. The critics and dependency theorists may label this cultural imperialism of the United States in the new era (*New York Times* 1982; Parenti 1989). Consequently, the dependency of developing countries on the West will likely be perpetuated, leading to a "neocolonization" of the developing nations of the South by the developed nations of the North.

Such a new global administrative system will no doubt have advantages as well as disadvantages for the developing countries of the global community. One advantage would be the amount of administrative and managerial expertise that these countries will gain through this new structurally integrated system of administration. Second, their administrators will be exposed to the explosive knowledge constantly advancing in the multidisciplinary field of public administration and management. Third, their administrative system will likely be modernized along with the global administrative system, with its apex being in the United States. Fourth, their public administration will resemble the American and other Western administrative systems. Finally, this may shift the blame of their administrative failures externally to the Western/American system. No excuse, of course, but a practical possibility!

The disadvantages of such a globally integrated public administration system will be many, including the high dependency of these countries on Western technology, knowledge, expertise, and other resources. Not all information will be shared with the developing countries; strategic pieces will no doubt be withheld as special privileges. Also, administrative colonization will mean cultural transformation through the internalization of external values, norms, and procedures that are often at conflict with the native traditions.

The Global Bureaucracy

The global coordination of this new global administrative system would also require a proliferation of the huge global bureaucracy characterized by diversity, extensive complexity, and significant interdependence. This global bureaucracy will probably be in two forms: an invisible one and a visible one.

The invisible bureaucracy is already in the making and will increasingly be developed into a full-fledged system around the complex web of economic, political, social, academic, cultural, and military relations between the United States and other nations, particularly the developing world. The U.S. Department of State, the C.I.A., the World Bank, IMF, U.S. AID, the multinational corporations and their subsidiaries, and other suprainternational organizations form such a global bureaucracy. Universities and colleges, sister cities, state governments, and other organizations have also been joining this bureaucracy. Their activities are generally coordinated and monitored by a complex system of communication, rules, laws, and regulations in the United States and other leading Western nations.

The second and visible global bureaucracy is the United Nations and its thousands of affiliated organizations and nonaffiliated associations created for a variety of purposes. Located in different parts of the globe, these U.N. organizations will likely continue to be expanded and more centralized to include more nations of the "global village" created and promoted by "the telecommunications and transport technologies" (Wilson 1994). More and more international issues, global problems and conflicts, and more global opportunities of diverse nature will likely be handled through these international organizations of the global bureaucracy. The United Nations at the apex of the visible global bureaucracy will be an important channel through which opportunities for research, development, and policy implementation will take place.

Implications for Public Administration Theory and Practice

The New World Order and the global public administration with a global bureaucracy discussed above will have major implications for public administration theory, education, and practice. Students and scholars of public administration will be learning to think more globally rather than parochially. American public administration theory has been characterized by "ethnocentrism" (Caiden 1991b; Farazmand 1994f; Riggs 1994b; Thayer 1981). As Caiden (1991b: 5) notes correctly, "even current attempts to reformulate American public administration theory despite their recognition of the global nature of the field still tend to be insular and myopic." American administrative theories and doctrines have often been "thwarted time and time again by aid recipients as being culturally imperialistic" (Caiden 1991b: 5).

However, the ideal of a global public administration is increasingly finding its way in the frame of mind among American social scientists, including public administration theorists (Caiden 1991b; Goodsell 1990; Riggs 1994b). Citing the tradition of international business, finance, and the military, Goodsell argues that "a newly globalized civilian public administration can do the same, if equipped with equivalent resources and mandate" (1990: 503). More and more textbooks in organization theory and management are treating sections on global aspects of business and public administration (Adler 1991; Daft 1992). Thinking globally enables public administration and organization theorists to understand better the field in general and American public administration in particular.

Another implication of this new global public administration will be the proliferation of research centers and other institutional arrangements in promoting research and development studies in a variety of public policy and public management subject areas. More universities are redirecting their focus of research activities on international and global aspects related to public policy and management. Experts on public administration, whether educators or private consultants, will be involved in research assignments and on a variety of training programs. This will likely broaden their understanding of and appreciation for other cultures and their administrative systems abroad.

As Heady (1991) notes, there is little known in the United States about the administrative features of small nations, such as the Scandinavian system of the Ombudsman. The new global administration will eventually make American theorists understand that there are historically rich traditions of excellent administrative theory development and practice of governance in other parts of the world, such as those found in the Middle East and Asia for millennia (Farazmand 1994b; Whyte 1957). Additionally, the former Soviet Union was managed by public administrators, and a great deal can be learned from them.

Still another implication of this new global public administration will be the vast opportunities that would be created by the global bureaucracies in the future. Training and development is one area in which numerous opportunities would be created. The global bureaucracy will be in need of expertise in a wide spectrum of fields and skills. The global bureaucracy will be an emerging organizational arrangement for the global public administration activity coordination in the future. Consequently, we might expect a new organizational person to emerge with a global I.D. for control purposes (Farazmand 1994b).

A significant characteristic of the global public administration will be its high degree of professionalism, diversity, and demographic representation. However, it will not be representative in terms of public policy, organizational decision-making, and managerial and leadership structures. Still another implication will be the changed nature of elite orientation in the global public administration with the big multinational corporations and the governmental officials in the United States at the top level of the hierarchy, to be followed by significant professional managers in the middle, and the key bureaucrat and business leaders of the developing countries at the bottom. The last group in the hierarchy will be the professional administrators and bureaucrats—public and private—around the globe (Farazmand 1994b).

The entire system of public administration around the globe will likely reflect the private, business/corporate interests and those of the dominant governments pursuing market-based policy interests. The elite orientation of the global public administration will be directly linked to the security and military-bureaucratic structure, as well as to the international corporate structure, which is highly concentrated and centralized. This would have serious implications for public administration in developed and developing nations, but it will be consistent with the New World Order. As corporations expand their global domains, so do their governments with larger and newer bureaucracies, civilian and military. They also require an expanding public administration to facilitate their operations and to protect their interests around the globe.

CONCLUSION

The New World Order has caused a restructuring and reshaping of the global power structure ever since the fall of the USSR and other socialist nations a few years ago. Under the two-world system of the Cold War era, superpower competition and rivalry had offered both advantages and disadvantages for peoples and nation-states around the globe. The entire world was divided between the two ideological, economic, military, political, and administrative orientations. Different nations sought alliance and protection from one superpower against the other. Generally, the capitalists and landowners had strong allies in the West under U.S. leadership, while the less advantaged and the poor of the urban and rural areas found moral and political support in the East. Caught in the middle were the professional public administrators whose job was to implement public policy decisions. Public administration grew fast and became highly professionalized during the twentieth century.

With the fall of the Eastern superpower, the only superpower is the United States, determining the parameters and conditions of the New World Order that has significant political, military, economic, social, and administrative implications for developed and developing nations. The globalized slogans of democratization, marketization, and privatization have had and will continue to have significant consequences for public administration in the developed and developing worlds. While offering many advantages to peoples and their social systems around the globe, these slogans will also have significant negative and even dangerous consequences for many developing nations. In the developed

world, the conservative ideology of the New World Order will ̦
enterprise of public administration as a growing, sound field of stuc

The emerging global public administration is based on a number of
adjustments or readjustments that have been taking place around tl
These readjustments have been in the forms of redefining the sc̨   ...u
boundaries of public and private sectors, of administrative reforms, of civil
service reforms, of organizational reconfiguration and restructuring, and many
more. The elite-oriented global bureaucracy will likely perform numerous
functions and act as a conduit of international problem solving, policy development, and policy implementation toward achieving the goals of the New
World Order. The emerging professionalized and elite-oriented global public
administration will have significant implications for public administration
theory and practice in developed and developing countries.

The implications of the New World Order and the emerging global public
administration will likely be more negative than positive for developing nations.
This is in part due to the aggravating economic and political situations that the
conservative New World Order will likely produce for the majority of the
population—the lower class and lower middle class of the urban and rural
areas—in developing countries. Pushing marketization and privatization, with
a globally dominant public administration model, will have a tendency to
empower further the ruling elites—the big capitalists, large landowners, big
corporate powers, and regimes that are too often corrupt, undemocratic, and
repressive. Such a scenario will likely fuel a new wave of revolutionary
upheavals, calling perhaps for another New World Order. A dialectical process
of change and continuity will continue.

NOTES

1. An excellent analysis of this subject is presented by David Gibbs in his paper "Private
Interests and Foreign Intervention: Toward a Business Conflict Model," presented at the 1991
Annual Conference of the American Political Science Association, Washington, D.C., August
1991.

2. Evidence shows that "three-fourths of U.S. foreign-assistance money remains in the U.S."
(Barry, Wood, and Preusch 1984: 159). According to AID administrator Peter Macpherson,
"Two-thirds of what we give comes back in 18 months in the form of purchases" (ibid.).

3. For more information on the concept "heterarchy," see Hedlund (1986) and Daft (1992:
238–243).

4

MANAGING THE ENVIRONMENT IN AN INTERDEPENDENT WORLD

RENU KHATOR

We live in a global village. Among the factors that force us to acknowledge the "villageness" of the globe, the most conspicuous is the environmental crisis. The nature, scope, and complexity of the environmental crisis are such that scholars and scientists now believe that it can be dealt with only at the "global" level. In the industrial growth era, advancements in technology and science afforded us the luxury of having a small world. Today, because of the looming environmental crisis, this luxury has turned into a necessity. We realize not only that the globe must be viewed as a single entity, but also that it must function as a village—realizing and honoring interrelationships—in order to survive. This ecological reality forces us to focus on the relationships among individual entities in the global village, rather than on the mere existence of the entities. For a world that is used to viewing itself as a sum of its parts, the idea of the whole, or that the whole is better than the sum of its parts, is an aberration. Globalization, as defined by Robertson (1987), is a process by which the world becomes a single place. The word "single" here does not denote the process of homogenization; instead, it is a characteristic that allows a common purpose, which Robertson refers to as culture, to emerge amid sustained diversity (Robertson 1987; Wallerstein 1987).

Scholars claim that environmental issues are at the center of any emerging world order (Caldwell 1991; Mathews 1991). This realization is now beyond rhetoric. Lynton Caldwell claims that "global economic and environmental issues have become major forces for international cooperation and have modified the scope of unilateral national policy" (3). Al Gore, in his book *Earth in the Balance*, claims that "we must make the rescue of the environment the central organizing principle of civilization" (1992: 269). Convinced of the centrality of these issues, some have even coined the term "the new ecological order" to describe the changing landscape of world relations.

Environmental issues are transnational issues that are invading national agendas and corroding traditional boundaries. Because of the process of globalization and the rising crisis of the environment, the distinctions between domestic and foreign, national and international, and private and public are fast disappearing. It is only natural that the invasion of transnational environmental issues into the American political and social agenda must affect the field of public administration. How has the field responded to globalization and environmentalism? At the micro level, several studies have tackled the issue, their focus being the effective management of environmental policies and careful analysis of agreed-upon policy designs. Under this general focus, some studied administrative behavior (Kaufman 1970; Paehlke and Torgerson 1990), others focused on management strategies (Henning and Mangun 1989; Jones 1975; Rabe 1986), and yet others targeted the role of actors and institutions in the administrative process (Clarke and McCool 1989; Game 1979; Lester 1980; Vogel 1986). However, most of them examined the environmental crisis as a problem that awaits resolution. In this guise, environmental forces served as dependent variables that we tried to understand, modify, and administer. What is needed now is an attempt to understand the ways in which the parameters of public administration themselves have been changed and are likely to be changed by the new trends of globalization and environmentalism. Here, the environment, its forces, and its global implications serve as antecedent variables, and the field of public administration itself becomes a responding variable. It is my contention that there is clearly a need to view American public administration in the global context and to understand the effects of the changing globe on the demands made on the field itself. There is clearly a need to globalize and environmentalize the orientation of public administration by internalizing these changes. This study argues that the environmental crisis, along with other globalizing forces, has changed the role of the nation-state, which in turn has changed the nature of public administration as a field of study.

ENVIRONMENTALISM, INTERDEPENDENCE, AND NATIONAL PREROGATIVES

The rise of environmentalism in the 1970s initiated an unprecedented shift in international power relations. The crisis, even in its infancy, challenged the foundations of national sovereignty and prerogatives. Several international organizations and agreements emerged in the 1970s and the 1980s, and national governments found that they were losing control over what were understood to be their domestic issues. Acid rain, ocean pollution, global warming, ozone depletion, and "dumping" started to become legitimate issues and to draw considerable attention, at least in the international forum. International treaties, even though labeled as "soft law," threatened the freedom that has traditionally been enjoyed by national governments.

By the early 1990s, the control over the environmental agenda had almost entirely shifted away from national governments to international organizations. Lynton Caldwell complained in 1984 that the environmental progress between 1972 and 1984 had not gone beyond superficiality and that forces destroying the environment were gaining, rather than losing momentum (1984: 260). His claim may still be true, but one must agree that a general international consensus on the environment has clearly emerged. The 1992 Earth Summit in Rio, while short on action, was not a peripheral event. President Bush's reluctance to attend the meeting was viewed harshly by the United States' own political and diplomatic allies. The actions and speeches of the U.S. administrators were scrutinized not just by the American public, but by the international public. The extent of the scrutiny was so intense that a leak regarding Environmental Protection Agency (EPA) chief Jim Reilly's disagreement with President Bush was reported and analyzed by the 8,000-member media in almost every member country. The Rio meeting and the reluctant appearance of the United States at it led many observers to conclude that the United States has lost its environmental, and perhaps even world, leadership. Many called for a new environmental order, and many others predicted a deeper divide between the North and the South. One thing discernible in the meeting was the change in terminology. The words of "helping out" and "foreign aid," reflecting unilateral relationships, had been replaced by "partnership" and "sharing burden," indicating the onset of a bilateral relationship between the developing and the developed world.

Commenting on the effects of environmentalism on world relations, Jessica Tuchman Mathews claimed in 1991 that "governments are already knowingly and unwittingly delegating power, both upward to international institutions and downward to nongovernmental organizations (NGOs) and the corporate sector" (34). Lynton Caldwell (1991) remarked on the similar loss in nation-states' power. He held two separate pulls responsible for this loss: the external pull of an emerging global economic-environmental order and the internal pull of pressures to decentralize authority. It is also my contention that the environmental crisis has undermined the power base of national governments by allowing their powers to be shifted to the international level on one hand and to the grass-roots level on the other. Over the years as the environmental crisis deepened, the governments found themselves trapped in an invisible web of responsibilities and duties. Subsequently, the governments delegated them, and in many cases were forced to delegate them, to others. This delegation of power, whether upward or downward, eventually eroded the parameters of authority and unilateralism within which national governments were used to functioning.

I would like to argue that the two responsibility swings, upward and downward, are the keys to understanding the changes that confront public administrators in the 1990s. The upward swing (from national to international units) is the result of three major factors: the magnitude of the environmental problem itself, the changing equation of "haves" and "have nots," and the breakup of the East-West axis. The downward swing (from governmental to nongovernmental units), on the other hand, is the indirect result of the emerging shift in societal values incited by the failures of economic rationality and the awakening of the grass roots (see Figure 2). Let us first examine these trends and then make an attempt to hypothesize the ways in which these trends may affect the context of American public administrators.

Global and Universal Magnitude

To a great extent, environmental issues are responsible for our acknowledgment of the single, interdependent global village. They, in the 1960s and 1970s, challenged the prevailing international economic order based on rapid industrial growth. These challenges were legitimized by several events that took place in the decade to follow. The 1984 poison gas leak in Bhopal, the 1986 radioactive explosion in Chernobyl, and the 1989 Exxon Valdez oil spill in Alaska crystallized the irrationality of the industrial growth order. These and other disasters precipitated the need for the development of a New World Order focusing on geophysical, rather than geopolitical or economic-political factors.

Environmental issues, indeed, encompass every aspect of life and, consequently, every aspect of a government's sphere. Local actions have global implications; global actions have local consequences. The clearing of Brazilian rain forests, the destruction of Asian mangroves, the erosion of Australian wetlands, the destruction of Laotian forests, acid rain in Canada, and the ozone hole over Antarctica are not problems of any single nation (Meadows, Meadows, and Randers 1992). They affect the survivability of the earth. No single country can be held responsible for environmentally destructive trends, nor can any one country be held liable for their reversal.

The magnitude of the problem itself is a humbling experience for most governments. The United States is no exception. After having spent $700 billion in the past twenty years on water and air pollution control alone, the American public is still faced with the dangerous levels of pollution (Hembra 1990). At the global level, the situation is even more dismal, despite the fact that over 130 international agencies exist to implement more than 150 environmentally oriented international treaties (French 1992: 155). It is estimated that by the year 2075, the ozone-destroying components of chlorofluoro-carbons (CFCs) will triple even with 100 percent participation in the Montreal Protocol, a treaty that many are reluctant even to sign (Shea 1991: 61).

Figure 2
Environmentalism and the Erosion of National Powers

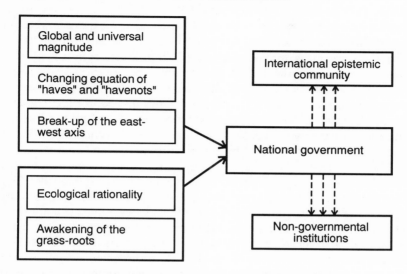

The Changing Equation of "Haves" and "Have Nots"

The environmental crisis has shattered the myth of Western superiority. It has questioned the ability of the West to manage its own affairs, let alone those of the Third World. The cleanup of nuclear sites in the United States alone, for instance, is expected to cost more than $300 billion—not an easy task for a country shouldering a budget deficit of the same amount (Postel 1992). Despite all the efforts, more than 150 million people in the United States still live in areas that are considered to be unhealthy by the U.S. Environmental Protection Agency (French 1991: 97).

If we consider natural resources to be at the center of human life, then we must raise the question: Who has these resources and who controls them? The increasing scarcity of natural resources is precipitating a subtle shift in power relations: a shift from the traditional "haves" to the new "haves," who were traditionally the "have nots." The traditional "haves" under the new ecological world order are turning into "have nots," and the previously classified "have nots" are emerging as the new "haves." The "haves," from the ecological point of view, include the economically poor yet ecologically rich countries of Asia, Africa, and South America. The "have nots," at the same time, comprise the economically rich yet ecologically stressed countries of Europe and North America. They are "have nots" because they either do not have the natural resources to spare, such as Japan, or cannot use what they have because of public pressure, such as the United States. This change in the power equation positions the disadvantaged countries of the Third

World on an equitable ground, the evidence of which is becoming increasingly clear with Brazil's insistence on "using" the Amazonian forests, unless the United States makes concessions on its outstanding debt, and India's insistence on not signing the Montreal Protocol unless expenses were provided by the West. Similarly, Agenda 21 of the Earth Summit '92, an 800-page document, is another example of Third World activism. Notably, Agenda 21 advocates the goal of sustainable development. However, it declares developed countries to be accountable partners in the process of achieving this goal. In addition, there is evidence that people are beginning to identify themselves with ecological commonness. "The Aral Sea Region," for instance, is used by the people of several ex-Soviet republics to identify their common suffering caused by the deterioration of the environment in the region. Similarly, "Amazonians" come from various countries, brought together by the commonness of the Amazonian rain forests (Gore 1992: 300).

The growing scarcity of natural resources can transform ecological resources into precious economic commodities. Even though developing countries have so far failed to establish an international environmental commodity market, the possibility of such an arrangement cannot be ruled out (Cooper 1991). A glimpse of this trend can be seen in the "debt-for-environment-swap" program, which allows indebted countries to preserve their environmental resources in return for not having to pay their financial debt. Similarly, China's and India's demand that developed countries establish a global Green Fund from which economic resource-starved countries can draw money to finance their ecological projects is another indication that developing countries are more than likely to act as "haves" in coming years.

The ecological dependence of developed countries on developing countries is propelled by the existence of the international "commons," such as the seas and the atmosphere. Although all countries receive benefits from their bounty, few countries, like Garrett Hardin's herdsmen, are interested in caring for them (1977). To ensure the protection of these commons, cooperation is needed from all user countries—small and big, rich and poor. Should developing countries be expected willingly to cooperate? Or will there be a need to "buy off" their cooperation with incentives? Clearly, developing countries may use their cooperation as a bargaining tool to seek better financial assistance from developed countries. It is notable that in the Rio conference, the delegates from developing countries were demanding, not pleading, that the cost of sustainable development in their homelands be borne by developed countries.

The Breakup of the East-West Axis

The 1980s witnessed a great historical shift when the communist fallout in the Soviet Union and Eastern Europe led to the breakup of the East-West axis in world relations. The decade of the 1990s, according to many, will experience the replacement of this axis by a new North-South axis (Ramakrishna 1990). On the old East-West axis, the world revolved around strategic interests. International relations were guided by hegemonic motives. With the end of the Cold War, these issues have become less important, if not totally irrelevant. The international agenda today is flooded with issues that pertain to ecology and economy, of which ecological concerns are a big part.

The new North-South axis is developing around geophysical interests. Issues and priorities are being shaped by the international epistemic communities formed around common ecological interests and expertise (Hass 1990). These communities nurture their strength on the commonality of the interest that they share and on the scientific information that they disseminate. They fill in the vacuum created by national governments and gain their credibility from the larger, international public. There are already indications that old strategic and industrial communities are coming under pressure, and oftentimes are forced, to transform themselves into new ecological communities. The 1989 Paris meeting of the G-7 Group, for instance, spent as much time deliberating on environmental issues as on economic issues. Since then, the share of environmental issues has increased despite the dismal economic performance in most member countries.

Clearly, environmental issues are expected to play a key role in defining future world relations. Nations will be called upon to accept outside interference and to rely on mutual cooperation. Old resistance will have to be met with a new sense of global responsibility. The events in 1972 leading to the scheduling of the United Nations' Conference on Human Environment reflected the traditional protectionism and mistrust when most Third World countries refused even to participate in the conference, claiming that it was a deliberate strategy designed by the industrialized West to impose its wishes on the rest of the world. (Caldwell 1972). However, as Caldwell notes, by the end of the 1980s, most countries had found a place for the environmental issue on their national agendas (Caldwell 1990). It must be acknowledged that this change in attitude came about partly because of the severity of the problem but also partly in lieu of any willingness by the West to accommodate "development" issues in the international environmental agenda. The coming years will witness a greater degree of adjustments and cooperation from both the poor and the rich.

Ecological Rationality

The economic rationality of cost-effectiveness and cost-benefit guided the affairs of the industrial growth era. It was assumed that as long as a government was economically rational, it would ensure the welfare of its citizens. Inherent in this notion was also the idea that the government or a similar authority was capable of playing the "referee." The government in its referee role was rational and was able to judge the rationality of social actions.

The environmental crisis, however, questioned the logic of the economic rationality as well as the ability of the government to be a rational actor. Economic rationality is impossible to achieve for a given action if the true costs and values involved in that action are not known. As the environmental crisis deepened, it became clear that the true value of ecological assets was impossible to assess. Thus came the notion of ecological rationality. People started to accept those costs that would otherwise be labeled irrational. Doomsday predictions created fear in the public, and public opinion surveys started to indicate that people were willing to pay an "irrational" price for their environment. In Canada, for instance, public opinion surveys indicated that 80 percent of the public was willing to pay 10 percent more for "environment-friendly" products.

As the basis of rationality was changing, another question had to be raised: Is the government capable of refereeing a game that is to be played with the rules of a new, ecological rationality? Voluminous research done in the field answered this question in the negative. Studies indicated the failure on the part of the government to administer the environment regardless of political arrangements. The result was a universal mistrust in the government's ability to manage the environment. The market had already shown its inability to be ecologically rational, and now the government was also turning out to be an inept referee. Clearly, a new medium had to be found. This vacuum was partially filled by the international epistemic community, but the rest fell on the shoulders of nongovernmental actors. The inclusion of nongovernmental actors altered the traditional practices of public policy-making and executing. The major alteration was that the process of decision-making became more tolerant of outside interference and, in many cases, allowed these outside forces to assume the lead.

Awakening of the Grass Roots

Environmentalism involves an unprecedented level of direct public participation. This participation becomes necessary when people find themselves increasingly frustrated with the established channels of public participation and search for alternatives. The most impressive of these are the grass-roots movements. Several of them have already carved a niche in the system; their strength was noted in the 1992 Earth Summit meeting, where they had organized a parallel platform and were able to use it to shape and preempt formal discussions in the meeting.

Similarly, the Chipko Aandolan in India, Greenpeace in Europe, and the Sierra Club in North America are also indicative of the strength and productivity of nongovernmental actors. Their strength typically lies in their easy accessibility to the people. Many stay within their political boundaries, but most reach out at least to form common alliances with their counterparts in other countries.

The grass-roots movements often play a double-edged role: First, they strengthen the hands of policy-makers by participating in the formulation of policies; once policies are in place, they play a watchdog role. Their ability to cut across national boundaries and collect financial and ideological support from the international public makes them effective in their surveillant role. Because of their size and vigor, the grass-roots movements can force a government to become accountable to its people as well as to the international epistemic community.

In brief, the environmental crisis has redefined national prerogatives: It has forced nations to lose their secluded sovereignties willingly and to realize their mutual dependence. It has coerced them to acknowledge their membership in the global village. According to Lynton Caldwell, "No other international movement—world peace included—engages so large a number of individual participants, so many and such diverse forms of cooperative effort, so broad a range of human skills and interests, and such complex interrelationships among governmental and non-governmental organizations" (1990: 311). In this context, the environmental crisis has brought us all a little closer.

ENVIRONMENTALISM AND GLOBAL FEDERALISM

The New World Order, with its emphasis on interdependence and geophysical interest, is giving rise to a new system of global federalism. This system can be envisioned as having at least three, and perhaps even more, layers of power hierarchy: international, national, and nonnational (or social). At the apex of the invisible organization is the environmental epistemic community (see Figure 3). Admittedly, there are several smaller epistemic subcommunities representing various aspects of the environment, such as the ozone layer, conservation, pollution, food, and energy. Nonetheless, at the ideological level, the subcommunities join hands to form a single environmental epistemic community. Because of the complex and interrelated nature of environmental issues, the international epistemic community can command a unique and powerful role in defining the international agenda.

The second tier of the global federal system is formed by individual national governments, which, despite being sovereign, are limited in using their sovereign authority. For instance, the Canadian government has the power to identify the problem of acid rain, but it has no authority to make the U.S. government acknowledge the problem. The international epistemic community is the primary source of influence and informal mediation in this situation. As most environmental problems are interdependent in temporal, spatial, and functional ways, national governments are continuously forced to yield to the international epistemic community. Today, more than 150 international treaties express the voice of that community. The treaties often involve a large number of sovereign nations: 129 are partners in the 1982 Law of the Sea Treaty; 124 in the 1972

Figure 3
Global Federalism and Lines of Penetration

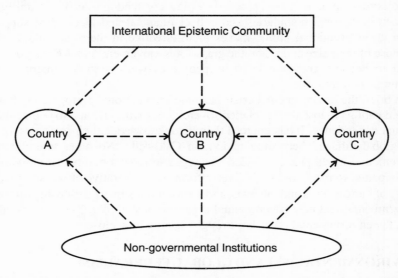

Biological and Toxic Weapons Treaty; 85 in the 1972 World Heritage Treaty; and 29 in the 1987 Protocol on Ozone Depleting Substances Treaty (World Resource Institute 1989: 348–349).

In theory, national governments possess the power to accept or reject the directives sent by the epistemic community; in reality, their powers are limited for a variety of reasons. A national government needs cooperation from other governments and such cooperation can often be worked out only in an international setting. Also, national governments often lack the basis to defy decisions taken by the epistemic community. Their reservoir for scientific information may be less than the collective reservoir possessed by the international community. More often than not, their own experts and scientists also belong to the international epistemic community and can be expected to be loyal to it for the sake of a common professional interest.

Regardless of their yielding position, national governments are the most critical link in the global federal system. They are responsible for carrying out decisions made by the epistemic community. They are also the medium through which the epistemic community collects and disseminates information. Without the willing consent of national governments, the epistemic community cannot obtain legitimacy. Up until recently, the environmental epistemic community had little credibility because it could not convince individual nations to comply with its decisions.

The third and last basic link of global federalism is formed by nongovernmental institutions such as grass-roots movements and organizations. They are at the societal level and are brought together by their common, altruistic, and nonpolitical interests. They differ from the international epistemic community in two important ways: first, they do not rely on expertise; second, unlike the community that is research-oriented, they are action-oriented. Often their activities are constrained by national physical borders, but in most cases they do not observe such borders. Even though their activities are aimed at local targets, their common ideological interests are broad. Consequently, their actions have a wide impact range. Consider the Blue Angel labeling program in Germany: over 3,500 products in fifty categories bear "eco" labels. The strategy is now being considered in other European countries as well as in Japan and the United States.

The nongovernmental actors link national governments to the public. It is through them that millions of people are able to participate in environmental activities. They provide a two-way channel of communication. On one hand, they reinterpret the directives of the international epistemic community to fit the needs of local communities. On the other, they translate public wishes to the government and to the international epistemic community.

ENVIRONMENTALISM, INTERDEPENDENCE, AND PUBLIC ADMINISTRATORS

How do public administrators fit into the emerging world order? Does the new order based on interdependence, geophysical interests, and global federalism affect the working environment of public administrators?

We can begin by identifying some key concepts that form the heart of public administration: hierarchy, rationalization, cost-effectiveness, cost-benefit, productivity enhancement, political-administrative dichotomy, local autonomy, equity, ethics, and representativeness are just a few to name. Clearly, these concepts are the byproducts of "industrial growth era thinking," which was directed by hegemonic motives, strategic interests, political hierarchies, and uncontrolled economic growth. Inherent in this thinking were the assumptions that the United States is a superpower and that America leads the world through its military might. The implication of this thinking was that public administrators should be trained to work in a context in which they were accountable only to their own immediate surroundings. They were not expected to respond to international forces.

As the New World Order takes shape, these concepts will begin to lose their validity. To say the least, they need to be reexamined and reassessed. Theories of administrative styles, culture, and structures need to be redefined and rearranged in order to be compatible with the changing world order. For public administrators, the New World Order could mean a drastic change in their tasks, expectations, and styles. At the very least, they must be prepared to function in the complex web of global federalism by accepting vertically sensitive, horizontally open, and diagonally responsive relationships.

With the help of the environmental issue, I will make an attempt here to highlight the areas where incompatibilities are becoming apparent.

Shifts in Administrative Context

The context of public administration itself is changing in the interdependent world. Today, public administrators are forced to work under a new set of multiple laws. The traditional dichotomy of politics and administration is no longer critical, since the scope of penetration is no longer just political. It is wider than before, and it stretches beyond one's own political system to include international laws and systems. As national governments open up to the pressures of the international epistemic community, all levels of governments and administrative organizations will become vulnerable. Here is an example to illustrate the point.

The U.S. government recently placed a ban on Mexican tuna on the grounds that it is being caught in a fashion that kills more dolphins than are allowed to U.S. fishermen. To fishermen and their local officials in Mexico, the complexity of the situation is overwhelming. They are supposed to observe not only what their government allows them and what the international community dictates to them, but also what the U.S. government, which is the importer of their catch, permits them. Although the GATT (General Agreement on Tariffs and Trade) called the U.S. ban unjust in September 1991, the pressure on Mexican fishermen has not lessened. Mexican fishermen must still show the evidence of compliance with the U.S. law because it is based on ecological morality. The U.S. demand has the backing of the international epistemic community.

Similarly, the complexity of EPA head Jim Reilly's job became clear during the 1992 Earth Summit, when he bowed to the international community and displayed his disagreement with President Bush in a personal memo. The memo, however, was leaked out, creating embarrassment for everyone involved. The traditional debate over public administration as a trustee or a delegate in this case suddenly got a third angle, as accountability to the international community also came into the picture. Questions still remain: Was Reilly being accountable to his president? Or was he being accountable to the American public? Or was he being accountable to the global village?

Undoubtedly, public administrators in coming years will be required to please not only their political masters but also the international epistemic community. This means that they will become more vulnerable than ever before. The hierarchical structure of bureaucratic organizations that so far has sheltered public administrators from accountability will no longer be able to protect them. In the future, at least in the environmental field, while formal orders will continue to come from their political bosses, informal pressures will come from all those levels to which their national governments have yielded or are yielding their powers.

Although the policies of the industrial growth era were built around nationalism, the call of the New World Order is necessarily denationalization and depoliticization (although not deculturalization). Efforts are being made to acknowledge the problems of nuclear arsenals, CFC use, coastal pollution, and atmospheric changes as "common" problems. While national and international agencies remain sensitive to individual sovereignties, the objective is to elevate common problems above national conflicts. It is not surprising that the management of the Soviet nuclear arsenal is considered to be more a responsibility of the United States than of the ex-Soviet republics. Similarly, the use of CFCs in the United States, mining in China, deforestation in Brazil, population growth in India, and drought in Bangladesh are also being denationalized in the sense that they are being deliberated in international forums. Denationalization would mean that public administrators in these countries must open their systems to outside interferences. At the same time, it would also mean that international forces must come out of the traditional donor-receiver mode of the industrial growth era and must learn to respect others' preferences (Mathews 1991).

Shifts in Administrative Style

Global interdependence will more than likely force public administrators to become balancers. In sharp contrast to their existing role as regulators, this new role will demand that they carry out their tasks through bargaining, negotiation, and cooperation. In a comparative study of national styles in the United States and Great Britain, David Vogel applauded the British for their environmental performance (1986). He argued that the British administrators performed better because British law allowed them flexibility to negotiate and bargain with polluting industries on a case-by-case basis. This, according to Vogel, yielded better results than the American style, which emphasized uniformity and strict adherence. In their balancing role, British inspectors were able to reconcile differences between economic priorities and environmental values at a substantially low cost to the society.

The balancing role of public administrators is even more critical in developing countries, where any slowdown in the economic growth rate is sure to bring drastic results. In most instances, nations pass conflicting policies under pressure. Administering the environment in Hong Kong, for instance, is a unique challenge for its administrators. Although comprehensive pollution control laws exist, administrators are expected to implement them so as not to adversely affect Hong Kong's competitive edge in the world market. Hong Kong's economy relies on its small-scale industries that work on small margins in a highly competitive market. Although these industries are known to be the major polluters, any action placing additional burdens on them can be a threat to the territory's economic survivability. Public administrators, in such circumstances, are called upon to use their judgment and act as balancers.

In the late 1980s, Hong Kong developed a two-way strategy to cope with the situation (Khator 1992b). The first was a bailout strategy under which existing industries were allotted a pollution quota that was 30 percent higher than their existing discharge levels. Unfortunately, this meant that the pollution level in the territory was only going to increase. The second strategy was a coproduction strategy, where public agencies themselves accepted the responsibility of custom-designing pollution control mechanisms for individual industries. The intent of the dual strategy was to allow the implementors to remain flexible. They could maintain a healthy balance by moving from one extreme to the other depending on market demands and resource availability.

What Hong Kong administrators were asked to do is also known as superoptimum administration. The call for superoptimum administration comes with the realization that zero-sum games are unhealthy for interdependent relationships. Superoptimum strategies promise all affected parties to be somewhat better off than before. Under economic globalization and interdependence, public administrators will be required to adopt administrative strategies that, other than coping with the wider magnitude, will also display an understanding of global trends and consequences. An example of global insensitivity lies in the management of hazardous waste in the United States in the 1980s. Under the prevailing industrial order, it was possible for the United States to export its garbage to another country as long as the receiving country was willing to accept it. The U.S. General Accounting Office estimates that one-fourth of all pesticides sent to the Third World were banned at home. According to Greenpeace, at least ten million tons of waste have been sent from the West to the countries of Eastern Europe and the Third World during the last six years (French 1992). Today, however, such practices are difficult to justify because the receiving countries are not seen as being better off, at least not ecologically. The 1988 saga of the *Khian Sea*'s round-the-world tour in search of a dumping ground for its cargo of trash is a proof of this shift.

As the society's attention moves from short-term benefits to long-term impacts, the job of public administrators, along with that of policy-makers, becomes more challenging. A good example is recycling. A superoptimum solution in recycling calls for strategies that can satisfy consumers' demand for quality, producers' demand for cheap material, society's demand for protection of natural resources, and processors' demand for operating profit. Policy-makers, in this field, have undermined the complexity of the situation by passing vague recycling laws that provide only a general framework. The responsibility of interpreting such laws, however, falls on the implementors, who must design programs that could satisfy all parties. This means that they must work on several fronts: changing consumption patterns, creating markets for recycled products, and promoting research on the collection and processing of recyclables.

Shifts in Administrative Goals

With interdependence, the existing goals of public administration also stand to lose their relevance. Under the industrial growth order, the goals of efficiency, representativeness, and productivity reigned. Under the new geophysical order, however, a shift from efficiency to effectiveness, from representativeness to responsiveness, and from productivity to sustainability seems unavoidable. If public administrators are going to be held accountable for results and not just for the process, then they will have to focus on effectiveness and responsiveness. In the Weberian style of bureaucracy, it was easy to overlook these goals. The social forestry program in India exemplifies the shift in question.

Social forestry was launched in India in 1980 with the help of the World Bank and several other international donor agencies (Khator 1991). The objective of social forestry was to preserve natural forests, while meeting the needs of the poor who depended on forests for their livelihood. Under the program, free seedlings were given to farmers and to the communities who were to plant, care, and use the product from them. It was later discovered, however, that most of the seedlings were made available to rich farmers who used them to convert their agricultural-crop farms into cash-crop farms. In more than 80 percent of the cases, the planted trees were eucalyptus, a plant that not only is disastrous to the soil but also useless in terms of generating fuel and fodder for the poor. In this case, efficiency and representativeness superseded effectiveness and responsiveness, because eucalyptus plants produced the best income opportunities and were in great demand. However, the end result was that natural forests could not be preserved; the rich got richer from cash crops, while the forest-dependent poor were still turning to natural forests to meet their daily needs.

Clearly, the goals of effectiveness and responsiveness place a different set of expectations on public administrators. They require public administrators to participate actively in political processes.

Rosemary O'Leary points to another area of potential conflict in terms of the new challenges for public administrators. Citing the case of *Lucas v. South Carolina Coastal Council*, in which the pivotal issue is whether the implementation of the South Carolina Beachfront Management Act was a regulatory taking, she claims that "the decision has the potential of settling the divisive issue of where regulation ends and taking begins" (O'Leary 1992). This and similar litigation signal a change in the job requirements of public administrators in the 1990s and beyond.

GLOBALIZING PUBLIC ADMINISTRATION

The New World Order based on global interdependence and geophysical interests requires redefinition of administrative style, context, and goals. It poses many new questions for research. Will a new administrative culture emerge from the new tasks assigned to public administrators? Will existing organizations provide answers to new challenges? Will there be a new way of arranging organizational structures? Will the New World Order necessitate the development of a new paradigm for public administration?

Fred W. Riggs noted in 1976 that "the new paradigm for public administration must be comparative, i.e., global, since the solution of the problems to which it addresses itself will require increasing communication between scholars and practitioners in all countries. The American dimension of these problems will surely come to be seen as a 'subfield' or a parochial aspect of the broader subject" (Riggs 1976: 652). Since the collapse of the CAG (Comparative Administration Group) in 1973, the soul of comparative public administration has really not been found (Heady 1991). It is my contention that the geophysical, interdependent, and global federal world order may just provide that new point of gravity. The time has come that global comparative models of public administration direct the primary field of public administration. Only the models based on comparative work can grasp the complexity of modern problems and the intricacies of modern public administration. They can promote interaction, cooperation, and mutual learning.

Existing frameworks of comparison, however, must also be reexamined. The classic model of administrative systems based on the Weberian understanding of a rational hierarchical bureaucracy is insufficient even for the countries of the North. The level of penetration in the interdependent world makes it impossible for public administrators to maintain a perfect hierarchy and to respond only to the legal rational authority. The "prismatic-sala" model of Riggs holds promise, but it is limited to structures and functions. In the unfolding world order, new frameworks of comparison must go beyond explaining; they should be able to help and guide the society toward new arrangements and better administration. They must reflect social shifts in values. They must avoid classifying nations into mutually exclusive categories, assuming that each category has a different center of gravity. After all, to function in an interdependent world is to function in a single, nonhierarchical world.

II

DEVELOPMENT ADMINISTRATION
Case Studies

5

NEOTERIC THEORIES FOR DEVELOPMENT ADMINISTRATION IN THE NEW WORLD ORDER

JEAN-CLAUDE GARCIA-ZAMOR

The problems of public administration in developing countries are so vastly different from those of the developed world that a new discipline, development administration, has emerged since the 1960s to study them. Although a large number of books and articles have been written on the subject, questions still persist as to whether such a discipline exists or is necessary.[1] Nevertheless, development has become a major focus of administrative activity in the countries of the Third World.[2] The industrialized societies have recognized the need for these countries to gear their administrative machinery to new developmental tasks and responsibilities. The mounting external debts of the Latin American, African, and Asian countries have lent a new urgency to the problems of administrative reorganization and reform.

In 1976, the Section on International and Comparative Administration (SICA) of the American Society for Public Administration (ASPA) published a paper entitled "Development Administration: Background, Terms, Concepts, Theories, and a New Approach." Its author, Richard W. Gable of the University of California at Davis, reviewed the basic literature in the field and traced the development of the concepts and practice from the U.S. experience with technical assistance and scholarly interest in comparative administration (Gable 1976: 1).

Gable's excellent paper presented a strategy for administrative change toward a "new" development administration. That new strategy was a tacit recognition that external assistance is indispensable for public organizations and institutions of the Third World. The earlier theories, most of them reviewed by Gable, were written by American scholars who had started or pursued their interests in the working of developing countries' administrative structures while bringing assistance sponsored by the United States or United Nations to these countries. These earlier theorists, all members of the Comparative Administration Group (CAG) led by Fred Riggs and operating within ASPA, were so convinced of the indispensability of foreign aid for the functioning of the Third World bureaucracies that they responded in a fashion consistent with that conviction when their own "external" funding from the Ford Foundation was terminated: CAG simply ceased to exist; fortunately, it was replaced by SICA. Although the termination of the Ford grant was the main reason for CAG's demise, many of the early theorists blame it on the lack of a clear definition of the parameters of the emerging field. Keith Henderson, Lee Sigelman, Garth N. Jones, Jamil E. Jreisat, and several others made that point in their writings (Heady 1984: 25–26). As that early period was one of searching for definition and identity, a variety of CAG writers, among them Jong S. Jun and Milton J. Esman, contributed enormously to the establishment of comparative and development administration as a distinct discipline. However, Fred Riggs and others were already questioning the relevance of the field in 1970. Garth N. Jones went even further. He criticized the U.S. Agency for International Development (AID) for its lack of viable doctrine and its policy of expediency. He viewed AID as overbureaucratized and lacking in imagination and risk-taking capability (Jones 1970).

Interestingly enough, the bureaucrats of the developing countries were the most vocal supporters of the dependency approach.[3] They questioned why capitalist development, such as had occurred in the United States and Western Europe, had not taken place in the Third World. In their efforts to obtain more and more foreign aid, they deliberately presented an image of being unable to cope by themselves with the tasks of development. Lacking in funding and strategies for responding to this challenge, international donors have limited their actions to timid innovations such as expounding the virtues of public participation in the planning and executing of projects (Garcia-Zamor 1985). However, a recent work by Derick W. Brinkerhoff, focusing on program management, draws some systematic lessons for improving the sustainability of development program performance (Brinkerhoff 1991).

Another factor that inhibited the development of the discipline was the inability of some American scholars to see the relevance of foreign aid to U.S. domestic programs. As early as 1969, John D. Montgomery compared the U.S. foreign aid program to its domestic aid program. He concluded that poverty and the promise of development are the common elements in programs of foreign and domestic aid. He also concluded that the foreign aid program had operational advantages over the fragmented domestic aid program and that the procedures developed by AID employed a higher level of programming skill than that available to other government agencies (Montgomery 1971: 469–470).

However, students at American universities have been reluctant to enroll in development administration seminars, viewing them as irrelevant to the core concerns of public administration. This attitude has prompted some scholars to emphasize similarities between the tasks of the developing countries' bureaucracies and those of poor municipal and county governments in the industrialized countries (Goodsell 1981). In both situations, the struggling bureaucracy finds itself dependent on external technical assistance and financing to develop projects and programs and to deliver services. While in the developing countries such external assistance is provided by international institutions such as the World Bank and the International Monetary Fund, as well as "donor countries," in the municipal and county governments of the United States the dependency is on state and federal assistance. In both cases the recipient governments are subjected to an array of restrictions that often limit the capability of their bureaucracies to give priority to the urgent needs of their communities. However, one thing is quite clear: The tasks of these bureaucracies to promote development would not be possible without outside assistance.

This decade has started with a dramatic change in the geopolitical alignment of the world, and this chapter will examine whether the existing approach to development administration should be revised to be more relevant to this New World Order.

THE NEW WORLD ORDER

After President George Bush coined the phrase "New World Order," he tried to articulate it in terms that would infuse a new sense of mission to America. He seemed to regard instability abroad as a danger for America.[4] Although President Bush wanted to continue the U.S. internationalist policies of the last forty-five years, Americans and the Congress tended to lurch between isolationism and idealism. But as the Cold War has wound down, there can be little doubt that a New World Order is emerging that creates challenges for the United States and other Western nations that might be equal to those that existed when world politics turned on the confrontation between East and West. Unfortunately, most of the attention has been focused on the major events that created the New World Order: the dramatic dismantling of the Berlin Wall, the fall of communism in Eastern Europe and in the former Soviet Union, and the resurgence from their remains of independent republics. It appears that the 1990s will see foreign aid both from the United States and from the other Western countries going primarily to help establish free market economies in the former communist countries.

An underlying concern in the West is the control of the Soviet nuclear arsenal. At the present time 80 percent of the Soviet strategic nuclear weapons are located in the Russian Republic, and the remainder are deployed in Ukraine, Byelorussia, and Kazakhstan. Tactical nuclear weapons are distributed more evenly across the republics. In 1991 the U.S. government provided $400 million for the dismantling of nuclear weapons deployed in Ukraine and Kazakhstan.

Although the bulk of U.S. foreign assistance has been provided only to five countries over the past decade,[5] many of the countries of Latin America, Africa, and Asia were receiving substantial U.S. assistance before the rise of the New World Order. These countries stand to lose a sizable portion of that aid. Other political developments are contributing to the diminishing interest being shown to these nations (Berg and Gordon 1989; Hellinger, Hellinger, and O'Regan 1988; Schraeder 1992).

In the New World Order, the former Soviet Union has become primarily a recipient of foreign aid rather than a donor (to Cuba, the Warsaw Pact countries, and African states leaning toward communism). Among the major donors, the individual Western European states might soon coordinate their strategies to operate within the new European Community. Thus, in the New World Order, this chapter identifies five major groups of recipients: (1) Latin America, (2) Africa, (3) Asia, (4) Eastern Europe, and (5) the former Soviet Union. Among the international donors, this chapter identifies three: (1) the United States, (2) the European Community, and (3) the World Bank. This new grouping of recipients and donors reflects the fact that, while the pool of recipients has grown considerably, the pool of donors has shrunk. More importantly, the new geopolitical alignment of some countries has shifted the interests and motivation of donors, who might want to relocate their grants to maximize the "return on their investments." Needless to say, in the face of this new reality, the bureaucracies of Latin America, Africa, and Asia—the traditional recipients of foreign aid—will need to design new approaches to development administration. Following is a brief review of recipients and donors in the New World Order.

THE MAJOR RECIPIENTS

Latin America

In 1980, twelve of the eighteen countries of Latin America were governed by military regimes. The United States often supported these regimes because of their fierce anticommunist stands. The free market system even flourished under some of them (e.g., Chile). However, with these countries now governed by democratically elected presidents and with the disappearance of the Soviet threat, U.S. economic assistance has shifted. The fear of communism has been superseded by the fear of drugs. The meager aid that was previously provided in the form of military assistance is now going to fight the perceived new regional threats to the vital interests of the United States: drug trafficking, massive immigration, and environmental degradation.[6] However, the bureaucracies of these countries continue to lack the resources needed to develop the projects that could counteract these new threats and improve social and economic conditions. In Brazil, one-third of the population lives in poverty while 1 percent controls 60 percent of the country's wealth. In Venezuela, currently about 43 percent of the population, compared with 18 percent in 1987, makes less than $130 a month. Considering the fact that an increase in oil revenue helped the Venezuelan economy to grow at an estimated rate of 9.2 percent in 1991, those statistics dramatize the polarization between the wealthy and the poor in Third World countries at a time when their economies seemed to be growing. The deteriorating economy prompted the Venezuelan military to attempt a coup in early 1993. Costa Rica has a foreign debt of $3.5 billion, in a country of only 3 million citizens, and is dependent on foreign credit to service that debt. Thus, the largest country of the region and two of the most stable ones have joined the others in increasing the uncertainty of the future of the poor in Latin America. With Castro's ability to pose a threat severely diminished by the events in Russia, the Sandinistas out of power, peace in Central America, and democracy prevailing in the region, Latin America stands to lose the priority for foreign developmental aid. Except for token gestures to Nicaragua and Panama, toward which the United States justly feels some responsibility, any aid going to the region will be targeted to curbing drug production and export.

Africa

Faced with the specter of pouring money into a bottomless pit, Western aid donors, together with the World Bank and the International Monetary Fund, have used the threat of a cutoff in financial support to encourage domestic disenchantment with state control of economic activity. Strengthened by the wave of democracy that swept through Eastern Europe and the end of the Cold War, Africans have been demanding changes in their political systems. A half-dozen leaders have been forced out of office during the past four years, and at least sixteen others have grudgingly legalized opposition parties. Unfortunately, unlike the people of the former Soviet Union, Africans do not have Western industrialized nations enthralled with their struggle, eager to pour billions of dollars into an effort to avert hunger that could threaten freedom in its infancy. The United Nations recently reported that Western efforts to help Africa shake off disease, debt, hunger, and endemic crises during the past five years have been a failure (*Miami Herald*, January 5, 1992: 23A). Africa might end up being the big loser in the New World Order. This is most unfortunate, especially as newly published data showed that their trade has worsened by almost 25 percentage points over the past decade (United Nations Development Programme 1991: 4).

The countries of Latin America and Africa, except for a few exceptions, have too little to offer and lack too much economic infrastructure to be able to use the New World Order to their advantage. For them, the New World Order will go the way the "New World Economic Order" went after it was promulgated in 1974.

Asia

Several of the countries of the region are emerging from their underdevelopment. Four of them—Taiwan, Hong Kong, Singapore, and South Korea—have benefited from their cheap labor and some value-added export strategies to dominate exports to other Asian countries as well as the rest of the world. South Korea is probably the first country to be successful in reversing its brain drain. Several of its citizens who have succeeded abroad have been enticed back to take top managerial positions in the private sector. These four countries have a disciplined workforce, but the key factor in their growth has been entrepreneurship. Their success has inspired other countries of the region to follow their path. A new foursome is already emerging to compete for a share in the export trade: Indonesia, Malaysia, Thailand, and, to a somewhat lesser extent, the Philippines. Some people believe that, as its political system has now stabilized, Vietnam may soon join them. The leader of the new pack is Thailand, which has the fastest-growing economy in the world—at about 10 percent a year. These nations' success, based on deeply ingrained cultural values, will be difficult to duplicate in the rest of the Third World. Nevertheless, lessons can be learned from it.

Japan is in a class by itself. It has a $41 billion trade surplus with the United States. It has established tariffs and marketing obstacles that make most American products extremely difficult to sell in Japan. In addition to their manufacturing excellence, the Japanese have utilized basic education as a source of economic power. As in the cases of South Korea and Singapore, domestic and external competition has very often spurred innovation, the diffusion of technology, and an efficient use of resources. These countries have established a global competitive advantage through the rigors of competition (World Bank 1991b: 7).

Asia will be better off in the New World Order since it may acquire new markets for its exports. Although the countries of the Pacific Rim are not yet significantly involved in foreign assistance, except for Japan,[7] they will probably end up dominating the world economy in the next decade. These Asian countries stand to benefit from the new geopolitical alignment in the world.

Eastern Europe

In 1989, the U.S. Congress passed the East European Democracy Act to help the emerging democracies of Eastern Europe. In the fiscal year 1990–1991, the United States provided assistance of $2.112 billion to Central and Eastern Europe. That assistance was primarily through grants, rather than debt forgiveness, long-term credits, and the like, which some other nations use, largely because the United States believed that the grants better protected the fragile economies of the region. This policy was based on what former U.S. secretary of state James Baker called the "new democratic differentiation." In 1991 and 1992, American programs were designed to support democratic and free market reforms and were tailored to meet the needs of the countries as they moved toward the following four objectives:

1. political pluralism, including free and fair elections
2. economic reforms through the development of a market economy, with a dynamic private sector
3. respect for internationally recognized human rights
4. the desire of the country to enter into a friendly relationship with the United States.

The United States is presently providing assistance in three broad areas, with a major priority in each to improve trade vital to the region's economic development:

Democratic Initiatives. This area accounted for 7 to 9 percent of assistance provided. Aid is granted to encourage the development of institutions and practices of democratic pluralistic societies, based on Western values of human rights and individual freedoms.

Economic Restructuring. About 70 percent of assistance went for the transformation of centrally planned economies into market-based economies that are led by the private sector and integrated into the world economy.

Quality of Life. Roughly 17 to 19 percent of assistance was for improving the basic quality of life through medical and food assistance (ACIPA 1991).[8]

The massive U.S. assistance toward consolidating democracy in Eastern Europe has had mixed immediate results. In the case of Poland, the privatization of small businesses has been a success. Seventy-five percent of shops and 43 percent of the construction industry are now in private hands. Private enterprise currently accounts for 30 percent of all economic activity, compared to 3 percent under communism. Eighty to 85 percent of industrial output, however, remains in the hands of some 7,000 state-owned factories. Almost all of these factories are money-losers, and at least 100 of them have gone completely bankrupt. Poland's gross domestic product, the main indicator of a nation's economic health, was expected to drop by 3.7 percent in 1991 (*Miami Herald*, December 1, 1991: 3L).

In Bulgaria, the situation is the same. It was the first former Warsaw Pact country to adopt a new constitution modeled on Western democratic principles, and it is the first to hold a second round of open, free elections. Bulgaria has also adopted one of the strictest economic reform packages in Eastern Europe. However, the nation is in serious economic trouble. Inflation in 1990 reached

400 percent, and many goods are in short supply. Unemployment has skyrocketed as inefficient state enterprises have shut their doors and laid off thousands of workers (*Miami Herald*, November 10, 1991: 6C).

The situation is similar in most of the Central and Eastern European countries. But U.S. officials are nevertheless optimistic. For one thing, despite these countries' economic woes, their populations have far stronger educational backgrounds than those of prior aid recipients. Therefore, results should come more quickly and be longer lasting. Officials are hoping that aid to the region might no longer be necessary by the end of the 1990s. That would be a welcome change for the donors, who have seen the past forty years of foreign assistance bearing very little fruit.

The Former Soviet Union

The demise of the Soviet Union and the emergence of the independent republics present a challenge to the Western world. A few statistics, gathered before the breakup of the central economy, hint at the depth of the crisis facing these new nations of 286 million people spread across eleven time zones. In the first six months of 1991, gross national product (GNP) fell 10 percent compared with the same period in 1990, hard-currency earnings plummeted with the drop in Soviet oil exports, and inflation ran at about 100 percent. The Soviet economy was in such a shambles in early 1991 that it was exhibiting some characteristics of Fred Riggs's prismatic model (Riggs 1964: 27–31), a mixture of raw superpower and Third World standards. In fact, it was only the massive nuclear arsenal of the Soviet Union that qualified it as a superpower. Those nuclear warheads became the focus of attention after the breakup of the country. The United States and the Western powers soon demanded their destruction as a condition for foreign aid. Indeed, most of the aid went to disabling and dismantling the former empire's nuclear arsenal. The former superpower was pushed by its former archenemy to accept such targeted aid to qualify for other urgent aid for medical and food supplies.

In 1991, some $400 million was given by Congress to channel assistance to Russia. As usual, as soon as the money was allocated, several government agencies were competing for a piece of the action. In early 1992, President Bush pledged to ask Congress to provide another $650 million in new technical assistance and humanitarian aid for the new republics. This new pledge raised total U.S. aid—in food credits and grants, medical and technical help, and nuclear disarmament assistance—to over $5 billion.[9] This is an extraordinary amount of money to stabilize a former enemy's system when one considers that the Marshall Plan, initiated to help former allies in war, cost just over $100 million in 1991 dollars. Also, in 1947 the United States was the richest nation in the world. Today it feels comparatively broke. This broad aid, however, will not necessarily endear the United States to the Soviet people. After a recent visit there, former secretary of state Henry Kissinger reported that he experienced an anti-American side of Russian nationalism when he met in Moscow with a group of "up-and-coming young Russians. They argued that the United States was taking advantage of the current situation, and that the term 'New World Order' was highly presumptuous because it assumed that Russia would no longer be a significant factor in world affairs" (Kissinger 1992).

THE MAJOR DONORS

The United States

Historically, U.S. foreign aid has always been motivated by national security concerns. When the Berlin Wall tumbled in the autumn of 1989, experts noted that the end of East-West conflict rendered the main regional threats to the vital interest of the United States not communism, but rather drug trafficking, massive immigration, and environmental degradation. Although the argument was advanced that the best way to counteract these threats was to improve social and economic conditions in donor countries, the sheer cost of doing so and the uncertainty of effective results have prompted the U.S. government to adopt alternative policies. Although it is obvious that the new massive aid to the Soviets will require the United States to prioritize anew its entire foreign aid program, no open initiative to do so has been aired by cautious bureaucrats. They fully understand that the name of the game is politics and they would rather leave it to the politicians (Congress). This is unfortunate because Congress's yearly brawl over the passage of the foreign aid bill has clearly demonstrated its incapacity to deal with such a topic in a dispassionate manner, with only the long-range best interests of the United States as the sole objective.

Some countries have argued recently that the United States should make more significant cuts in its defense budget to allocate much-needed funds to other domestic and foreign programs. In September 1991, the Brookings Institution recommended in a report that, with the end of the Cold War, the United States should slash its military budget by up to 50 percent annually over the coming decade, well beyond the cuts planned by the Defense Department. The report called on the Defense Department to retool its defense investments in light of the nation's new "one superpower status." According to calculations by the privately financed Center for Defense Information, however, after a slight election-year dip to $281 billion (from $284 billion), military funding will increase steadily in current dollars each year until 1997.

In 1991–1992, other urgent economic problems prevented the United States from focusing in any significant way on foreign assistance except for that to the Soviet republics and Eastern Europe. The U.S. economy was in shambles. The country was pinned down by a recession. Unemployment lines were getting longer. In desperation, President Bush was embracing a once-shunned notion, "industrial policy," to stem the nation's shrinking technological edge.[10] In the meantime, new figures released by the U.S. Commerce Department in July 1991 did nothing to change the underlying shift of the United States from its standing as the world's largest creditor country as recently as 1983 to that of the world's largest debtor nation. To complicate even further the bleak economic outlook, a U.S. State Department conference in 1991 predicted that the United States will continue to depend heavily on Middle East oil through the 1990s. A Bush administration eighteen-month study for a new American energy strategy concluded that no feasible combination of domestic or foreign energy policy options can fully relieve the United States of the risks of oil dependency in the next two decades.

The European Community

In December 1991, the twelve nations of the European Community took their boldest step toward creating a united Europe. They approved two wide-ranging treaties that will create a single European currency and move the member countries toward common defense, foreign, and economic policies. It is too early to tell how that will affect the individual countries' present foreign assistance programs. But a logical assumption is that a portion of that external aid will need to be diverted to level off the economies of the less-affluent members of the community. At the present time, Germany is the biggest donor. It has been generous toward the remnants of the former Soviet empire. As in the case of the United States, however, it has acted in its own interests as well by paying Moscow to remove Soviet troops from German soil. Also, Germany, like the United States, faces a financial slump. Germany's five leading economic think tanks produced their grimmest forecasts in years, warning of prolonged budget deficits and rising unemployment, growing government debts, and shrinking trade surplus (*Miami Herald*, November 4, 1991: 11A).

The European Community has become a trading bloc richer than the United States, with 350 million people and an estimated gross national product of $6 trillion, compared with a population of roughly 250 million and a GNP of about $5.7 trillion for the United States. Nevertheless, future admission of other small and poor nations into the community will lessen its ability to help Third World countries. Eventually, even the Eastern European countries are expected to join. The attitude of the new Europe to the outside world will be deeply affected, as the countries start turning their backs on the Third World to develop instead a European destiny.

The World Bank

There is little doubt that no other institutions, or countries, possess the combination of money and expertise possessed by the World Bank and its sister institution the International Monetary Fund. The two institutions were created to help restore the economies of Western Europe after World War II. They later funneled more and more of their resources into the development and growth of Latin America, Africa, and Asia and, later, into an international war on poverty. However, with both institutions girding for the massive job of helping Eastern Europe and the former Soviet Union, the Third World countries rightly fear that those nations will draw funds and staff away from traditional recipients.

In its 1991 World Development report, the bank suggests three approaches by which the industrial countries and multilateral agencies, including the bank itself, can strengthen development prospects in developing countries: (1) increase financial support, (2) support policy reform, and (3) encourage sustainable growth. However, no solid figures accompanied the prescribed enhancement in the quantity and quality of external financial assistance. Furthermore, the report clearly states that the developing countries' prospects are principally in their own hands. To assure the benefits of better external conditions, the bank recommends that developing countries undertake domestic reforms in these areas: (1) invest in people, (2) improve the climate for enterprise, (3) open economies to international trade and investment, and (4) get macroeconomic policy right (World Bank 1991b: 11). These approaches alone will not succeed, because in the New World Order the developing countries' funding is not being withheld only because of their lack of compliance with structural adjustment programs. The situation is a shifting of the interest of donors from traditional recipients to new ones who offer prospects of a better "political and economic return on their investments."

NEW DECADE, NEW GOALS, NEW APPROACHES

Despite all the talk about a New World Order, those who look for very radical changes in the international strategy for the 1990s will be disappointed. The New World Order strategy does emphasize programs and funding that will consolidate the emerging democracies. As in the past, the solidification of the status quo has always been more appealing than the creation of new conditions. None of the strategic players in the technical assistance area played a role in the events that brought down communism. Those events came about as a result of internal changes provoked by new domestic policies of the countries involved. Therefore, the Third World bureaucracies should learn from that new experience and deemphasize their dependence on foreign technical assistance to create real changes in the Third World. Despite new goals and new approaches that regularly have been announced at the beginning of each decade since 1940, the only dramatic change that occurred in Africa and Asia that was provoked by external policies has been the geographical repartition of the two continents into a series of independent states.

The creation of new international forums where meaningful North-South dialogues could take place has not narrowed the gap between the First and the Third Worlds. The World Bank, the International Monetary Fund, and to a certain extent even the regional financial institutions have not allowed the Third World countries to escape the domination of the West. The voting power of the Western nations in these institutions gives them an absolute majority to rule them. At the United Nations, the one-nation/one-vote system in the General Assembly has allowed the emerging countries to have some impact in the programs and strategies of the United Nations Development Programme (UNDP), even though the money still comes from the West. In addition, it is a matter of legal dispute to what extent any U.N. or UNDP plan is binding on the member countries.[11]

What then is the solution to the problem of underdevelopment? What kind of policies can realistically be made at the bureaucratic level? This chapter suggests a series of new approaches. Not all of them can be initiated in the bureaucracies. Some vital approaches must come from the political leadership of the Third World countries. Then, and only then, will the bureaucracies be able to play a meaningful role in facilitating their implementation. If and when these new approaches are initiated, international donor aid might become crucial in their successful completion. Therefore, the approaches prescribed in this chapter are deemphasizing the present total reliance on external initiatives and replacing it with new strategies conceived by the political leadership of the Third World countries.

Again and again the structural adjustment programs strongly encouraged by the International Monetary Fund (IMF) and supported by the World Bank have proven politically and socially disastrous for many Third World countries. These outside prescriptions conceived at headquarters in Washington, D.C., often fail to recognize the marked differences that exist among Third World countries. Domestic conditions vary so much from one country to another that the economic recipes for development conceived abroad will always risk failure unless they are flexible enough to allow broad fixes.[12] Nothing illustrates better the contrast between UNDP on one hand and the IMF and the World Bank on the other in their approaches to development strategies than a quick comparison between their 1991 annual reports. Although the president of the World Bank stated in the foreword of its report that "markets alone generally do not ensure that people, especially the poorest, receive adequate education, health care, nutrition, and access to family planning" (World Bank 1991b: iii), an overview of the report failed to reveal any strategy to address that issue. By contrast, the UNDP report clearly stated that "the lack of political commitment, not of financial resources, is often the real cause of human neglect" (United Nations Development Programme 1991: 1). The UNDP report primarily addresses financing human development through a restriction of national budgets and international aid. The report concludes that much current spending is misdirected and inefficiently used.

The concept of human development was first introduced in the 1990 UNDP report. For years, economists, politicians, and development planners have measured per-capita income to chart year-to-year progress within a country. As a result, a great deal of national development activity was focused on economic growth, often neglecting the human dimension of development. As a new way to measure human development, a team of leading scholars created a new Human Development Index (HDI) for UNDP. It revealed that even countries of a low per-capita GNP may rank higher on the HDI. In comparison, countries with high per-capita GNP may still have low rates of human development. The difference lies in the way national leaders set their priorities and allocate government funds and in the degree of freedom that citizens enjoy to act on their choices and influence their own lives. The triple-component Human Development Index considers life expectancy as one component not only for its own value but also because it speaks to health care delivery and the ability of people to live long enough to achieve goals. The second component, literacy, not only helps people to get and keep jobs but also assists them in understanding their surroundings and culture. The third one, purchasing power (per-capita income adjusted to account for national differences in exchange rates, tariffs, and tradeable goods), demonstrates the relative ability to buy commodities and meet basic needs (World Bank 1991b: 5–6).

This chapter suggests four new approaches to guide the task of development administration practitioners: (1) population control, (2) indigenous democratization, (3) regional alliances, and (4) reversal of the brain drain flow.

Population Control: The Missing Strategy

Although global population growth still strains natural resources and exceeds the world's ability to provide jobs and decent living standards, the U.S. government, owing to its fear of antiabortion forces, refuses to contribute to the United Nations Population Fund or to support domestic or foreign family-planning programs. In Latin America and the Caribbean, 44 percent of the labor force is unemployed or underemployed. In many countries of Africa and Asia, the situation is similar or worse. It is almost tragic how curtly and vaguely some Western countries deal with the most serious human problem of all, the population increase. Even the North-South program for survival, better known as the Brandt Report, managed to skip the issue entirely despite devoting long sections to hunger and food and suggesting a program of priorities (Brandt 1981). Prior to the Brandt Report's publication, the much-heralded "New International Economic Order" failed to address the subject (United Nations 1974).[13] One reason for such omissions was probably the assumption that the world population would grow at a much slower rate than it actually did. Advances in public health and medical care have in fact led to a rate of population growth twice or three times as great as the one predicted in the 1960s.

Only the Pearson Commission, at the behest of the World Bank, has presented a well-reasoned document on overall development strategy. The commission recommended as early as 1969 that the World Bank in consultation with the World Health Organization should sponsor a broad international program for channeling, coordinating, and financing research in the field of contraception and control of human fertility (Esman 1991; Jackson 1969; Martin 1969; Pearson 1969; Peterson 1970).

The focus of development administrators on this problem is imperative in the New World Order when development assistance resources are becoming more restricted and scarcer.[14] Furthermore, effects of rapid population growth in the developing countries include potentially irreversible stresses on the land and other natural resources and increasing inadequacies in human services. The problem of rampant population growth in the Third World is exacerbated because it is occurring in areas where available resources are inadequate to accommodate this increase. Tropical rain forest countries are particularly vulnerable to obstacles to sustainable development, according to one expert. This is due in part to the conduciveness of moderate climates to high population, coupled with the unique characteristics of tropical rain forests—fragile and complex ecosystems developed over millions of years that, once destroyed, cannot be returned to their original diversity and complexity (Baldi 1989).

Population growth has to be carefully controlled so that growth will be slow enough to allow for the adjustment of land use practices, human services, and economic development. Rapid and uncontrolled growth is occurring in many developing countries because of declining death rates due to improved living conditions and health care, combined with high birth rates and lower infant mortality. Population control is still the missing strategy in the planning of development administrators. With the formidable reduction in the dollar amount of foreign aid in the New World Order, population control should be one of the priorities when development administrators reconsider their strategies.

Indigenous Democratization

The Western powers have been constantly pressuring the Third World countries to hold free elections. In the late 1970s, President Carter's democracy activism paved the way for the two succeeding Republican presidents. At the present time all the governments of South America have been elected; and twenty-five African nations, about one-half of the total, are either democratic or committed to democratic changes. However, these democracies have not been indigenous, and often the poor have not profited from them. Somehow, the elites of these countries have managed again to fool the Western countries into continuing their financial assistance to them by staging democratic "coups." In Peru, for example, there is a copy of the constitution in every telephone book. But the middle and upper classes effectively circumvent the law, and the judges are corrupt, ill-educated, and inept. *Habeas corpus* is ignored. The poor are marginalized and disdained (*Miami Herald*, January 29, 1992: 11A). In February 1992, another South American country, Venezuela, with thirty-four years of two-party democracy and the highest rate of economic growth, was threatened by an unsuccessful coup. Instead of celebrating, the majority of the Venezuelans in the slum areas of the capital were sad because of the failure of the coup and the consolidation of democracy. The democratic system had fomented generalized corruption that has helped a few well-connected Venezuelans make fabulous fortunes in recent years (*Miami Herald*, February 6, 1992: 19A). Other countries of Latin America and the rest of the Third World are exhibiting the same phenomenon. The advance of democracy in Africa also has occurred because Western donors have been requiring it as a condition for their loans. Although in some cases democracy breeds prosperity and produces stability, it has not brought social progress. Only if the poor are as well protected as the rich and share in the progress that the rich usually monopolize will they care about the virtues of democracy.

An indigenous democracy should:

- encourage public participation in development planning and management
- view local initiatives as something positive for development
- have a national bureaucracy that accepts participatory methods as an avenue to the economies of scale that are sought
- have coordination at the national level to allow the government to formulate coherent development strategies
- have coordination at the local level to allow development agents to discuss among themselves the technical and physical inputs required by their programs, the implications their programs have for each other's activities, or any sequencing of activities that could make everyone's task easier
- hold public servants and other government officials accountable. "Accountability is the foundation of any governing process. At the very roots of democracy lie the requirements for public responsibility and accountability of ministers and public servants" (Jabbra and Dwivedi 1989: 8)
- close the gap that usually exists between the national and local governments. In developing countries most government resources are concentrated in the capital. There is a total lack of administrative manpower, even poorly trained manpower, in other areas of the country. This gap between the national and local governments is constantly widening. An indigenous democracy should work at reversing it.

The world is presently on a democracy binge. But the triumph of democracy will not affect the poor if it is not indigenous and is limited to free elections. The Western nations have developed their democracies over centuries in the framework of popular participation and prosperity. But democracy by itself does not necessarily bring prosperity if the democratically elected government does not choose the right policies. In Asia, for example, the pattern seems to be the reverse: South Korea, Taiwan, and Singapore all built up booming economies under regimes that tolerate little opposition (Auchincloss 1992: 28). As another writer said appropriately, "Democracy means more than not killing voters on election day" (Matthews 1991).

Regional Alliances

Latin America has taken the lead in forging regional alliances to further economic integration. The trend has been recognized by the developed nations (the European Community). The Andean group became a reality in January 1992 after twenty-three years of false starts, when the free trade zone agreement among Venezuela, Colombia, Ecuador, Bolivia, and Peru became effective. The five countries established common tariffs and unitary customs and also agreed to ban weapons of mass destruction. The formation of the Andean group was propelled by progress in negotiations among Mexico, Canada, and the United States to sign a free trade agreement. At the signing of the Andean agreement, one of the five presidents invoked the Bolivarian vision by saying, "After 1993, we'll practically become a single country" (*Miami Herald*, December 11, 1991: 20A). The Rio group of Latin American countries is a reincarnation of the defunct Contadora group, formed in 1982 by Colombia, Mexico, Panama, and Venezuela to mediate Central American conflicts. A support group of Argentina, Peru, Brazil, and Uruguay was organized a year later. In 1986, the countries came together as the Group of Eight, emulating the international trend of forming economic blocs. Since then Chile, Bolivia, Ecuador, and Paraguay have joined the group, which is not a formal trading bloc.

President Bush's "Initiative for the Americas," announced in June 1990 and expected to open U.S. markets to Latin products, gave further impetus to the revived Latin American interest in regional integration. Indeed, Rio member nations agreed in 1991 to designate the existing Association for Latin American Integration (ALADI) as the major institution for efforts that could lead to the establishment of a Latin American common market. The backbone of the Rio group's efforts is two fledgling subregional blocs: the Group of Three, consisting of Mexico, Venezuela, and Colombia; and the Southern Cone Common Market (MERCOSUR), which includes Argentina, Brazil, Paraguay, and Uruguay. The Rio group is appealing for the European community to consider major investments in the region and for the participation of the European Investment

Bank in development plans. Europe is more attractive to the group because, unlike the United States, it does not demand that the countries establish a particular economic program in exchange for economic cooperation (*Miami Herald*, April 11, 1991: 16A).

In Asia, there is an alliance among Singapore, Malaysia, Indonesia, Thailand, Brunei, and the Philippines—the Association of South East Asian Nations (ASEAN)—but it was established primarily because of political and security concerns. However, ASEAN has increased trading among its members and coordinated trading outside the group.

Africa has been the continent with the most regional alliances, perhaps in recognition of the idea that the states are too small and not viable. Most of these alliances are not very effective. The preindependence East African Community was a solid economic union, but it deteriorated and finally disappeared after the British left. Present regional alliances include a customs union between the six central African states of Gabon, Chad, Cameroon, Central African Republic, Equatorial Guinea, and Congo-Brazzaville; another customs union between the four southern African states of Botswana, Lesotho, Swaziland, and southern Africa; an association between the four Indian Ocean states of Madagascar, Reunion, Mauritius, and the Seychelles; and a North African Association with Morocco, Tunisia, and Algeria. Most of these alliances are not real trade or economic pacts. In fact, they have very specific and sectoral objectives. For example, the South African Coordination Conference, with more than ten members, is primarily concerned in developing alternative communications for avoiding linkage with South Africa. Only the West African Community, with more than a dozen members and a formal secretariat and headquarters in Lome, has the kind of broad economic objectives of ASEAN and the Andean group. However, it has never really functioned effectively.

The proliferation of regional alliances will not aid development if it does not lead the way to reduced dependency. In the area of research and development, where most small poor countries are not doing well, individual countries' efforts should be coordinated and linked. Some of these small countries cannot pay their researchers, cover minimum maintenance cost, or buy equipment. The most advanced developing countries in the area of science and technology (e.g., Barbados, Costa Rica, Botswana, and Zimbabwe, in the group of small nations) should take a leading role with the countries in their regions to reduce their dependency on Western nations' technology (Segal 1990: 224).

The donors should initiate more regional projects instead of extending their country-level activities. These regional programs, when multiplied, will help the developing countries develop economic linkages and diminish their dependency on the developed nations.[15]

Reversal of the Brain Drain Flow

Brain drain has always been one of the big obstacles to development in the Third World. Recently, however, several countries have been recruiting their own nationals who have been successful abroad. The Asian countries, especially South Korea, have been quite active in doing so. Unfortunately, most developing countries do not have the capacity to attract their expatriates back. The new strategy suggested here is only for countries with solid economic prospects.

Several Latin American countries are now trying to get skilled workers from the former Soviet bloc. Five southern Latin American countries are involved in the program: Argentina, Venezuela, Uruguay, Paraguay, and Bolivia. These countries know that Russia and Eastern Europe have a surplus of hospital equipment maintenance technicians, electrical engineers, construction foremen, and plumbers, and they happen to have a shortage of such experts. After studies showed that between 2.5 million and 10 million Russians and Eastern Europeans could flood Western Europe in coming years because of growing economic trouble at home, Argentina's government made a formal request to the European community to help finance the resettlement of a hundred thousand such experts in Argentina. Venezuela has already approved a project to bring in ten thousand of them (*Miami Herald*, February 12, 1992: 1A).

The four approaches suggested in this chapter may not be entirely new, and the list is definitely not exhaustive. The four approaches, however, if jointly executed, could be a good strategy to enable Third World development administrators to succeed despite the inevitable neglect they will experience from donors in the New World Order. These macro approaches should be reinforced by sectoral strategies (especially in the sectors of health, education, and agriculture) and "realistic" structural adjustment of the economies. In all cases the commitment for reform from the political leaders and the management capacity of the public sector as a whole will be major and crucial factors in the success or failure of development efforts.

NOTES

1. Some of the earlier theories developed by the author of this chapter dealt with the inner work of development administration (Garcia-Zamor 1968, 1973, 1990).

2. It is commonplace to refer to the underdeveloped countries of Asia, Africa, and Latin America as the "Third World." The "Second World" used to be the communist countries. It is not certain whether this term will still apply to the few remaining communist nations. The "First World" comprises the United States, Canada, and Western Europe.

3. The attitude of these bureaucrats was in sharp contrast with that of leftist nationalists, who viewed dependency as an obstacle to political development. The debate over dependency theory has been rich in content and relevant in application (Chilcote 1982).

4. UNESCO Director General Frederico Mayor Zaragoza remarked in early 1992 that the term "New World Order" is being abused and is meaningless. He reminded an interviewer that

Benito Mussolini was the first leader to use it. He also stated that the world had a "New World Order" since 1948 when the Universal Declaration of Human Rights was promulgated, and supposedly a "New World Economic Order" since 1974, but rich countries just ignore them (*Miami Herald*, January 31, 1992: 17A).

5. However, an increasingly large fraction of the program has been in the form of military assistance, which provides weapons and defense services to friendly foreign countries on a grant basis. At the beginning of the Reagan administration, this form of assistance totaled $110 million. By 1987 it totaled $950 million. For example, the military assistance to Spain, Turkey, and Portugal increased by 200 percent between 1980 and 1985. Comparing the 1978 foreign assistance program with the 1987 program, military assistance increased from 26 percent to 36 percent of the entire program while resources devoted to development assistance declined from 21 percent of the total to 15 percent, and food assistance declined from 14 percent to 10 percent (Hamilton 1988).

6. Even in the case of environmental degradation in which the industrialized societies' interests are at stake, the United States has been slow to play a leading role. An important United Nations–sponsored meeting, the Earth Summit, took place in June 1992 in Rio de Janeiro, Brazil, to debate how to resolve environmental crises such as global warming, forest destruction, and ocean contamination. Although more than 100 heads of state had committed themselves to attend, President Bush reluctantly decided only at the last minute to accept the invitation. A main reason for his coyness was concern that developing countries, led by China and India, would press the United States and other wealthy nations for large and unrealistic funding transfers to the Third World to pay for environmental programs (*Miami Herald*, February 11, 1992: 7A).

7. Japan is already a leading source of foreign assistance, which comprises about 1 percent of its gross national product, approximately the same percentage that Japan spends on defense. By comparison, the United States devotes about 8 percent of its GNP to its world role, unfortunately almost all of it going to the far-flung military effort. If Japan could be persuaded to spend more on global leadership—say, 5 percent of its GNP—the result would be a vast increase in assistance to poorer countries (*Newsweek*, November 25, 1991: 47)

8. For the fiscal year 1991–1992 U.S. assistance to Eastern Europe was focusing on national public administration. Previous efforts were centered on ways of improving local or regional administration. The American Consortium of Public Administration (ACIPA) has developed an unsolicited proposal to establish and operate an International Public Service Executive Corps (IPSEC) to provide public administration technical assistance services to Central and Eastern European governments.

9. The U.S. pledge was made at the conclusion of a two-day international conference called by President Bush to coordinate worldwide aid to the former Soviet Union. The conference was held in Washington, D.C., in early January 1992. Representatives of forty-seven nations and seven international organizations reported at the meeting the formation of "action plans," to ensure orderly shipments and distribution of food and medicine and to ensure the coordination of help to solve housing and energy shortages. The wealthy Arab nations of Saudi Arabia, Kuwait, and the United Arab Emirates have pledged an additional $4 billion in Soviet relief. Such an extraordinary amount of foreign assistance had never been contemplated to lift the Third World nations out of their misery.

10. The High Performance Computing Act was signed by President Bush in December 1991. It authorizes eight federal agencies to spend $638 million to develop hardware and software for a teraflop computer capable of performing one trillion computations a second. At the same time, Energy Secretary James Watkins announced that the government's 726 national laboratories— facilities that spend more than $20 billion annually, mostly on weapons research—will now be available for joint research projects with private businesses.

11. When national governments felt that a U.N. plan made a negative impact on them, they had always distanced themselves from it. In the early 1960s when the Soviet Union and France disapproved of U.N. Secretary General Dag Hammarskjold's Congo Operation, they simply ceased to pay their annual dues to prevent any part of their money from going toward the financing of that operation.

12. A policy and scholarly consensus is emerging on reducing the role of the state in the economy, but with relatively little consideration of its meaning and potential consequences. Thomas J. Biersteker (1990) of the University of Southern California published an article distinguishing six different forms of state economic intervention. He combined them to characterize different national economic regimes. IMF and World Bank recommendations for policy reform are then identified, and the consequences of those recommendations are assessed for different forms of economic intervention.

13. The "New International Economic Order" was adopted by the United Nations in 1974 to encourage the transfer of resources from the poor to the rich. It had numerous supporters in the Third World and some of the specialized agencies of the United Nations. In the more developed countries, however, it was popular only among nongovernmental organizations. Two American scholars, William Loehr and John Powelson, have published an interesting book on the pitfalls of the New International Economic Order (Loehr and Powelson 1983).

14. Colombia has been an exception and one of the Third World's greatest success stories in family planning, driving down its birth rate from an average of six children per woman in 1970 to 2.2 children at present.

15. Interregional projects will not, however, meet these objectives, because they take place in countries that have totally different kinds of economies and are geographically too remote from each other. Of course, these projects were not initiated for that purpose. For example, one of UNDP's interregional projects is in the field of public administration. It covers Africa, Asia and the Pacific, Latin America and the Caribbean, and Arab states and Europe. Its overall goal is to assist countries in these regions in improving their public sectors by enhancing the management capabilities of their governments.

6

DILEMMAS OF DEVELOPMENT ADMINISTRATION IN THE GLOBAL VILLAGE
The Case of Colombia

FERREL HEADY

As a member of the contemporary global village, Colombia inevitably benefits from the advantages and suffers from the disadvantages that have their origin in its network of relationships with other nation-states. This has complicated the problems of Colombia's political leaders in trying to carry out plans for national development.

POSITIVE DEVELOPMENTAL ATTRIBUTES

Colombia is a nation with attributes holding promise for progress toward attainment of developmental objectives. It is the fourth largest country in Latin America, over 440,000 square miles in area (one and two-thirds the size of Texas, four-fifths the size of Alaska). It is located strategically in the northwestern part of the South American continent at the base of the Isthmus of Panama, with frontage on both the Pacific and the Caribbean. It is varied geographically, with flat coastal areas, a highland region of mountain ranges and valleys, and eastern plains with drainage to the Orinoco and Amazon rivers. Its natural resources include numerous agricultural crops (both legal, such as coffee, bananas, and flowers, and illegal, such as marijuana and cocaine), petroleum products, emeralds, and hydroelectric sites.

The Colombian population totals almost 35 million, making it the most populous country in South America after Brazil, and is growing at a rate of 1.8 percent annually. Life expectancy at birth is just under seventy years. Colombians are predominantly (about 75 percent) mestizos or mulattoes of mixed blood, with only small groups of whites, Indians, and blacks, making them one of the most integrated populations in the hemisphere and sparing the country from serious ethnic tensions. Spanish is the language of most people, and illiteracy is under 20 percent. The dominant religion is Roman Catholicism, but numerous other creeds are represented as well. Urbanization of the population has been increasing at a rapid rate, from 57 percent in 1951 to over 70 percent today. Thirty cities now have 100,000 or more inhabitants, with over 5 million in Bogotá, and Medellín, Cali, and Barranquilla ranging in descending order from 2.5 million to 1.3 million.

The Colombian economy during most of the 1970s experienced a growth rate in real gross domestic product (GDP) of over 6 percent. Beginning in 1976 the country ceased receiving economic assistance from the United States. During the 1980s, GDP growth declined because of combined internal and external factors, bottoming out in 1982 at 1 percent, but then it jumped back to over 5 percent in 1985 and 1986, in response to government-initiated adjustments in trade policy, currency devaluation, and budget and fiscal reforms. During the early 1990s, the growth rate has again been between 4 percent and 5 percent, encouraging plans announced in 1991 for a three-year "peaceful revolution" aimed at lifting a quarter of the nation's poor above the poverty level, improving the quality of rural life, and eliminating urban illiteracy.

Politically, Colombia has had a checkered history, but for the last two decades it has maintained a competitive democratic system (Dix 1987; Roa Suarez 1992; Rodriguez 1985), with control alternating between the Liberal and Conservative parties. The current president is Cesar Gaviria Trujillo, a Liberal serving a four-year term ending in 1994. The Liberals also have majorities in both houses of the legislature.

In addition to this achievement of a functioning democracy, Colombia has been engaged during the last few years in an impressive array of activities to reform both its political and administrative systems.

The most significant of these reforms was adoption of a new constitution that went into effect in mid-1991 (*Constitución Política de Colombia 1991* 1992). Following a referendum in 1990, the much-amended 1886 constitution was extensively revised by a constituent assembly operating without limits on what could be considered. The basic presidential system was retained, but numerous less fundamental changes were accepted. Among these were several reforms, previously considered but not put into effect for one reason or another, affecting existing institutions (including the legislature, the attorney general, the supreme court of justice, and the constitutional court). A second category of reforms added new features, including elimination of reference to the traditional two-party system and recognition of a multiparty system, removal of the last constitutional vestiges of the old 1957–1974 National Front political arrangements, recognition of legal equality for all religious sects, and adoption of a set of mechanisms for direct citizen participation in the making of policy decisions through devices such as referenda and initiatives. A third category consisted of reforms not seriously considered previously, such as election of all members of the Senate by popular vote, a runoff if needed in the election of the president, adoption of a bill of rights, creation of an office of public defender, introduction of the "tutela" as a form of legal action to secure guaranteed rights, and formalization of constituent assemblies for future constitutional reforms.

This constitutional revision has laid the foundation for a program of administrative reforms, many still in the planning stage but with some already in place.

One major thrust of the new constitution and of the announced program of the current government is toward greater privatization and decentralization of programs now administered by the central government. For example, numerous articles in Title II, Chapter 2, of the revised document deal with social, economic, and cultural rights, and Article 366 in Title XII states that the general welfare and betterment of the quality of life are social ends of the state.

Leadership during the Gaviria administration in implementation of these reforms is in the hands of Jorge García González, presidential adviser for state modernization, who has articulated a program of change from an existing system that he describes as closed, protectionist, interventionist, and centralized to a system designed to be open, internationalized, deregulated, and decentralized politically, financially, and administratively (García González 1993). This redefinition of the role of the state contemplates privatization of some functions and lifting of detailed constraints in many others, calling in turn for policy changes regarding, for example, foreign commerce, customs, labor relations, and the operation of ports, railroads, and highways. This transformation is viewed realistically not as a single action or decision, but as a gradual process requiring sustained official commitment and public support.

In most areas, realization of these objectives seems to be more prospective than actual. In at least one instance—the proposed sale of Telecom, the government-operated communications system—a major change was initiated early in 1992 and then aborted, allegedly because of inadequate public debate and unclear definition of objectives and means (Child 1992). Significant progress is being made in some fields, however, particularly in public health and social welfare, as detailed by Antonio Yepes Parra (1991) and Martha Laverde de Orjuela (1991).

Structural reform of the administrative machinery is identified by García González as one of the requirements for modernization. Title VII of the constitution, dealing with the executive branch, provides for major administrative agencies (ministries and administrative departments) established by law to function under the president as chief of state, head of government, and highest administrative authority. Currently there are fourteen ministries plus several administrative departments (including, for example, the Administrative Department of the Public Service). Transitory Article 20 of the new constitution calls for the establishment of a study commission for reorganizing public administration and for the adoption within eighteen months of the effective date of the constitution (that is, early 1993) of plans to eliminate, merge, or restructure entities in the executive branch.

The public service is declared by the constitution to be a career service unless otherwise provided in the constitution or by law, with members selected by competitive examination and without regard to political affiliation and prohibited (without prejudice to their free exercise of suffrage rights) from taking part in the activities of political parties and movements and in political controversies (Title V, Chapter 1, Articles 125, 127). A National Civil Service Commission is to be set up to protect members of this career service (Article 130).

Past efforts to reform public administration or to extend the merit principle in the Colombian civil service have proved to be disappointing (Ruffing-Hilliard 1991; Vidal Perdomo 1982), and only minimal progress has been made to date in implementing these constitutional mandates, although García González stresses the need for "professionalization of public servants, in such a way as to restore an authentic administrative career service, based on merit and promotion for efficiency and fulfillment of duties" (1993: 62).

Nevertheless, preliminary steps have been taken to carry out some of these objectives. In 1991, initiatives from the president's office resulted in the completion and publication of two major planning documents, one offering a strategy for optimizing the social productivity of public resources (Comisión Presidencial para la Reforma 1991) and the other mapping out a new regimen for public administration (Consejería para la Modernización del Estado 1991).

The reorganization commission was duly set up before the end of 1991 (with three members designated by the Council of State, plus one cabinet minister, the head of the national department of planning, the presidential adviser for modernization of the state, and the mayor of Bogotá), and made a preliminary report to the Council of Ministers on March 30, 1992. A presidential directive was issued the following August (Presidencia de la República de Colombia 1992). The directive presented an analysis of the provisions of the new constitution that ought to be taken into account in restructuring identified general objectives (such as decentralization, rationalization, and simplification to assure greater efficacy and efficiency) and assigning responsibility to various officials and agencies for preparing proposals, supporting documentation, and drafts of implementing decrees. All of these assignments were intended to assist the reorganization commission during the six-month period remaining in the constitutional time schedule for completion of its work. However, by early 1993 no final recommendations had been issued. With regard to the constitutional directives concerning the civil service, a major step was taken in April 1992, when the president, acting on the basis of authority conferred by language in Article 189 of the constitution to specify functions and fix salaries and emoluments of central government employees, issued Decree No. 643 (*Carta Administrativa* 1992). This document specified functions and minimum requisites for these employees by hierarchical level (directive, advisory, executive, professional, technical, administrative, and operative, plus a number of specialist categories). The functional expectations for each category were laid out in detail. With respect to requisites, those in the directive category in the lower grades, for example, must have as a minimum a university degree and two years of professional experience, with those in higher grades requiring more advanced or postgraduate education or additional years of experience. At the other end of the spectrum, employees in the operative group at the lowest grades may have as few as five years of basic primary education. What other moves may be in the offing for improvements in the selection of public administration personnel were unclear early in 1993.

NEGATIVE FACTORS AFFECTING DEVELOPMENT

Counteracting these positive indicators for development are some even more powerful factors inhibiting progress until they can be either eliminated or minimized (Behar and Villa Salcedo 1991; Galán 1991; Landazábal Reyes 1990; Marulanda 1990).

One set of inhibitors stems from inequalities among groups in Colombian society. Colombia has had and continues to have a severe maldistribution of wealth, with little movement toward more economic equity. Inflation is a continuing phenomenon, fluctuating between 20 percent and 30 percent annually during the last decade. Unemployment is above 12 percent and is not declining. Markets for Colombia's main legal exports—coffee, bananas, and petroleum products—are dropping or stagnant. Foreign debt is low by regional standards, but reducing it depends on growth in exports and conservative fiscal management. These economic inequities are mirrored to a lesser degree in social and political life.

An overwhelmingly negative contributor to developmental prospects is the prevalence of "La Violencia" in Colombia, both historically and currently. Violence as a fact of life is the product of past and present forces in Colombian society. Sharing the Latin American record of political instability during much of the time since independence, Colombia can trace its political rivalries to the contrasting philosophies of Simón Bolívar and Francisco de Paula Santander, the national heroes of the struggle for independence. Bolívar was an advocate of centralism and unification, Santander of decentralization and federalism. These two political currents were formalized by the mid-1800s in the Conservative and Liberal parties, patterned respectively on the beliefs of Bolívar and Santander. Fierce rivalry between these groupings has been a constant in the country's political history. During the nineteenth century the result was more than fifty insurrections, eight civil wars, and a succession of name changes and constitutions for the country, culminating in 1899 with more than 100,000 deaths during the War of a Thousand Days.

After the early decades of this century were relatively quiet, an even more destructive civil war broke out in 1948, with a death toll of 300,000 before a military intervention in 1953 by General Gustavo Rojas Pinilla imposed a forced pacification. Following this atypical four-year military dictatorship, the two major parties entered into a pact to establish the National Front, which lasted from 1957 until 1974. This pact provided for alternating the presidency every four years and sharing equally in government at all levels. The National Front succeeded in paving the way for a resumption of open political competition, which began with the 1974 presidential election and has continued up to the present.

Nevertheless, reliance on violence persists as a dominant characteristic of two other movements that have impacted negatively on Colombia's development beginning with the years of civil conflict at mid-century: persistent insurgencies by radical guerrilla groups and the emergence of powerful cartels engaged in illegal drug trafficking.

Contemporary armed insurgent groups advocating drastic political and societal reforms can be traced to the turmoil of the 1940s and 1950s and the later imposition of relative public order under the military dictatorship and the National Front pact between the mainstream Liberal and Conservative parties. This restricted pattern of political participation was unacceptable to a variety of dissidents who had gained experience in guerrilla warfare during the more violent years. These groups share a leftist political ideology, but they have never succeeded in uniting under common leadership for a cohesive plan of action, although they have formed an umbrella organization, the Simón Bolívar Coordinating Board (CGSB) for the conduct of on-and-off-again negotiations with the government (Pizarro 1990). The current major insurgent groups are the Colombia Revolutionary Armed Forces (FARC), which is the oldest and now the most numerous, the National Liberation Army (ELN), once the largest and most militant with close earlier ties to the Cuban revolution, and the Popular Army of Liberation (EPL), originally pro-Chinese and inspired by Maoist political doctrines. An earlier fourth major participant, the April 19 Movement (M-19), which carried out a dramatic takeover of the Palace of Justice in Bogotá in 1985, was demobilized in 1990. Former members now form a party represented in the national legislature and have even served in the cabinet during the current administration.

Estimates in mid-1992 were that approximately 8,000 combatants were active on behalf of the various guerrilla forces. Even with this relatively small number, their ability to disrupt normal living conditions has been tremendous. Obvious targets are the major oil pipelines, electric power lines, railways, and highways. One main petroleum line has been dynamited at least 300 times since its construction in 1985. During a single month in the fall of 1992, the two most important lines were blown up at least a dozen times, forcing the country to import oil for the first time in almost a decade to meet national energy needs. Downing of power lines, plus other factors such as lower than average rainfall and slower than expected progress on new hydroelectric projects, brought about a nationwide rationing of electric power in the spring of 1992, with electricity usually cut off five hours per day. Barricading or destruction of railways and highways is a frequent occurrence, as is occupation of entire villages for brief periods of time. Massacres of security personnel and ordinary citizens, particularly in rural areas, are reported on a daily basis. A summary compilation issued in 1992 concluded that the toll had increased by 20 percent over 1991 and that the monthly average had reached twelve massacres, with sixty-one resulting deaths. In just one episode early in November 1992, twenty-six police officers were killed and two others wounded in an attack by the FARC on guards at an oil well near the Ecuadoran border. Many of the dead are victims of kidnappings of individuals by guerrillas for ransom that was not paid on demand by relatives or friends. An additional cost of insurrection is the exaction of tribute from campesinos, miners, foresters, and others in large areas of the country in de facto control of guerrilla forces. For example, documents captured by security forces indicated that in 1991 the ELN alone had extorted $30 million in this fashion.

Illegal international trafficking in drugs (particularly marijuana and cocaine) is the second source of lawlessness and violence. Because of its proximity to the United States, where the main consumer demand exists, and its advantages in access to producers within its own borders and in neighboring countries (particularly Bolivia and Peru), Colombia inevitably has emerged as the global center for such activities. The marijuana trade was of most importance earlier, but during the 1970s the cocaine industry overtook it and quickly developed into the major partner, controlling in recent years an estimated 80 percent of the world cocaine market. With this expansion has come increasing sophistication in the growing, processing, and exportation of cocaine; greater centralization, closer control, and more secrecy and security in their operations by the drug leaders; and the realization of immense profits by the cartels they organized (estimated as at least ten billion a year in U.S. dollars). The primary cartels have been headquartered in the cities of Medellín and more recently Cali, the second and third largest metropolitan centers in the country.

The boom years for the cartels came in the early 1980s, peaking in 1982 and 1983. A campaign against the drug trade launched in 1983 by President Belisario Betancur led in 1984 to open warfare between the cartels and government forces, with many of the most prominent and effective opponents of the cartels being liquidated during the next few years, including kidnapping of the son of a former national president and assassination of the country's attorney general in 1988. Probably the most devastating blow came in 1989 with the murder during a campaign rally of Luis Carlos Galán, Liberal party candidate for the presidency and the expected winner in the upcoming 1990 election.

Meanwhile, cartel leaders had gained great wealth, power, and influence, backed up by a willingness to resort to violent methods to protect their turf.

Among the best known were Jorge Luis Ochoa, Carlos Lehder Rivas, and especially Pablo Emilio Escobar. The government has had only very limited success in trying to apprehend and punish them. It did succeed in capturing Lehder early in 1987 and extraditing him to the United States. Ochoa was captured toward the end of that same year, but his extradition was overturned by the Supreme Court, and he was set free after only one month in a Colombian prison. In 1991, Escobar entered into an agreement to give himself up and was placed in a special prison in his home town of Envigado, near Medellín. He escaped in July 1992, under questionable circumstances, from what was then revealed to be a luxury facility built to his own specifications and enabling him to continue directing cartel operations. In March 1993, he was still at large, despite a massive manhunt launched after his escape and the offer of huge cash awards for his apprehension.

This standoff between Escobar and the authorities has contributed to a new wave of violence from the narcotraffic cartels, directed primarily at police and military officers. During a period of less than three weeks in the fall of 1992, thirty-four police officers were killed, presumably under orders from the Medellín cartel, which reportedly offered 2,000 U.S. dollars for each officer killed, bringing the total to more than fifty-five since July, and about thirty bombings took place in Medellín and other cities in the department of Antioquia against banks and other civilian installations, killing at least six people.

Early in December 1992, because of either guerrilla or cartel actions, crucial equipment was destroyed at five airports around the country, a car bomb exploded outside a stadium in Medellín following a soccer game, high-powered bombs exploded almost simultaneously in Bogotá at four major hotels, and seven political party offices were bombed in Medellín. Collaboration or coordination in these antigovernment campaigns is only the latest in a long series of alliances or joint undertakings by insurgent and drug groups, which often are operating in the same areas and find it mutually beneficial to cooperate in acts of terrorism or exaction of tribute from individuals or groups incapable of resisting effectively. Both are well enough established and possess enough power to expand their activities well beyond their original objectives. Thus guerrillas are often accused of having "forsaken Marx for Mammon," and drug operators have branched out into other kinds of illegal activities.

GOVERNMENTAL RESPONSES

To these more and more open and widespread acts of defiance and terrorism, the Gaviria government has responded in a series of actions beginning in the summer of 1992. In July, all members of Gaviria's cabinet resigned at his request. This had been a mixed group consisting of eight members from Gaviria's Liberal Party, four from the Conservative Party, and one from the M-19 Democratic Alliance. Six Liberal ministers were retained, as was the foreign affairs minister affiliated with one of the Conservative Party factions. Four new appointees were Liberals, two were Conservatives, and one was supposed to represent the M-19 Democratic Alliance, although there was some dispute as to whether he actually was approved for the appointment by M-19 party leaders. Clearly the intent was to produce a cabinet more identified with Gaviria's own party and presumably more responsive to his leadership. In an address at the opening of a new session of Congress on July 21, President Gaviria (1992) revealed plans for a "social revolution" to reduce poverty, improve levels of education, and lessen social disequilibrium. He also said that there would be no more unfruitful dialogue with guerrilla groups and announced the creation of a mobile brigade to maintain order in regions with greatest unrest. This was supplemented in a statement the following month by Horacio Serpa Uribe, the presidential adviser for peace negotiations, expressing skepticism about the resumption of peace talks on October 31, as previously scheduled. Also in August, a special task force for Morality and Efficiency in Public Administration (Misión para la Moralización y Eficiencia de la Administración Pública 1992) issued its report, with a series of proposals for dealing with corrupt practices among public officials and imposing disciplinary sanctions and penalties against wrongdoers. At about the same time, the National Electoral Council officially revoked legal status for eleven political parties, including the Colombian Communist Party, for failing to receive the constitutionally required minimum number of votes in municipal elections held the previous March (*Notisur*, September 1, 1992).

On November 8, in view of the failure to recapture Escobar and the stepped-up terrorist campaigns by both guerrillas and drug traffickers, President Gaviria felt compelled to declare a state of emergency and suspended constitutional rights and guarantees for a ninety-day period. He declared that his emergency measures would "attack the guerrilla leadership, finances, and operational capability and urban networks, and take on the criminal wave of narcoterrorism in Medellín" (*Facts on File*, November 26, 1992: 899–900).

The declaration of emergency, promulgated in accordance with a provision of the 1991 constitution, authorized Gaviria to issue directives against terrorism without legislative or judicial approval. Among the measures adopted were these: a prohibition against the broadcast over government-controlled airwaves of interviews with antigovernment leaders or publicizing of their communiques; ineligibility for carrying out public contracts for domestic companies that had paid protection money to guerrillas or drug traffickers and a bar to doing business in Colombia against foreign companies implicated in protection schemes; dismissal of local officials maintaining contacts with outlaw groups; administration by the central government of oil revenues from wells located in areas of rebel strength; assumption of investigative powers by armed forces in rural areas, subject to accountability to central government officials; offer of rewards for the capture of two named guerrilla leaders (one from ELN and one from FARC), in addition to the rewards already offered for capture of Escobar; increased security for members of the armed forces and police; and establishment of a witness-protection program to encourage testimony against drug traffickers and insurgents.

These emergency decrees were supported by 75 percent of the Colombian public in opinion polls and were endorsed by many business, religious, political, and ranching leaders. A group of fifty Colombian artists and intellectuals, led by Gabriel García Marquez, called on the rebel groups to abandon armed violence. However, some union leaders expressed fears that basic human freedoms might be denied if the emergency policies were applied in a blanket fashion; later in the month, the M-19 Democratic Alliance announced its decision to withdraw from the government coalition because of disagreements with Gaviria's policies, and its representative in the cabinet (the minister of health) submitted his resignation (*Notisur*, December 15, 1992).

In another significant action on November 12, the government replaced the chairman of the joint chiefs of staff and the commanders of all three branches of the armed forces—army, navy, and air force. An official statement was issued that these shifts reflected only a normal shuffling of posts and were unrelated to the declaration of emergency, but unofficial sources reported that Defense Minister Rafael Pardo preferred to appoint his own commanders to replace those who had been appointed by the previous government. Shortly afterward, a special Senate investigating committee that had been probing the escape of Escobar placed major responsibility on the general who had been in command of the army brigade in Medellín at the time. Political responsibility was assigned to several former officials—the minister and deputy minister of the Ministry of Justice, the director of prisons, and the director of the Envigado jail, all of whom had been removed from their posts shortly after the escape (*Notisur*, November 11, 1992).

In a prompt follow-up to the emergency declaration, subsequent to a meeting of local, regional, and federal security personnel, Interior Minister Humberto de la Calle beefed up police and military patrols in the city of Medellín, adding eighty military and three hundred police officials for increased security (*Notisur*, December 12, 1992).

These and other efforts to bolster the antiterrorism campaign did produce results, although at the price of renewed terrorist attacks. Early in December, police captured the ELN's third in command. A number of Escobar's close associates were also either killed or captured late in 1992.

Early in January 1993, official reports summarized the depressing record for the year 1992 (*Notisur*, January 12, 1993). Throughout the country, 27,100 people had been murdered, an 8 percent increase over 1991. The city of Medellín alone accounted for 6,622 of these victims. Rebel violence had also increased, with a total of 1,100 terrorist attacks, compared to 926 the year before. The only decline was in the number of kidnapping cases, from 1,717 to

1,136; but it was noted that only about 40 percent of all abductions are reported to the police.

Late in December and early in January, new emergency security decrees were issued by the government, designed to improve police income and retirement benefits, ease eligibility requirements for police service, guarantee insurance payments for public transportation drivers operating in guerrilla zones, and restrict the use of weapons, portable communications equipment, and armored vehicles. Also early in the year, the second in command of the Popular Liberation Army (EPL) was captured, and a new elite military unit composed of 5,000 individuals drawn from the armed forces and the national police was formed to focus on capture of the heads of the two other main insurgent groups—the Revolutionary Armed Forces of Colombia (FARC) and the National Liberation Army (ELN)—and increased rewards were announced for information leading to their arrest (*Notisur*, January 12, 1993).

In mid-January, newly appointed Interior Minister Fabio Villegas announced that Escobar, in an eight-page letter delivered to authorities by his wife, had made new demands as conditions for his surrender, including that he be held in a police training school in a Medellín suburb and that about seventy other previously incarcerated Medellín cartel members be relocated there. He also demanded that his guards be drawn not from the police but from the air force, the navy, or some international organization. Moreover, he asked, "What would the government think about having a car bomb made up of 10,000 kilograms of dynamite explode in the attorney general's office?" (Attorney General Gustavo de Greiff had repeatedly refused to negotiate with Escobar and had demanded that he surrender without any conditions.) In response, Villegas stated that Escobar was simply trying to confuse the public by attempting to divert attention from the crimes he had committed and that the government would not recognize his actions as "political" (*Notisur*, January 19, 1993).

Within a week of the threat from Escobar, a powerful car bomb exploded in a residential area of northern Bogotá, damaging buildings, knocking out electricity over a wide area, and injuring eighteen people. Three other bomb attacks took place in Bogotá and nearby towns as well, and police confiscated 1.5 metric tons of dynamite at a ranch southeast of Bogotá. In response to these events, security forces were placed on alert and began around-the-clock patrols on Bogotá streets (*Notisur*, January 26, 1993). Despite these measures, a wave of car bombings continued in Bogotá, including one in the downtown area that killed twenty-one people (including three children) and injured seventy-seven. In the Medellín area, two explosions occurred in the city and another at a ranch belonging to Escobar's mother, and four corpses were found on the streets with signs indicating that the killings were for acceptance of government compensation in exchange for information on drug traffickers (*Notisur*, February 2, 1993). A new phenomenon appeared as this pattern of violence escalated—the emergence of vigilante groups dedicated to vengeance against Escobar and his elimination. One was identified as "Victims of Pablo Escobar" (PEPES as abbreviated in Spanish), and a second as "Free COLOMBIA" (COLOMBIA Libre). PEPES claimed responsibility for various bomb attacks in the Medellín vicinity, especially on properties belonging to Escobar or members of his family, and for the murder of as many as forty of his associates. COLOMBIA Libre disavowed violent methods but was reported as wanting to coordinate activities with PEPES to eliminate Escobar.

The official response to the emergence of these organizations was negative, despite the shared objective of opposition to Escobar. For instance, the mayor of Medellín said that they would "only add to the violence currently engulfing the country." The Inter-American Human Rights Commission strongly condemned the growing wave of violence, stating that it created an atmosphere of terror and threatened directly the right of Colombians to life, security, and personal integrity.

A more positive development for the authorities was the surrender to police on February 18 of Carlos Alzate Urquijo, who was viewed as the mastermind of Escobar's terrorist activities, responsible for organizing more than seventy assassinations of police officers and numerous bomb explosions in several cities. He stated that he wanted to take advantage of reduced sentences for drug traffickers and rebels who collaborated with officials.

Meanwhile, the Colombian government issued a report on the first ninety-day period of emergency and announced its decision to extend the state of emergency for an additional ninety days, until early May. The report stated that a total of 180 bombings had occurred in major cities, and that 124 civilians and 97 members of government security forces had been killed in rebel- or narco-initiated violence. On the other hand, government forces had captured twenty-five rebel leaders and had killed at least ten high-level members of the Medellín drug cartel. The government also announced plans for carrying out a program to provide land to members of four former rebel groups that had signed peace treaties with the government and whose members had been pardoned of crimes committed before their demobilization. The grants, totaling about 17,000 hectares, were intended, according to the director of the National Agrarian Institute, to convince these former rebels "to take up farming and turn their backs forever on revolutionary warfare" (*Notisur*, February 16 and 23, 1993).

Thus, the Colombian government has made inroads against both the guerrillas and the drug cartels, provoking violent reactions from both of its challengers, without breaking the long-standing impasse. Meanwhile, most other kinds of governmental initiatives have had to be postponed, including sustained attention to developmental program objectives.

COLOMBIA AS A SEMISOVEREIGN STATE

The current reality seems to be that Colombia is a state that is only semi-sovereign, with the government sharing its political powers and control over much of the nation's territory with two competing groups that have divergent objectives and motivations but often act in alliance against the state as their common foe. As Colombian journalist Cecilia Rodriguez (1992) put it, following the escape of Escobar, "The government can no longer pretend to be in control."

Moreover, the resulting dilemmas facing state political and administrative leaders cannot be dealt with solely and completely by them, because these dilemmas arise from the circumstances of Colombia's role in the network of interactions among societies in what has become essentially one global village. Depending on circumstances, domestic forces can seek to take advantage of desirable opportunities and to accommodate themselves to unwelcome external pressures, but escape from this global village is impossible.

Unfortunately, from the Colombian point of view the national options are limited at best because of uncontrollable realities of geography, size, and history. The most intimate and closest relationships for Colombia, of course, are with its Latin American neighbors, particularly the other Andean countries—Venezuela, Ecuador, and Peru. It has strong historic, cultural, and religious ties with Spain and other countries of Western Europe. Among the nations in this hemisphere, only the United States is a major world power, making it the dominant external influence for all of its neighbors. Although among the larger and better-endowed countries of all of Latin America, Colombia always has been and will continue to be subject to hegemonic pressures from the United States because of proximity, relative size, and the hemispheric pecking order (Ardila 1991; Pardo and Tokatlian 1988; Randall 1992). The loss of Panama during a period of internal strife is an ever-present reminder of the enduring power relationships between the two countries, even in an era of good relations. At the same time, of course, the United States is a natural ally in world politics and the major market for Colombian products, offering the main hope for realization of Colombian prospects for future development.

Of more relevance to Colombia's current problems is the direct and crucial impact of external factors on the rise and persistence of both the internal threats now being faced by the state in Colombia. Neither guerrilla insurgency nor illegal drug trafficking would have reached their current dimensions without motivation, support, and protection from outside. Prospects for success in coping with each of these disruptive forces, particularly the latter, are problematic as long as these external ties continue.

With regard to the threat of guerrilla insurrection, keeping in mind the domestic circumstances that provide the seedbed for rebellion, the external links have been to countries of what was the Second World—to Castro's Cuba, to the former Soviet Union, and to Communist China. Marxism-Leninism, sometimes with Maoist overtones, has provided the base of political ideology for Colombian insurgent groups in this century.

With the collapse of the Soviet Union and the linked loss of ability by Cuba to export its revolution, with the defeat at the polls of the Sandinistas in Nicaragua, and with the peace accord reached among rival factions to end the civil war in El Salvador, external sources of support for Colombian insurgents have greatly diminished, with very little indication that they will be revived in the near future.

This enforced necessity to stand on their own feet with few outside allies, combined with their continuing inability to coordinate their programs of disruption, has made the guerrilla groups in Colombia considerably more vulnerable to government efforts to defeat, weaken, or demobilize them. The outcome remains uncertain, in view of the continuing costs of terrorist attacks and intimidating threats to individuals and groups, but some progress is being made. In essence, the prospects for success in dealing with insurgencies are considerably brighter now than they were earlier because of the weakening of these ties between guerrillas and external sympathizers and supporters.

With regard to the narcotraffic problem, the situation is quite different. The illegal drug business is attractive to potential profiteers because of the immense foreign market, particularly in the United States, for Colombian producers and distributors. Colombia, because of its proximity to this market and its geographical location as a conduit between South America and areas to the north—in the Caribbean, in Central America, and in North America—cannot escape from this threat to its ability to manage its own affairs. Cecilia Rodriguez (1992) quotes Colombian columnist Antonio Caballero: "The United States invented drug use on a grand scale. The United States turned a killer like Pablo Escobar into the most powerful man in Colombia." She adds that this "is not much solace for a tormented country," but "perhaps it relieves an ounce of the burden we carry simply for being Colombian." In sum, the temptations and opportunities to resist government regulations and controls over illegal drugs are tremendous, as the rise of the Medellín and Cali cartels has demonstrated. The government faces multiple handicaps in trying simultaneously to cope with local drug syndicate leaders, with their allies abroad, and with their agents inside the government itself because of intimidation, infiltration, and bribery. Moreover, when the Colombian government accepts enforcement aid from the United States (as it has, for example, in the destruction of crops, in the interception of drug shipments, and in efforts to recapture Escobar after his escape from prison), it must then address popular resentment against this dependency on external assistance as evidence of limited sovereignty.

Certainly, as long as Escobar remains at large, even if his resources have been diminished, Colombia cannot expect to emerge the winner in this contest with a semisovereign drug conglomerate and its foreign allies. Even if he is caught and reimprisoned without conditions, the outcome will still remain uncertain because of the long-standing circumstances of Colombia's role in the global village.

Colombia is an extreme example of the common predicament of developing countries with restricted control over their own futures, even when their potential for development is high and they are making vigorous efforts to realize this potential.

7

DEVELOPMENT MANAGEMENT IN THE GLOBAL VILLAGE
Lessons Learned from Working with the Transition in Mozambique

LAWRENCE S. GRAHAM

An important issue facing public administration today concerns restructuring governments in developing countries in such a way that they can respond more effectively to internal and external market forces. The structural adjustments entailed in such endeavors are especially acute in countries emerging from experiments with state socialism where prior economic and political institutions were dismantled in favor of Soviet and Eastern European models. However, the resources needed for such initiatives and available in the international community for such undertakings are limited in that no single country has the capacity today to act unilaterally. This is especially the case in sub-Saharan Africa, where the enormity of the development tasks exceeds the resources of individual donors. As a consequence, much of the work being done today in development management involves negotiating and leveraging cooperative efforts within the donor community in conjunction with national governments in transition. Because this process is particularly well advanced in Mozambique, Mozambique constitutes a theoretically relevant case study of how development management initiatives in these countries can provide insight into the new conditions that must be responded to as well as the new patterns emerging in international cooperation. In this setting old-style dependency relationships are disappearing, and in their place new interdependencies are appearing that are focusing attention at the regional level in such a way that prior national boundaries are being superseded as much from without as from within. Key

This chapter is a revised version of material published in Lawrence S. Graham, "The Dilemmas of Managing Transitions in Weak States: The Case of Mozambique," *Public Administration and Development* 13, no. 4 (October 1993): 409–22. Reprinted by permission of John Wiley & Sons, Ltd.

items in the policy agendas in these cases range from enterprise restructuring in the public and private sectors to decentralization and deconcentration work in development programs and projects, as governments are having to respond to pressures and demands radically different from those that they have had to face in the immediate past.

THE INTERNATIONAL SETTING

To date, four very different patterns (or models) have emerged in the economic and political transitions under way. These have embraced (1) government-initiated economic liberalization prior to undertaking fundamental political change (incorporating groups acting outside the state); (2) radical political change undertaken by opposition groups seizing control of the state through coup or abdication of those holding authority (in which economic reforms ensue according to the political preferences of those taking control); (3) negotiated transitions in which reformist forces in the ruling coalition reach out to the opposition and craft a pact conducive to the construction of a new political center (while prevailing economic choices remain in force); and (4) the convergence of democratization and market-oriented reform movements (where leaders in newly constituted open regimes based on regularly held elections seek to build market economies). Mozambique belongs to the first of these.

In examining an African case such as that of Mozambique, it is as important to be aware of the policy implications of the model selected as it is to understand the conjunctural factors conditioning policy choices and how they shape attempts to consolidate reforms. Because there is a hiatus between the academic literature on transitions, which emphasizes the richness of each case and calls attention to general historical patterns, and donor initiatives, geared to technical analysis and the design of appropriate economic and social programs, it is especially appropriate in the case of Mozambique to attempt to fit together the two processes and to isolate instances where there are convergences and where political initiatives and socioeconomic endeavors are working at cross purposes. There are two reasons for adopting such a perspective. First, the transition model pursued needs to be linked much more closely to questions of policy than has been the case in the past. Both the country case material and the technical reports currently available on a variety of countries now make it possible to identify much more clearly successful matches between policy preferences and the design of strategies linked to effective program performance. Second, sensitivity to the timing of transitions and the wider conjunctural setting influencing new regimes in the making can heighten awareness of the factors limiting and encouraging the formation and consolidation of democratic governments and market economies.

Case histories to date, combining the comparative politics literature and the technical assistance literature, are possible in at least three contexts: Southern

Europe during the mid-1970s (in which the cases of Greece and Portugal diverge markedly from the experience of Spain); South America throughout the 1980s (in which the cases of Argentina, Uruguay, and Chile differ greatly from those of Brazil, Bolivia, and Peru); and Eastern Europe in the early 1990s (in which Poland, the former Czechoslovakia, and Hungary warrant contrast with Romania, Bulgaria, and Albania). While the successor states of the Soviet Union certainly merit consideration also, the changes there are so recent and the context so ill-defined that they, along with the Yugoslav republics, must be excluded because of the fluidity of their current situations.

If Mozambique is approached from this wider perspective and compared with the foregoing, what has been occurring there since 1987 is economic liberalization, coupled with cautious experimentation with political reform. In this particular setting, in which extensive donor support has been the vehicle through which economic liberalization has been financed, increasing the capacity of the central government to implement economic and social policy has become a necessary corollary. Compared with the transitions from centrally planned economies elsewhere, what is particularly distinctive about Mozambique's experience is its illustration of how economic reform and the restructuring of the state apparatus can proceed ahead in the midst of prolonged conflict and unresolved social issues sustaining internal warfare. At the same time, if the sum total of this experience is evaluated holistically and if its implication for the distribution of political power within Mozambique is fully understood, then it should not be too difficult to understand why donor emphasis on strategies linked to decentralization and strengthening local initiatives outside government have been the subject of great debate and open to much criticism.

Accompanying this process has been a gradual opening up of politics. Consequently, today it is much easier to analyze differences in policy perspectives among the groups vying for power. These include the debate within Frelimo (Front for the Liberation of Mozambique) between social democrats and Marxist-Leninists, within the state between reformers and those with a vested interest in the status quo, and outside the state between advocates of moderate change and a more radical restructuring of state and society (Hanlon 1984, 1991).

There is yet another respect in which the particulars of the Mozambican case are instructive for our understanding of political and economic transitions generally. An implicit assumption in the comparative-politics transitions literature, in case studies of Southern Europe and South America (O'Donnell, Schmitter, and Whitehead 1986), is that changes in economic relationships have inevitable consequences for politics. Although that literature distinguishes between economic liberalization and political democratization, it generally assumes that the former is linked in one way or another to the latter, that is, that one cannot have economic liberalization without ultimately producing the conditions for a democratic opening. This argument has been developed most fully in examining the Spanish transition and in arguing for the relevance of Spain's experience by extension into the Latin American area (notably the case of Brazil) and into Eastern Europe (especially in the case of Hungary). However, when the experience of other world areas is added, that is not necessarily the case. Especially pertinent here is the introduction of policy reform and structural adjustment perspectives. When one contrasts World Bank papers and policies for Mozambique with the negative assessment of the overall impact of donor assistance in that country (as illustrated most clearly by Hanlon), what these conflicting perspectives dramatize is the need for greater attention to the synchronization of public policy, broadly conceived of as the analysis of what governments do, with the design of particular programs and projects intended to ameliorate socioeconomic conditions in order to achieve sustained impact in attending to a country's developmental needs. Seen from this perspective, the Mozambican case becomes theoretically relevant in a very concrete way as an instance in which current debates over alternative development programs and projects come into specific focus in terms of how best to alleviate the conditions of poverty and suffering rought about by natural disasters and sustained, institutionalized violence.

If one will utilize the periodization suggested by Hanlon (1991) for chartering the course of Mozambique since independence, and if that perspective is combined with specific instances of bilateral and multilateral donor assistance, the economic and political changes that have been going on since 1984 raise serious questions about the extent to which the government of the Republic of Mozambique (GRM) has guided the process as opposed to external actors dictating the direction of change through the use of conditionalities. Further complicating the transition in Mozambique is the debate over political liberalization, between those who see recent political developments as an extension of economic liberalization, devoid of any significant interest on the part of government in opening up the political process to political groups it cannot control, and those in the opposition, who argue that Renamo (Mozambique National Resistance) cannot be expected to honor the agreement to lay down the use of arms over the long term unless the debate over the extent of economic, political, and social change is expanded beyond the limits imposed by the government. It is at this point that governmental and international policy-makers face a dilemma. To move ahead with policy reform and further structural adjustments, the government must be able to count on a state apparatus sufficiently strong to ensure that government officials in the capital as well as in the provinces will follow central government policy preferences by converting general guidelines and priorities into specific sets of programmatic and project-oriented undertakings that can be implemented at the subnational level, in regions outside the core urban areas of Maputo and Beira. Yet, under present conditions, to decentralize effectively and to permit activities outside the state to take on a life of their own (notably in social policy, where for the past ten years the international nongovernmental organizational community has been setting the effective agenda) is likely toaccelerate the process of state disintegration and thereby defeat the state- and nation-building endeavors that have been going on since 1975 in the constitution of an independent Mozambique. It is this dimension that differentiates Mozambican experience most clearly from the other leading instance of economic liberalization and controlled political reform, that of Mexico. If changes under the former have been limited at the implementation stage because of weak state structures (especially at the grass-roots level), the latter has succeeded up until now precisely because of the strength of the state in the center as well as in the periphery and the reciprocal penetration of official party and public bureaucracy structures by Mexican officialdom. Now that a peace accord has entered into effect between Frelimo and Renamo, as of October 1, 1992, it remains to be seen if policy-makers interested in promoting civil accord and bringing an end to guerrilla warfare throughout the country will be more successful in the case of Mozambique than has been the case with Angola.

BACKGROUND: REVIEW OF THE COUNTRY SITUATION

Three sets of experiences have conditioned the transition under way in Mozambique and warrant consideration in the elaboration of any strategy designed to strengthen the capacity of the government to implement development policies.

First, one must take into account the cohesiveness of the original Frelimo movement and its ability to transform state and society in the aftermath of the Portuguese exodus. In assessing the current situation, one should not forget the political success achieved in consolidating a new regime in 1975–1980. From this vantage point, the issue to be confronted in the 1990s is how to maintain the cohesiveness of this fragile new state and to leverage further socioeconomic reforms without contributing to the disintegration of a state apparatus that has maintained unity in the place of considerable diversity and without encouraging separatism among ethnic groups alienated by fifteen years of Frelimo rule.

Second, the commitment to centralized command economic initiatives overrode all other development policy considerations in the aftermath of independence. The principal economic difficulty confronting Mozambique in 1981–1986 lay not in dismantling the prior economic model but in constructing a new economy that could supplant the underdeveloped, externally dependent, mixed economy inherited at independence. Limited economic success during the early 1970s in attending to Mozambique's developmental needs under colonialism is to be contrasted with economic failure in the early 1980s in establishing the foundations of a new economy fueled by extensive economic and technical support from the Soviet Union, the Eastern European republics, and Cuba. It is against the background of this failure of state socialism that

Mozambique's accord with the International Monetary Fund (IMF) and the World Bank in 1984, the economic restructuring between 1984 and 1986, the Economic Rehabilitation Program (1987–1990), and the revival of markets in the 1990s are to be contrasted.

Third, offsetting the attempt to create a centralized state and a command economy has been the reality of Mozambique's linguistic and ethnic diversity. The fragmentation of Mozambican society, as a consequence of Frelimo's failure to develop a concept of nationalism sufficient to offset the country's ethnic diversity, and the shift in the core of the opposition movement from white resistance (the Mozambican National Resistance Movement) to internal ethnic conflict within African society (in which Renamo has maximized tribal differences and antagonisms) have placed severe constraints on the capacity of the government to implement its development policies. Although conflict permeated the countryside throughout the 1960s and the 1970s, by the 1980s the devastation produced by civil war, combined with the impact of severe drought, brought the country to a standstill. This situation is to be contrasted with the initial success achieved by Frelimo with innovative social policy and the educational and health reforms implemented through donor assistance provided principally by the Nordic countries. Increasingly, during the 1980s, Mozambique became a country in which the government controlled only the cities and where, as a consequence, rural inhabitants fleeing the randomness of guerrilla attacks and the uncertainty surrounding life in the countryside clustered around major urban centers. In this regard, the current issue in decentralization is how to move beyond these constraints and expand social services beyond their current concentration in Maputo and Beira.

REVIEW OF GOVERNMENT REFORM POLICY AND PROGRAMS

Rapidly deteriorating economic and social conditions in 1981–1986 generated a situation in which the leadership came to question the model of state socialism it had embraced at independence. In the interaction between the state and the donor community, the decision by the GRM to rebuild its economic and political ties with the West, while retaining commitment to its particular version of African socialism, shaped the setting into which the World Bank stepped in 1987 in recommending and in having accepted its economic rehabilitation program for Mozambique.

Available U.N. and World Bank documents[1] all concur on one basic point regarding Mozambique at this time: Despite considerable economic potential and extensive donor support, it continued to rank among the poorest countries in the world. Poorly and unevenly developed under the Portuguese as a consequence of their own resource constraints, Mozambique was a country characterized by great economic and social disparities at independence in 1975.

Given the cohesiveness of the leadership that assumed power and the extent of external assistance made available for funding a wide range of development programs, Mozambique's first five years as a sovereign nation were centered around the construction of a socialist state and economy and the inauguration of new activities in health and education to benefit the poor majority.

Sustaining Mozambique's new social and economic programs, however, has proven to be far more difficult than designing and undertaking innovative policy initiatives. After what appeared to be successful ventures in such areas as health and education, what transpired during the 1980s were extended crisis and the breakdown in newly developed social services. Simultaneously, the GRM had to face prolonged economic decline, breakdown of what little social and economic infrastructure it already had in place, a series of natural disasters, and ever-increasing insecurity as organized violence spread throughout the countryside. In contrast, once a series of accords with the IMF and the World Bank were in place, the Economic Rehabilitation Program (ERP) undertaken by the GRM, with the support of the World Bank, from 1987 through 1990, had considerable initial success in arresting the country's economic deterioration. The problems encountered in structural adjustment policy since, however, have not been notably different from those encountered elsewhere, for instance, in Bolivia. Success in bringing greater order to economic and financial management and planning does not constitute a sufficient prior condition to engender and sustain new economic growth.

Various statistics cited in materials published by the United Nations Development Programme (UNDP) and the World Bank substantiate the seriousness of the country's economic and social conditions at the time economic reforms were initiated. Per-capita income had remained low, at an estimated $150 per year. Compared with 1980, by 1986 the gross domestic product (GDP) had declined 40 percent, with exports amounting to less than one-fifth of imports. By 1988, over 40 percent of the population was suffering acute hardship due to the cumulative effects of drought and insecurity (World Bank n.d. "Mozambique: Proposed US$900 million"). As a consequence, the breakthrough in development envisaged at the end of the 1970s did not take place. Around 65 percent of the population, estimated to be some 10 million people, continued to live under conditions of absolute poverty. More than 1.6 million persons had been displaced by the war. Yet another 2.4 million were experiencing serious food shortages in rural areas, while the 2.6 million people calculated to be living in urban areas depended almost entirely on imported food supplies for their survival (United Nations Development Programme 1988a: 17). The problem today is that after five years of structural adjustment and improving conditions of life for the more affluent, especially in Maputo, none of these basic conditions has been altered.

Even though socioeconomic data vary greatly in their extent of accuracy and according to source and perspective, insight into the country's manpower problems, the mixed results achieved since independence in education and health, and the extent of the setbacks experienced during the early 1980s can be captured readily by consulting these materials. They discuss how the exit of Portuguese nationals at independence removed virtually the entire educated population that had manned the middle and upper ranges of the colonial bureaucracy and had run the economy. For example, of the 487 technicians employed in the finance ministry (a comparatively well-run and well-managed entity), only thirteen remained after independence. Outside Maputo, all twenty-eight regional finance offices were left unattended with the departure of the Portuguese (United Nations Development Programme 1988b: 63–64). Remaining in a land filled with abandoned farms, commercial and manufacturing enterprises, and transportation facilities over which the state assumed tutelage by default was an African population poorly prepared for self-rule, with but 7 percent literacy and little or no experience in government or enterprise management.

In this setting, education became perforce an immediate priority and resources were made available to attack educational needs. Thus, in the first five years after independence, school enrollments underwent dramatic increases and the country's illiteracy rate decreased, dropping from 93 percent at independence to 70 percent in 1980. Indicative of the changes achieved in education are these figures: a tripling of enrollments in primary schools (where 90 percent of the school-age population was located), from 350,000 in 1975 to 1.3 million by 1980; an expansion of secondary school enrollments, from the 15,000 last recorded in 1960 before independence to 103,000 in 1980; and a dramatic improvement in the numbers of teachers and teaching ratios—from the 10,281 primary teachers reported in 1960, with a ratio of 65.3 students per teacher, to 20,275 teachers at all levels in 1980—at first with a much higher teaching ratio of 73.8 students per teacher in 1980 and later a much-improved one of 54.4 students per teacher in 1984 (United Nations Development Programme 1988b: 9).

Since the mid-1980s, however, retaining these enrollment levels and enhancing the ability of this educational system to produce more skilled manpower have proven to be enormously difficult, in a society in which, according to the 1980 census, 85.2 percent of the active population were in agriculture; 6.2 percent were employed in industry; 2.1, in commerce; and a scant 0.6, in education and cultural activities. For example, a Swedish International Development Agency (SIDA/ASDI) report issued in May 1987 reported that, of 3,698 primary and 111 secondary schools located in the country's five northern provinces, 2,202 in the former category and twenty-one in the latter were no longer operating because of security problems affecting over 350,000 students. In addition, in the country as a whole, less than 5 percent of those enrolled in primary schools were completing their first four grades in four years. And, out of 1,000 first graders, only forty-four were entering the fifth grade. Equally serious was the situation in secondary education where high failure, repetition of school years, and dropouts continued to plague a school system in which 55 percent of the teachers were considered to be undertrained (United Nations Development Programme 1988b: vi–vii).

In health programs, likewise, Mozambique made real progress during the late 1970s. Yet, seen from the perspective of the 1990s, the results have been modest and the needs remain great. Immediately after independence, with the support of the Nordic countries and Italy, the country successfully developed both a broadly based primary health care system and an essential drugs program. But, if currently available basic health indicators are used, results in terms of sustained impact are much less impressive. Life expectancy still ranges between forty and forty-three years; infant mortality stands at 30 to 40 percent; and, as violence has continued to spread throughout the countryside, 17 percent of the primary health facilities built since independence no longer function (World Bank 1989: II–77).

The cumulative effect of this situation has been to convince donors of the need to reorient development priorities toward greater concern with the social dimensions of development policies.

> The collapse of domestic food production, the reduced access to basic social services and educational facilities in terms of housing, sanitary facilities and water, medical services and educational facilities, the decline of recurrent public expenditures in these basic social areas, are all elements that feed the persistence of such a wide phenomenon of national poverty. (United Nations Development Programme 1988a: 18)

Given the seriousness of this situation, at the November 1989 meeting of the Consultative Group for Mozambique, donors agreed that poverty alleviation would be the focal point for future development programs. Since then, far greater attention has been devoted to the adoption of an integrated approach, one in which agricultural, health, and educational activities have received major attention (United Nations Development Programme 1988a: 18–19).

It is against this background of severe financial constraints and deteriorating social conditions that the success of the government's three-year Economic Rehabilitation Program needs to be highlighted, for it is generally recognized in the materials reviewed that success has been achieved through this program in reversing the economic decline experienced at the beginning of the decade. Indicative of this recovery are GDP growth rates of some 4 percent in 1987 and 1988, despite continued difficulties with organized violence in major sections of the country. Accordingly, of three UNDP country programs developed since 1977, the Third Country Program (CP) has been the most ambitious, with funding levels increasing from US$21,745,000 to US$66,009,000, making it the second largest UNDP program in Africa. Central to this plan are the concerns of overall institutional development, greater coordination of individual pro-grammatic activities in key sectors, and the enhancement of activities designed to develop skilled manpower in such a way as to achieve greater success in promoting self-sustaining growth (United Nations Development Programme 1989b: 51–55).

However, the generally positive impression created by these materials must be contrasted with the serious problems identified from 1990 onward in random interviewing and field trips conducted outside Maputo in four UNDP missions oriented to sampling grass-roots opinions and attitudes in the provinces.[2] This is especially the case if viewpoints communicated by government officials working at the provincial level with social policy in the bureaucratic arena defined as social action *(acção social)* and in touch with disadvantaged groups *(população vulnerável)* are to be taken into account. The conditionality requirements imposed to leverage economic change have so permeated the social milieu outside Maputo as to convince increasingly large numbers of nationals that a donor community dominated by IMF and World Bank requirements is increasingly incapable of responding to an ethnically diverse African majority for whom the last five years have brought no appreciable amelioration in the struggle to survive. In such a setting provincial officials have become paralyzed by countervailing pressures from administrative superiors and donors who call the shots and from an impoverished citizenry faced with enormous health hazards and the uncertainties of day-to-day life. For them, survival becomes linked to passivity and the avoidance of action on donor-guided assistance or central government policies with which they are not in accord.

Public Sector Profile

In restructuring state, society, and the economy in Mozambique after independence, the crucial public choices were those made at the Third Frelimo Congress in 1977, at which time a state socialist model was adopted. This can be seen in the commitments made to a centrally planned economy, the continuation of single-party rule, and the construction of a hierarchically structured state with the capacity to reach down to the grass roots and incorporate into the new order the resources and needs of rural communities. Subsequently, national and local elections designed to ratify these changes were held in 1978; new local council legislation was enacted, through which old-style Camaras (municipal councils) were replaced with Central Executive Committees; and districts—as intermediate units of governance between provinces and community-based organizations—were recognized as the basic planning units within the structure of a single, integrated national budget (World Bank n.d. "Local government administration": 25).

Since that time, nevertheless, rather than construction of the strong state envisioned as an essential part of this transition to socialism, Mozambican reality has not been all that different from many other developing countries: What exists is a weak state with a very limited capacity for implementing and giving meaningful content to the economic and social policies it has sought to enact. Over the years, three essential institutional issues have continued to plague the new system and undercut its revolutionary commitments. First is poor donor coordination (a component that has been of great import since the outset as the resources with which to develop the country have had to come from abroad). In the absence of organizational coherency, overlapping and repetitive development initiatives have become commonplace. Second, efficient and effective allocation of the resources with which the GRM has had to work has proven to be ephemeral (as the centrally planned economic and political model it adopted, once transferred into an African context, reproduced there the redundancies and the rigidities so often present elsewhere in other centrally planned economies and centrally directed polities). Third, no easy solution has been found for reducing unit costs, since the planning, budgeting, and public expenditure control mechanisms in place and the personnel responsible for their execution have not had the capacity to perform the tasks assigned them.

Recognition of these deficiencies underlies the National System of International Cooperation (inaugurated under Presidential Decree No. 27, of May 15, 1989, and Legislative Decree No. 18, of July 7, 1989). Similarly, awareness of this situation has reinforced continued use of the Consultative Group mechanism, under the leadership of the World Bank (as reflected especially in its third meeting of November 1989). Even more important in assessing these difficulties and recommending a plan for action are the recommendations contained in the World Bank's *Mozambique: Public Expenditure Review* of September 5, 1989.

The net results of fifteen years of state socialism (1975–1990) have been an excessively large public sector in which the central government consumes around 50 percent of GDP and the parastatal sector, another 20 percent (World Bank 1989: i–ii). Given the weight of the public sector in the economy and the size of its consumption of scarce resources, a key component of the UNDP and the World Bank reviews conducted in 1988 and 1989 (United Nations Development Programme 1988b; World Bank 1989) was the attention given to institutional issues, reduction in public sector size through structural adjustments and privatization, and the introduction of greater system autonomy not only in permitting market forces to function more freely in determining supply and demand but also in allowing local communities greater freedom in collecting and allocating local revenues in accord with local development priorities. These points are best summed up in this NATCAP statement:

that the strengthening of institutions is the single greatest contribution that T.C. [technical cooperation] can make in Mozambique's present situation, and of the various elements that go into this, none are more important than (a) staff upgrading, and (b) the generation of information for policy makers and administrators that is reliable, relevant and timely. (United Nations Development Programme 1988b: vi)

The State Apparatus

Central in all these discussions of how to restructure the GRM in order to generate greater productivity and to coordinate development policies and programs more effectively are eight central government institutions: four of which are sectoral organizations—the ministries of Agriculture, Labor, and Education as well as the State Secretariat for Food and Light Industry (SEILA)—and four of which are coordination- and control-oriented entities—the National Planning Commission (NPC), the Ministry of Finance (MINFIN), the Bank of Mozambique (BM), and the Ministry of Cooperation (MINCOOP). Attention to the latter four has been recognized as essential to any successful action in economic management, especially in targeting their personnel for immediate upgrading and increased professional staff and in generating more timely and accurate basic economic data.

While the NPC, MINFIN, BM, and MINCOOP are better endowed with professional staff than other governmental entities, the thinness of their staff is reflected in these findings: A survey of these organizations plus the labor ministry revealed that only 3 percent (seventy-two persons) had higher education degrees; 65 percent had completed only the basic educational cycle and had received less than nine years of schooling; another 26 percent had completed the ninth year, while just over 6 percent had finished high school (United Nations Development Programme 1988b: xiii). Despite the sketchiness of these data, we know even less of the specific manpower needs of the remaining sectoral organizations, except for frequent reference to shortages in professional staff, constant personnel turnover, and excessive overall employment coupled with noncompetitive salaries for retaining more skilled personnel.

Even more critical in assessing institutional capacity for implementing economic and social policy is the field administration structure of these organizations. The limited information available on the topic makes continual reference to its inadequacies and points out that, when present, local offices are subject to overlapping and competing administrative and political controls that stifle their programs and activities. Yet, without adequate representation outside Maputo and sufficient professional staff to oversee programmatic activities at the regional and local level, there is little likelihood that the majority of the population will ever be reached. Regardless of ample recommendations to the contrary, the majority of those capable of acting in these areas within the government and within the donor community continue to favor top-down strategies and to undercut initiatives designed to empower provincial and local officials to resolve a larger portion of their development needs at the local level.

Insight into the enormity of these problems can be seen in the 1987 profile prepared of agricultural ministry personnel. Out of a total of 132,989 employees in central services, research activities, and state-owned enterprises, 83,719 were illiterate; 38,355 had received four years of education, and 10,527 had completed six years (United Nations Development Programme 1988b: 84). Yet another sample, this one of the Bank of Mozambique (generally recognized as one of the best-staffed public organizations), revealed that of 1,681 employees distributed throughout the country, only eighteen had university degrees, and they were confined to Maputo. Of the 101 who had high school degrees, eighty-five were employed in this capital city. Of the remaining 1,526 staff members with nine years or less of education, 839 worked in Maputo and 723 worked in the provinces (United Nations Development Programme 1988b: 61).

An equally critical bottleneck in obtaining more flexible and responsive governmental services is local government. Despite the rhetoric of involving citizens at the grass-roots level and more responsive governance attentive to local needs, what has evolved (in ways not dissimilar from experience accumulated elsewhere under state socialism) has been a hierarchical, centrally controlled state apparatus with a single, unitary national budget through which funds are then redistributed at the provincial and district level. Current territorial administrative arrangements consist of ten provinces, 128 districts, and 394 administrative posts, with smaller locality designations of *bairro* (neighborhood) and *aldeia* (village) applying to rural and urban areas. These designations have remained largely unchanged in moving from colony to independent state. Urban administration, however, has undergone considerable modification through the establishment of City Executive Councils (CECs). Paralleling state socialist practices elsewhere, at each level chief executive officers combined with people's assemblies comprise subnational units of government. Likewise, regional and local political controls paralleling the state administrative apparatus have been set up, and practices of dual supervision have been introduced.

Theoretically speaking, even though there have been major changes in formal administrative arrangements, one should be aware of the fact that the practice of dual supervision in the administration of governmental services was already in place at independence. The primary change that has occurred here is in executive style, in the movement away from the vesting of authority in the hands of single executives, toward collective leadership. More importantly, what has occurred in the practice of city administration has been considerable expansion in the range of activities executed, most notably in the responsibility given to local organizations of governance for matters related to the local economy and local planning activities. Nevertheless, for all these rhetorical innovations in expanding the scope of government at the regional and local level, decision-making and resource allocation have remained essentially central government decisions. If in theory people have become more involved in politics and government at the subnational level through party participation and expanded representation of local interests, in practice centralized rule—albeit with a very different social and economic agenda—has continued. Compounding this situation is poor communication between center and periphery. The breakdown of previous social, political, and economic linkages (which always have been limited and fragile) has meant that the separation between Maputo and isolated villages (*aldeias*) continues unabated. Seen from below and from the vantage point of local citizens, the state as represented by government officials in Maputo and their delegates at the subnational level has remained as distant as ever. Thus, today, when one examines state structures and the capacity of government to implement policy in the periphery, one encounters a paradoxical situation. Insofar as political structures are concerned in areas under government control, communication between center and periphery is quite effective when Frelimo-based ties are utilized. But because this model is essentially a politicized command model, when government services are involved, provincial officials usually find themselves immobilized by requirements and customs that instruct them to await central government orders and local officials find themselves marginalized in the whole process. As the trappings of state socialism are being removed, however, what is most curious of all is how much of the centralism characteristic of the Portuguese state and identification with Prime Minister António Salazar's economic reforms to control, rather than to program, remained intact.

REVIEW OF RESPONSES WITHIN THE U.N. SYSTEM

The first attempt made at entering the subnational arena by working directly with provincial governors and local administrators arose out of a request for assistance from the Ministry of State Administration (Ministério de Administração Estatal, MAE). In a December 1989 letter from MAE minister Jose Oscar Monteiro to UNDP resident representative Charles Henry Larsimont, MAE requested assistance under the terms of the new UNDP Management Development Programme (MDP). In that letter Minister Monteiro noted that, while the ministry was receiving Swedish International Development Agency (SIDA) assistance in the implementation of a human resources management system and in training public employees in the central ministries, he wished to strengthen the overall operations of the ministry more generally by enabling it to fulfill its mandate as a state organization responsible for relations between central and local authorities (United Nations Development Programme 1989a).

By the time a mission was fielded in May 1990 a new resident representative (Peter Simkin) was in place and a broader mandate had emerged for UNDP work in Mozambique: that new projects be interfaced more effectively with ongoing U.N. work within the country and that priority be given to decentralization. In addition, conditions had also changed within the ministry. The anticipated departure of the current minister coupled with the redefinition of the ministry's mandate in a way compatible with the abandonment of state socialism led middle-level personnel to seek to separate more clearly donor work within the ministry along the lines of its division into two national directorates, one responsible for public personnel at the national level (the Direcção Nacional da Função Pública) and the other responsible for local government authorities (the Direcção Nacional de Administração Local). Adding further complexity to this situation was the expectation that this mission also respond to new thinking within the development community favoring greater donor coordination, but for which there were no clear guidelines as to how this was to be achieved. UNDP headquarters envisioned using its authority to leverage the programming of activities by sector and to move country operations away from isolated, project-specific activities. The issue at stake here was how to find a more appropriate mechanism for accomplishing this in such a way that the UNDP/Mozambique could achieve greater interagency cooperation, within the U.N. system as well as among bilateral donors.

What is instructive about the protracted discussions that ensued among individuals in the UNDP in New York, the local UNDP office, MAE officials, and other donors involved in MAE activities is that each set of interests had a different mandate in mind. From the standpoint of the UNDP/Maputo, what they saw in UNDP/New York assistance was management support that could be tied to their broader goal of facilitating GRM acceptance of UNDP/NATCAP recommendations and reinforce their general program priority of decentralizing both donor assistance and GRM activities. On the MAE side, the message sent from the very first meeting was their desire for immediate assistance in meeting a single priority: the establishment of more effective control, supervision, and performance standards over local government personnel. These MAE people saw such work as an essential first step in attacking the more general problem of how to attain greater coordination in public personnel policies in response to the president's mandate to revitalize local institutions, when most senior oficials in Maputo-based line ministries and state secretariats were engaged in the bureaucratic game of decentralization to centralize their own operations more effectively.

This particular task—how to achieve greater coherency in government programs at the subnational level—in the weak state that pervades Mozambique proved to be very difficult to pin down in terms of identifying a concrete initiative, developing a specific project, and assuring results. A clear-cut choice was posed from the outset. If UNDP/New York assistance was to be provided within the financial limits imposed of not exceeding one million dollars in expenditures for management work, either attention would have to be focused on central ministry needs (and thereby enter the morass of competing and overlapping donor initiatives already under way, some within the MAE and others running parallel to it and outside), or attention would have to be directed to the subnational level (whereby central office tasks would be redefined by developing new perceptions and responses in local government). The advantage of the former lay in the attention that might be given to reinforcing the World Bank's work in improved economic management. MDP (Management Development Programme) inputs could then be more easily defined in terms of the much narrower, more precise, and traditional thinking of classical public administration. Or, it could engage in the more risky and innovative domain of responding to President Chissano's interest in revitalizing local institutions and the UNDP/Maputo's interest in decentralizing development programs by bringing to both a distinctive management component.

After more than a year of debating priorities in local government assistance through the MAE, the conclusion reached by mid-1991 was that it would be more productive for such assistance to be directed at decentralization work and funded initially through country funds controlled by the UNDP/Maputo. In such a context, the format used was that of a three-year project, focused on local officials under the authority of MAE's National Directorate for Local Administration, with the expectation that the MDP in New York would become involved in the second and third years and that the question of how to achieve greater impact on the ministry as a whole would be reopened at that time (World Bank 1991a). Whether or not exploratory work that stretched over a year and a half could achieve the necessary impact was further conditioned by another internal governmental debate. This entailed the comprehensiveness of the constitutional revisions under way. Involved here were serious differences over the extent to which the government should move away from a centralized, regulatory state toward a more open, pluralist state attentive to the divergent needs and desires of various ethnic groups, located within a heterogeneous set of provinces whose goals and priorities were, more often than not, at odds with those dictated from Maputo. By the end of 1992 this was resolved by the president's decision to push ahead with economic and political liberalization and by an agreement between Frelimo and Renamo that a cease-fire would take effect the first of October, with national elections following in 1993.

While such contingencies precluded effective programming of local government work, even with a time span extending from September 1991 to March 1993, the lessons learned from this particular initiative suggest that in the future decentralization initiatives and work with subnational officials must be much more sensitive to political realities within the country as a whole. To date, except for this initiative, which was focused on governors and local administrators in the northern provinces of Cabo Delgado, Niassa, and Nampula, decentralization activities have been guided by competing sets of interests in Maputo-based public organizations and random projects concentrated in Beira, Nampula City, and Nacala.

As Mozambique's transition moves ahead, few if any current central government and donor initiatives are prepared to deal with the reality of the tenuousness of Maputo's control over the north or the interior. The alienation experienced among northern ethnic groups—for example, the Makonde and the Macua—as well as those in the center—for example, the Shona—will increasingly become relevant as the government attempts to open up both state and society. The north's perception of the state apparatus is one dominated by southern ethnic groups, as much in Maputo as in important governmental bureaucratic appointments made throughout national territory.

CONCLUSIONS

Although there is little donor interest in changing the present Consultative Group mechanism, when one engages issues in social policy and the political accords necessary to achieve peace, the more open agenda made possible through a Donors' Round Table with its potential for removing conditionality requirements in the areas of social and political policy suggests some interesting prospects for Mozambique. In this regard, a negotiated settlement that can hold and the issue of how to accelerate the conflict resolution process raise the question of what is likely to be an appropriate country strategy for transcending the present impasse. To accomplish such goals, greater integration of political policy (conflict resolution), economic policy (market revitalization), and social policy (concern with the human conditions produced by wartime suffering and poverty) must somehow be attempted. For all the weaknesses inherent within the U.N. system, it is difficult to conceive how this will be possible without permitting the UNDP to become a more effective independent actor, both in coordinating the initiatives of independent U.N. agencies and facilitating closer cooperation among bilateral donors. There is no area more sensitive at the present moment than social policy. While this is an area where the likelihood of a strong reaction among groups endeavoring to speak for the poor majority is yet premature, it is one that must be reckoned with as political controls are relaxed. Thus, even though the UNDP's role is a restricted one and its effectiveness depends on its ability to broker consensus and accord among independent organizations, the time has come for greater attention to coordination and the introduction of concepts of strategic planning and management through more careful programming of social policy. Such policy reform is essential in a country with very great and deeply rooted cleavages, in which few effective inroads have been made in transcending the frustration and the despair that come from thirty years of lving continuously in the midst of conflict and uncertainty.

NOTES

1. Several U.N. and World Bank documents were consulted for this study. The noticeable United Nations Development Programme documents in this context are Development Co-operation Report 1988 for Mozambique (1988); Technical Assistance Policies and Requirements

in Mozambique: A UNDP/NATCAP Report (1988); and Report of the Mid-term Review of the Third Country Programme (1987–1991). Among the most significant World Bank (Africa Region) documents are Local Government Administration and Finances in Mozambique: Preliminary Review (not dated); The Municipal Development Program for Sub-Sahara Africa—A Partnership for Building Local Government Capacity (African Technical Department and the Economic Development Institute 1991); Supervision of Second Rehabilitation Credit (1841–MOZ)/ Preparation of Consultative Group Meeting/ Back to Office Report (Tcheyan Memorandum, not dated). In addition, some government documents were also of significance: Fundação do Desenvolvimento Administrativo (FUNDAP) advisers at the Ministério da Administração Estatal published in November 1988 a document entitled "Fortalecimento Organizacional do Ministério da Administração Estatal: Primeira Fase: Diagnóstico (Relatório Preliminar)." The Ministry of the Environment, Finland, team working with the Ministry of State Administration (Mozambique) published a report in December 1991, "Nacala Integrated Urban Development Project, Mozambique." The Swedish International Development Agency's memorandum dated May 26, 1988, entitled "Support for Public Administration in Mozambique" and the World Bank Seminar on Local Government to be held in Maputo in September 1988 were also insightful.

2. Several UNDP consultant reports written by Lawrence Graham reveal this: Management Development Programme Report Concerning Assistance to the Government of Mozambique (June 1990); Management Development Project Identification for the Government of Mozambique and the United Nations Development Programme (October 6, 1990); A Management Development Approach to Local Government in Mozambique (March 7, 1991); Final Report: Mid-Term Review of Project MOZ/91/002, A Management Development Approach to Local Government (January 26, 1992); and Programming Social Policy in Mozambique with Special Attention to Capacity and Institution Building in the State Secretariat for Social Action (January 26, 1992). Several other consultant reports are also important: Public Sector Management Desk-Study of Mozambique (April 16, 1990); Aide Memoire: Management Development Programme Assistance to the Ministry of State Administration (May 22, 1990); and Consultant Report: Diagnostic Needs Mission in Support of the Secretary of State for Social Action, Maputo, Mozambique (May 27, 1991).

8

INSTITUTIONALIZING AN ETHIC OF CHANGE
Case Studies from East Germany and the United States

MARGARET F. REID

The global transformations now under way are only the most recent manifestation of processes that have been ongoing since the 1960s. These have been called post-industrialism, global interdependence, a new international economic order (Brunner 1976), and many other names (Rosenau 1990). Common to all of these approaches is an increased recognition of the complexity of human concerns and the enormity of transformations affecting all societies around the globe.

Normative qualities are conspicuously absent from the discussion of historical forces that shape organizational restructuring and administrative practices (Zucker 1988). An ideology of development, rooted in the economic, cultural, and political traditions of the West, has swept the globe, obliterating the emergence of alternate worldviews. The collapse of socialist societies and the resurgence of market-oriented approaches merely heighten the vacuous nature and lack of direction in the study of this important phenomenon (Archer 1988, 1990).

This chapter directs attention to a significant aspect of this change process that both so-called developed and developing countries must face: an ethic to guide models of change and the people involved in the restructuring of their institutions to respond to this change. In an era of massive transformations, the analysis of change can no longer be confined to a single organization or any one management practice. Rather, as this study argues, such a framework must advance an understanding of the institutional nature of change, which involves social construction of choices—whether material or symbolic—that form the basis of all innovations. This approach has the added advantage of forcing a search for comparative frames of reference not limited to particular policy domains or specific countries (Dwivedi and Henderson 1990).

Moving away from a technostructural approach of the past to a total systems perspective calls for a revised thinking. As a starting point, it requires the development of alternate *gestalts* or mental models with contingent sets of assumptions that can guide the search for a revamped ethic of change (Senge 1990). A dynamic framework of change—a framework that has applicability beyond the narrow confines of an organization—must address itself first and foremost to the values driving the change.

The framework advocated here views change as a continuum ranging from massive transformations to minor adjustments in authoritative or decisional patterns. At the one polar end are the transformational changes that I label here as *metamorphic* changes. Changes on the other polar end are called *isomorphic* changes (DiMaggio and Powell 1983; Hawley 1968).

The proposed framework does not advocate a search for a uniform explanation of all types of changes. Change is a complex process that does not follow a linear or predetermined path. Systemic conditions are often too unique to allow for generalized prescriptions (Brinkerhoff 1991; Brinkerhoff and Goldsmith 1990; Hage and Finsterbusch 1987). The uniqueness of most changes at the micro level limits our ability to suggest uniform models and approaches to change. Nonetheless, it is possible to identify common paths for both metamorphic and isomorphic changes.

In the following section, I discuss the arenas, paths, and types of changes in an effort to build a framework for comparison. The subsequent section offers two case studies that have been analyzed within the proposed framework.

ARENAS OF CHANGE

Change, as viewed here, occurs in one or more of the following three arenas: institutional framework, exchange mechanisms, and rules of engagement that guide individual and collective choices. Change achieves its acceptance only if its effects in the three arenas are in relative consonance with one another. If there are discrepancies in the relationships between institutional framework and exchange mechanisms or institutional framework and rules of engagement, the outcome can only be conflict (Laughlin 1991; Matthews 1986).

Change in the *institutional framework* refers to the structural transformation of social, legal, and political integrating devices, such as a constitution, economic exchange arrangements (e.g., markets), as well as religions or ideologies. Institutions themselves are social ordering devices to "reduce uncertainty by establishing a stable (but not necessarily efficient) structure to human interaction" (North 1990: 6). They constitute the legitimation devices for the system by determining access, the nature of distribution of national resources, knowledge, skills, and the loci of decision-making referred to by Brint and Karabel (1991) as "structural power."

The formal and informal mechanisms that bind the institutions of a system together and result in an institutional framework are here referred to as the *exchange mechanisms*. They include such formalized modes of interactions and exchange as bureaucracies, firms, parties or unions, and governance structures. They also encompass organizational capacities such as leadership, problem solving, decision-making ability, and communication devices. When institutions change, these capacities must change as well. The adaptability and flexibility of these capacities contribute significantly to a system's ability to deal with change. They also shape and modify the speed at which change occurs.

Finally, *rules of engagement* are those procedures that determine behavioral or role-based limitations within exchange relationships (Leblebici 1985). Socially constructed and sanctioned, they define the rights and responsibilities of individuals and organizations to exercise choices in different settings. Examples of these rules include social codes of ethics and conduct as well as legal and economic rules and regulations.

CHANGE PATHS

All changes pass through three stages that influence their ultimate outcome: initiation, implementation, and routinization. Depending on the type of change involved, one stage may become more important than others. For instance, some changes may focus on initiation as opposed to implementation, while others may stress implementation rather than routinization. Changes usually undergo a series of oscillations until an agreement over the nature and dynamics of the choices is reached.

For choices to be considered both legitimate and implementable, they require congruence of meaning for the arenas in which they are employed. In other words, the path from implementation to routinization is not a direct or incontrovertible one. Prolonged imbalances in the systemic arena, often a result of massive uncertainties about the cost and benefits of choices, can delay commitment to outcomes. Changes in the institutional framework are likely to be resisted when rules and exchange mechanisms are also in flux or begin to unravel. The inability of decision-makers to build a strong enough support for the intended change may easily derail any legitimate effort for change. This is particularly true for developmental changes in which the uncertainties about outcomes are especially pronounced. All developmental outcomes (as long as they are not imposed) are eventually the result of formal or informal negotiations over envisioned choices.

TYPES OF CHANGE

Metamorphic or transformational change is different from isomorphic change, for the latter presumes the legitimacy of both the institutional framework that must eventually sanction the change, and organizational capacities that must in the end implement it (DiMaggio and Powell 1983; Galaskiewitz and Burt 1991; Gow 1992). Metamorphic and isomorphic changes also differ with respect to the strategies that each one employs (refer to Figure 4). The two types of change and their attributes are discussed below.

Isomorphic Changes

Change paths can be very different, as Hinings and Greenwood (1989) point out. After an initial impulse that initiates the transformation, changes are likely to follow a process of homogenizing organizational structures, processes, and practices in order to minimize transaction costs (DiMaggio and Powell 1983). Laws, regulations, professionalization, and dominant organizations in a particular field are the forces that promote such a process. However, if this process is driven too far the result may be massive dysfunction of organizational form, escalating in the extreme to a cycle of metamorphic change. This outcome occurs when periodic changes in the exchange mechanisms are suppressed. In other words, if choices are severely constrained, then pressure can build to the point that metamorphic change becomes inevitable.

The more prevalent reasons for isomorphic change to occur rest in the recognition of performance gaps in the decisional or resource allocation systems (Yin 1978). These can result in intolerable burdens on existing exchange mechanisms and the organizational structures supporting them. The emergence of some prominent collective actors calling for a reorientation or a widely publicized crisis is often a good indicator of an impending change (Pettigrew 1985; Warren 1984). It is their ability to convince others that change is legitimate and is needed that determines whether the change will be symbolic or substantive (Weiss 1988). Symbolic change may be adopted when available choices are not clearly defined and the paths leading to their implementation are uncertain.

Isomorphic changes can require rapid or gradual transformation. As Figure 5 indicates, pressure on institutional frameworks, exchange mechanisms, and rules of engagement can vary, depending on whether a change is rapid or gradual. When change occurs at a rapid speed, the pressure on the rules of engagement is quite intense. Institutional frameworks are initially spared because the rapidity of the change demands an immediate result. Eventually, the institutions also feel pressure; however, it is more severe on rules and exchange mechanisms. Gradual change dynamics differ somewhat. They heavily rely on contagion as a vehicle for diffusing change. Such a process involves rationalization of organizational structures, homogenization of roles and behaviors, or professionalization. While pressures on the rules of engagement are quite high, pressures exerted on the institutional framework remain low.

Figure 4
Model of Contradictions Conducive to Metamorphic or Isomorphic Change

Arena of Change	Metamorphic Change	Isomorphic Change
Institutional framework	Ongoing, unresolved interinstitutional contradictions	Erosion of the connective power of metaphors, strategic orientations
Exchange mechanisms	Environmental pressures, high level of sectoral cleavages leading to disjointed transactions in resource mobilization and deployment	Expansion of rationalized structures through interorganizational networks limiting available choices
Rules of engagement	Value conflicts, means-ends decoupling through social deconstruction of rules	Occupational socialization, homogenization of rules

Metamorphic Changes

Metamorphic change assumes a fundamental reorientation of ideas, practices, and procedures leading to a total reconfiguration of institutional linkage patterns. The speed of the change depends on a number of factors: (1) external pressures for change when the system is perceived by others as an impediment to stability; (2) internal pressures as a result of vast social and economic inequities in resource and power distribution, producing massive transaction costs to the system; and (3) severe restrictions on discourse about alternative arrangements and choices, placing pressure on existing exchange mechanisms to cope with problems that they were not created for.

Regardless of their nature, metamorphic changes are not singular events; they are continuous processes. Although they often require a major crisis to jolt inertial forces into action, the pressure for change generally exists prior to it. An initial response to this pressure can range from repression to cooptation. If the crisis is perceived to be legitimate, response can include both real and symbolic actions (Weiss 1988). If decision-making environments are fraught with high levels of uncertainty, scarce or disputed resources, or lack of legitimacy, the more likely response is a symbolic one that suggests that the need for change has been acknowledged.

Transformational change seems to occur more rapidly with the onset of rationalized, secular societal structures, such as the emergence of professions, institutionalized technologies, bureaucratization, and the like (Meyer and Rowan 1991). Organizations provide the formal foundations, communication metaphors, and institutional rules by which change gains acceptance. In Middle Eastern countries, for example, the processes of change have been challenged because institutional legitimation has not occurred (Middle East Report 1992). Islam's value system is incompatible with many of the organizational and

Figure 5
Hypothesized Change Paths: Isomorphic Change
Pressures Exerted on Three Arenas under Alternate Change Conditions

Stages of Change	Rapid Transformation	Gradual Transformation
Institutional framework		
Initiation	Medium	Low
Implementation	Low	Low
Routinization	Low	Low
Exchange mechanisms		
Initiation	High	Medium
Implementation	High	Medium
Routinization	Medium	Medium
Rules of engagement		
Initiation	High	High
Implementation	High	High
Routinization	High	Medium

rule-based changes being introduced. This partially explains continued crises in this part of the world.

As Figure 6 describes, the pressure of change is most intense on institutional frameworks and rules of engagement during metamorphic change. In contrast to the situation during isomorphic change, exchange mechanisms during transformational changes are pressured the least. The actual change paths are a reflection of the choice set of attempted changes and the time constraints acting on the decision-makers. Rapid transformation exerts higher pressures on the institutional framework and forces behavioral adjustments. In both rapid and gradual change conditions, exchange mechanisms display the greatest difficulty in dealing with the uncertainties in their environment.

The following sections provide illustrations of how the proposed approach might be applied to the analysis of two very different settings: the search for reinstitutionalization in the former East Germany and the use of public-private partnerships to enhance and diversify economic development efforts in the United States.

METAMORPHIC CHANGE: EAST GERMANY'S FAILED ATTEMPTS AT *PLANVERVOLLKOMMNUNG* (PLAN PERFECTING)

The current turmoil pervading all countries of eastern Europe is indicative of the degree of change that has taken place during the last decade. The fundamental institutional deficiencies of *perestroika* as well as the failed reform efforts in East Germany in the late 1970s and early 1980s are suggestive of the magnitude of change needed to produce functioning market-based political economies (MBPE).

Figure 6
Hypothesized Change Paths: Metamorphic Change
Pressures Exerted on Three Arenas under Alternate Change Conditions

Stages of Change	Rapid Transformation	Gradual Transformation
Institutional framework		
Initiation	High	Medium
Implementation	High	Medium
Routinization	Low	Low
Exchange mechanisms		
Initiation	High	High
Implementation	Medium	Medium
Routinization	Medium	Low
Rules of engagement		
Initiation	High	High
Implementation	High	High
Routinization	Medium	Medium

The term MBPE is advanced here for reasons indigenous to the polities under discussion. Fully developed market systems that are prevalent in Western nations have no realistic chance of soon materializing in Eastern and Central European countries (Brabant 1992). Centrally planned systems cannot privatize their economies without embracing massive changes at all levels: institutional framework, exchange mechanisms, and rules of engagement. The case of the former German Democratic Republic (GDR) represents an interesting example of resistance toward a transformational change. The government, instead, favored gradual adjustments, which eventually caused the collapse of the regime (Bryson and Melzer 1991).

In May 1981, the GDR government announced at its Tenth Party Congress that its primary objective had shifted to rationalizing its scarce resources. With this announcement, it became abundantly clear that the reforms of the 1970s (related to decentralization) had become irrelevant (Collier 1987). Two options were now available to governmental decision-makers. One was to establish a socialist market economy in which the price system would be reformed but other aspects of the socialist value structure would continue, as in Hungary[1] or Yugoslavia. The other was to preserve the current economic and social linking mechanisms by introducing changes in the rules of engagement and the economic exchange mechanisms, that is, with major changes in the managerial, organizational, and coordinating devices.

The conservative East German government preferred the latter path, that of *Planvervollkommnung*, or plan perfecting. This avenue was considered preferable, as it assumed that associated uncertainties could be confined to what was considered a manageable area of reform. It was believed that the introduction of further decentralization and price reform could create social and political uncertainties that the government could not control.

In reference to the three arenas discussed earlier, the changes that the GDR government focused on were as follows: (1) rationalization of economic resources through better coordination of planning mechanisms and plan implementation (exchange mechanisms); (2) centralization of implementation decisions and production responsibilities at the Kombinat (combine) level (exchange mechanisms); and (3) improvements in financial and accounting devices to allow for more effective implementation and monitoring of plan objectives (rules of engagement).[2]

Quite clearly, the correction of deficiencies in process-structure linkages was the main target of the proposed reforms. Devolving strategic planning responsibilities to the combine level (a combination of business and political interests) allowed the government to exact greater coordination and flexibility at the production level while retaining its centralized supervisory powers. Similarly, the responsibilities for communications improvements were also "decentralized" and delegated to the combine level. The expectation was that communications would experience significant improvements in speed, conflict avoidance or settlement, and resource acquisition and exchanges. Furthermore, it was also assumed that an added benefit would result in the form of heightened motivation, as combine directors would assume greater discretion in vital areas of decision-making.

Needless to say, finance and accounting mechanisms had to be adjusted to accommodate the changes related to decentralization. The GDR government established a complex system of public finance (Buck 1987). The key components of the new system emphasized centrally fixed "costs" (such as cost reduction and cost discipline), "economic accounting systems," "price" (calculating more carefully cost-price relationships), and monitoring of performance through newly created agencies.

Instilling greater entrepreneurial vigor without compromising the principles of central control was one of the main goals of *Planvervollkommnung*. Concerns over improving the quality of products targeted for exports were triggered by the inability of the production units to be internationally competitive. So far, as most of the production output was exported to CMEA (Council for Mutual Economic Assistance) countries, enterprise managers did not have to worry about the competition from higher-quality Western and Asian products, nor did they need to be concerned about dealing with the fundamentally different transactional regimes (market economies) of the West.[3]

By shifting the responsibility for product improvements to the combine level, it was hoped that desired outcomes could be achieved more rapidly. Rewards and incentives were addressed vaguely in public statements. The assumption was that, as "socialist managers," combine directors and employees were given sufficient responsibilities to achieve higher production levels and better quality even with reduced resources. After 1985 (1986–1990 Five Year Plan), experiments with greater self-management and financial discretion for production investments were also aimed at a similar goal (Bryson and Melzer 1991; Collier 1987; Cornelsen 1988).

Despite these improvements, a number of serious problems emerged. The inappropriate pricing system continued to distort managerial, organizational, and procedural deficiencies of the system as a whole. There is no doubt that improvements were realized through the experimentation that took place during the 1980s. The susceptibility of the GDR to external influences remained largely unrecognized or understated by GDR officials. The GDR planners failed to relay the significance of these pressures to the combine directors and lower-level production managers whose eyes still remained fixed on the annually prescribed goals of the central plan. The cross-pressures of centralization and decentralization could never be reconciled. Furthermore, as the efforts to "empower" lower-level managers accelerated, monitoring and control by the ministries also increased, defeating the intended effect of greater self-management. The resulting transaction costs, in terms of stifling entrepreneurial vigor, motivation, and accountability, led to the system's eventual collapse.

The discrepancies in the existing institutional framework and the attempts to reform operational aspects of plan implementation eventually came to a conflict. Democratic traditions rely on the legitimacy of their institutions. Under the old regime in the GDR, this linkage was only made pro forma through the notion of "democratic socialism." As a result, the GDR suffered: (1) insufficient credibility to conduct authoritative exchanges, which led to the weakening of contractual arrangements; (2) a lack of trust in the viability of collective rules of engagement, which increased the need for other, third-party intervention; (3) a larger number of rules and regulations and greater monitoring activities to assure compliance; and (4) opportunistic behavior by individual and organizational actors, which resulted in pervasive uncertainty about accepted modes of conduct in a transitional environment.

The legacy continued to present major obstacles to the rapid metamorphic changes attempted by the German government (Kemme 1991; *Marktwirtschaft* 1991; Walker 1991). With a new institutional framework in place and the rudiments of transaction mechanisms initiated, the main tasks now lie in implementing and routinizing changes that have occurred too rapidly to be accepted.

The failure of the German government to recognize fully the need for coordination and balance among the three arenas—institutional framework, exchange mechanisms, and rules of engagement—may have serious ramifications for the new German *Länder* (states). For the imposed institutional framework to be internalized, mechanisms other than diffusion through contagion must be used in the initial stages until appropriate rationalized structures and professional networks have evolved. In the interim, a real danger exists: Judicial systems and changes introduced by the *Treuhandanstalt*, the privatization agency, may not have the desired effects. Consequently, efforts to institutionalize new meanings, values, and norms—both inside and outside organizations—may run into the inertial forces of old behaviors, patterns of interactions, and social control. The overly narrow focus on economic and technical improvements marginalizes the importance of institutional changes needed to weather the transformation.

In conclusion, the collapse of the East German economy reflects a far deeper problem: the failure of institutions to adapt. According to North (1991: 97), institutions "limit the set of choices and the transaction and production costs . . . institutions control the incentive structure of the economy." When institutional frameworks fail to provide meaningful gestalts for the organizational arrangements created in their support, human actors will be deprived of critical references. The system encounters periodic cycles of crises and selective interventions that eventually either culminate in a fundamental restructuring or precipitate its collapse.

ISOMORPHIC CHANGE: PUBLIC-PRIVATE PARTNERSHIPS IN THE UNITED STATES

The "rise of the entrepreneurial state" in the United States (Eisinger 1988) has raised a puzzling array of questions about the social and economic values that the traditional, neoclassical economic theory espouses. At the very minimum, it is agreed that an uneven development has occurred in American urban areas (Perlman 1992). The call for more "entrepreneurialism" as a means to redress the unevenness encompasses both the public and private sectors, as they clamor for greater flexibility, effectiveness, and efficiency in the delivery of products and services. The assumptions underlying entrepreneurialism are rarely questioned because, as Friedland and Robertson (1990) point out, because the entrepreneurial activities take place in a market environment, they are assumed to be efficient by definition. Recent history, however, shows that neither markets nor the firms operating in a market context can always, or even regularly, produce economically or socially desirable outcomes (Brooks 1984; Giloth 1988; Krumholz 1991).

The move toward incorporating "market"-like practices or operating the public sector more like a market[4] is an example of isomorphic change or change by contagion. Rather than challenging the prevailing system in its entirety, the idea of public-private partnership sanctions the current ideological environment and calls for minor, gradual adjustments within this prevailing framework.

To what extent do isomorphic changes succeed? The advocacy of public-private partnerships (PPPs) in the United States as a tool to redress uneven development is taking place in the context of a market-defined institutional framework. It has its own costs and benefits. The emphasis on market as an institutional framework necessarily undermines the values of other institutions such as the "local state" (Smith 1988) or the church. Public-private partnerships cannot be examined in a vacuum; they are a response to other major changes in the U.S. political economy. First, in recent years capital, especially international capital, has become increasingly mobile. Consequently, the "entrepreneurial state" is now forced to be more aggressive in forging alliances with private entrepreneurs in order to retain capital in local jurisdictions and maintain growth. Second, urban areas are faced with steadily diminishing resource bases and growing social and economic disparities between the urban core and suburbia. The result of this trend is the loss of the sense of community, pitting suburbs against the inner city and affluent against poor, in an ever-increasing spiral of decline (Perlman 1992).

Public-private partnerships are examples of new choices in organizational arrangements. They represent a response to the forces of decentralization and a devolution of responsibilities, not only from the federal to the local government but also from the public to the private and nonprofit sectors. They are also attempts at coordinating the potentially centrifugal forces of the marketplace in order to benefit local areas (Fosler 1992). In this process, however, values shift increasingly to those of the market: "Application of rational-actor models has been extended from the business firm to institutions such as the household and the state. . . . Households and states are interpreted as market analogues" (Friedland and Robertson 1990: 19).[5] Nonetheless, public-private partnerships are only a transitional phenomenon unless political and institutional choices can also be sufficiently articulated.

To understand the importance of these changes, apart from their potential economic significance, it is useful to couch them in a broader institutional context. The ineffectiveness of past governmental arrangements in preventing the decline of U.S. urban areas must raise fundamental questions about the value of "community" (Milofski 1988). Indeed, as Brooks has argued, "Community is an important public value, and its loss . . . is as serious a 'negative externality' of economic growth as environmental pollution or industrial accidents" (1984: 11).

The well-meant partnership efforts that are now under way are to some degree intended to bring the adversarial groups of the past together: government, the private sector, the nonprofit sector, and neighborhood organizations (Eisinger 1988; Wolman and Ledebur 1984). The current reform efforts are directed primarily to "empower" local levels of governments to recapture a sense of "community" in order to forestall a larger institutional crisis.

The nature and scope of isomorphic change can be understood with the help of Enterprise Zones (EZs). The idea of EZs clearly illustrates the problems and limitations of public-private partnership as a vehicle for change. Introduced by the Reagan administration in its first term and never passed by Congress, EZ legislation has now been adopted by about three-fourths of all states. EZs were originally designed as "federal, supply side, anti-regulatory, conservative-Re-publican" programs to attract "new, small business to the inner city" (Wolf 1990). Their mission and nature quickly changed, however. They assumed the character of public-private partnerships with a considerable role, both financial and managerial, in the public sector and were endorsed by the proponents of all political stripes. The existing programs place as much emphasis on attracting new firms as preserving the jobs that are already there. Zones have now expanded beyond the inner city to the suburbs and into rural areas as well. For many areas they have become a central element in their local economic development strategies. The rapid adoption of the zone concept demonstrates two issues with respect to the diffusion of change: EZs were able to capitalize on an economic climate in which a broad-based understanding of economic development goals had already been achieved, especially at the symbolic level. Furthermore, with early adopters leading the way, others quickly followed in order to capitalize on the perceived political and economic benefits of the zones for their areas. In this case, contagion was the prime vehicle to diffuse the change throughout the system. Although local EZ managements differ consid-erably, the general features of the zones are roughly comparable: targeting distressed neighborhoods—areas of high unemployment or population losses—coupled with offering incentives to spur business creation or retention. EZs were created to provide conditions for growth and to reduce barriers to private entrepreneurial activities.

Overall, the performance of these zones is debatable (Green 1991). As most zones' performance was initially poorly monitored, accurate data on job crea-tion and retention, new investment, and hiring of disadvantaged workers are not available (Papke 1988). Some critics of the zones contend that they have failed to address the underlying problems besetting urban areas. According to these critics, they continue to concentrate power in the hands of a few and provide only a token assistance to the rest.

The pervasive acceptance of the legitimacy of EZs illustrates the power of diffusion. A similar logic has been applied to other areas of economic development, such as trade export promotion, where we can witness similar contagion effects. On the other hand, the ongoing discussion of the efficacy of public-private partnerships may reflect the limits of change through contagion. The homogenization of all organizational exchange mechanisms exemplified in the pervasive slogan "to run government more like a busi-ness" may have resulted in the elimination of choices of discourse and the blurring of boundaries between the public and the private realm to the point that they are now merely symbolic (Bozeman 1987). If public agencies become no more than the extensions of the private sector, the welfare of the community as a whole is not preserved. Moreover, the very notion of community is threatened. If indeed the rise of the entrepreneurial state has contributed to the weakening of broader interest articulation, it effectively has eliminated a forum for public discourse. The search for "community" may have been abandoned.

This example provides an illustration of the limited usefulness of isomorphic changes in addressing complex problems. Should the current trend of devolution of tasks to the local level continue, the search for new institutional responses to the inadequate match of urban responsibilities and local constitutional powers may eventually trigger changes in the U.S. federal system. However, the need for massive institutional readjustments will only come to the fore when the systemic capacities to cope with crises can no longer be handled by isomorphic changes. This point has not been reached at the current stage—or at least its recognition has not.

CONCLUSION

This chapter outlines the core elements of a framework for an ethic of change that eliminates the artificial boundaries between development in developing and developed countries. It also emphasizes the need to devise a framework that conceptualizes change as an essential ingredient of institutional environments in an era of increasing globalization. If development is conceptualized as an ongoing process of change, the central question will be one of the extent, the nature, and the speed of change processes rather than one of developing versus developed countries. Examining change in common areas—the institutional framework, exchange mechanisms, and rules of engagement—creates a framework that avoids the pitfalls of an overgeneralized model without surrendering the need for rigorous comparative examination. Such a model also needs to account for change paths taken and the speed with which change proceeds. These factors are critical in the evaluation of respective local conditions.

Both examples illustrate the fundamental differences between metamorphic and isomorphic changes. Although the former requires a realignment in all three arenas, the latter is more likely to be confined to changes in rules and exchange mechanisms, using contagion as a vehicle for propagation throughout the system.

Further empirical studies must refine and test the outlines of these models when applied to varying conditions. The massive changes in Eastern and Central Europe provide a challenging field in which to examine the dynamics and paths of metamorphic change. On the other hand, changes in Western Europe are beginning to display the characteristics of contagion and homogenization—homogenization of rules and exchange mechanisms within the overall objective of retaining institutional harmony.

NOTES

1. The East German government's efforts to pursue *Planvervollkommnung* can be viewed as outright rejection of Hungarian-style reforms (Kornai 1986).

2. Industrial or agricultural *kombinate* (combines) were giant-size production units to allow for vertical and horizontal integration of production facilities. For an excellent discussion see Bryson and Melzer (1987).

3. There were a few exceptions, however. Exports of machinery, chemicals, and other products were increasing during the 1970s and parts of the 1980s. Several joint ventures with West German firms near the end of the decade signified further efforts to strengthen investment capacities, but to no avail.

4. What exactly this market consists of is rarely clear; presumably, it consists of public goods.

5. In this context, it is of interest to note Karl Polanyi's work of some forty years ago. He wrote that "to allow the market mechanisms to be the sole director of the fate of all human beings and their natural environment, indeed, even of the amount and use of purchasing power, would result in the demolition of society" (1944: 73).

BIBLIOGRAPHY

ACIPA (American Consortium for International Public Administration). 1991. Minutes of governing board meeting of December 9.

Adler, Nancy. 1991. *International dimensions of organizational behavior.* Boston: Kent Publishing Co.

Archer, Margaret S. 1988. *Culture and agency.* New York: Cambridge University Press.

———. 1990. Theory, culture and post-industrial society. In Mike Featherstone, ed., *Global culture.* Newbury Park, Calif.: Sage, pp. 97–120.

Ardila, Martha. 1991. *Cambio de Norte?: Momentos críticos de la política exterior Colombiana.* Bogotá: Tercer Mundo Editores.

Arrow, Kenneth. 1963. *Social choice and individual values.* New York: Wiley.

Ascher, Kate. 1987. *The politics of privatisation: Contracting out public services.* New York: St. Martin's Press.

Auchincloss, Kenneth. 1992. Limits of democracy. *Newsweek,* January 21: 25–30.

Baldi, Patricia. 1989. Address to the 1989 Society for International Development (Washington Chapter) annual conference. May 10.

Barry, Tom, Beth Wood, and Deb Preusch. 1984. *The other side of paradise.* New York: Grove Press.

Behar, Olga, and Ricardo Villa Salcedo. 1991. *Penumbra en el Capitolio.* Bogotá: Planeta Colombiana Editorial.

Berg, Robert J., and David F. Gordon. 1989. *Cooperation for international development: The United States and the Third World in the 1990s.* Boulder, Colo.: Lynne Rienner Publishers.

Biersteker, Thomas J. 1990. Reducing the role of the state in the economy: A conceptual exploration of IMF and World Bank prescriptions. *International Studies Quarterly* 34(4): 477–492.

Bill, James. 1984. *Politics in the Middle East,* 2d ed. Boston: Little, Brown and Co.

Binder, Leonard. 1962. *Iran: Political development in a changing society.* Los Angeles: University of California Press.

Bozeman, Barry. 1987. *All organizations are public: Bridging public and private organizational theories*. San Francisco: Jossey-Bass.

Brabant, Jozef M. van. 1992. *Privatizing Eastern Europe*. Dordrecht, Netherlands: Kluwer Academic.

Brandt, Willy. 1981. *North-South: A program for survival*. Cambridge, Mass.: MIT Press.

Brinkerhoff, Derick W. 1991. *Improving development program performance: Guidelines for managers*. Boulder, Colo.: Westview Press.

Brinkerhoff, Derick W., and Arthur A. Goldsmith, eds. 1990. *Institutional sustainability in agriculture and rural development*. New York: Praeger.

Brint, Steven, and Jerome Karabel. 1991. Institutional transformations. In Walter W. Powell and Paul J. DiMaggio, eds., *The new institutionalism in organization analysis*. Chicago: University of Chicago Press, pp. 337–360.

Brooks, Harvey. 1984. Seeking equity and efficiency: Public and private roles. In Harvey Brooks, Lance Liebman, and Corinne S. Schelling, eds., *Public-Private Partnership*. Cambridge, Mass.: Ballinger, pp. 3–30.

Brunner, Karl. 1976. The new international economic order: A chapter in a protracted confrontation. *Orbis* (Spring): 103–121.

Bryant, Coralie, and Louise G. White. 1982. *Managing development in the third world*. Boulder, Colo.: Westview Press.

Bryson, Phillip J., and Manfred Melzer. 1987. The Kombinat in GDR economic organisation. In Ian Jeffries and Manfred Melzer, eds., *The East German economy*. London: Croom Helm, pp. 51–68.

———. 1991. *The end of the East German economy*. New York: St. Martin's Press.

Brzezinski, Zbigniew. 1986. *Game plan: The geostrategic framework for the conduct of the U.S.-Soviet contest*. Boston: Atlantic Monthly Press.

Buchanan, James, and Gordon Tullock. 1962. *The calculus of consent*. Ann Arbor: University of Michigan Press.

Buck, Hannsjörg F. 1987. The GDR financial system. In Ian Jeffries and Manfred Melzer, eds., *The East German economy*. London: Croom Helm, pp. 149–201.

Caiden, Gerald. 1991a. Administrative reform. In Ali Farazmand, ed., *Handbook of comparative and development public administration*. New York: Marcel Dekker, Chapter 27.

———. 1991b. Getting at the essence of the administrative state. Paper presented at the Fourth Annual Symposium of the Public Administration Theory Network. George Washington University, Washington, D.C., March 21.

———. 1991c. *Administrative reform comes of age*. Berlin: Walter De Gruyter.

Caldwell, Lynton K. 1972. *In defense of earth: International protection of the biosphere*. Bloomington: Indiana University Press.

———. 1984. *International environmental policy: Emergence and dimensions*. Durham, N.C.: Duke University Press.

———. 1990. *International environmental policy*. Durham, N.C.: Duke University Press.

———. 1991. International response to environmental issues. *International Studies Notes* 16(1): 3–7.

Campbell, Colin S. J. 1986. *Managing the presidency*. Pittsburgh: University of Pittsburgh Press.

Carino, Ledivina. 1991. Regime change, the bureaucracy, and political development. In Ali Farazmand, ed., *Handbook of comparative and development public administration*. New York: Marcel Dekker, Chapter 54.

Carta Administrativa. 1992. *Revista del Departamento del Servicio Civil*. Marzo-Abril, 69: 51–60.

Chapman, Richard A. 1970. *The higher civil service in Britain*. London: Constable.

Chilcote, Ronald H. 1982. *Dependency and Marxism: Toward a resolution of the debate.* Boulder, Colo.: Westview Press.

Child, Jorge. 1992. El otro papel del Estado. *El Espectador*, 8 Noviembre, 3B.

Clarke, J. N., and D. McCool. 1989. *Staking out the terrain: Power differentials among natural resource management agencies.* Albany: State University of New York Press.

Collier, Irwin L. 1987. The GDR Five-Year Plan 1986–1990. *Comparative Economic Studies* 29(2): 39–53.

Comisión Presidencial para la Reforma de la Administración Pública del Estado Colombiano. 1991. *Informe final.* Preparado por Marino Tadeo Henao Ospina, Secretario Técnico de la Comisión. Bogotá: Centro de Publicaciones, Escuela Superior de Administración Publicá.

Consejería para la Modernización del Estado. 1991. *El nuevo régimen de la administración pública.* Bogotá: Ser Impresores.

Constitución política de Colombia 1991. 1992. 2da. Edición. Bogotá: Escuela Superior de Administración Pública, Departmento Administrativo del Servicio Pública, República de Colombia.

Cook, Paul, and Colin Kirkpatrick. 1988. *Privatization in less developed countries.* NewYork: St. Martin's Press.

Cooper, Richard N. 1991. The world economic climate. In Jessica Tuchman Mathews, ed., *Preserving the global environment.* New York: Norton, pp. 227–235.

Cornelsen, D. 1988. Die lage der DDR Wirtschaft zur Jahreswende. *DIW Wochenberichte*, February 4.

Cowan, Gray. 1990. *Privatization in the developing world.* New York: Praeger.

Crenson, Matthew A. 1975. *The federal machine: Beginnings of bureaucracy in Jacksonian America.* Baltimore: Johns Hopkins University Press.

Daft, Richard. 1992. *Organizational theory and design*, 4th ed. NewYork: West Publishing Co.

Dahl, Robert A. 1947. The science of public administration: Three problems. *Public Administration Review* 7: 1–13.

———. 1970. *After the revolution.* New Haven: Yale University Press.

———. 1971. *Polyarchy: Participation and opposition.* New Haven: Yale University Press.

de Orjuela, Martha Laverde. 1991. Avances de la descentralización del sector salud en el pais. *Salud y Gerencia*, Boletín de la Unidad de Desarrollo de Sistemas de Salud, Universidad Javeriana, Bogotá, 7: 1, 9–10.

DeGregori, Thomas. 1974. Caveat emptor: A critique of the emerging paradigm of public choice. *Administration and Society* 6: 2.

Diamant, Alfred. 1960. The relevance of comparative politics to the study of comparative administration. *Administrative Science Quarterly* 5: 87–112.

Diamond, Larry, Juan Linz, and Seymour Martin Lipset, eds. 1990. *Politics in developing countries: Comparing experiences with democracy.* Boulder, Colo.: Lynne Rienner Publishers.

Dillman, David. 1994. The Thatcher agenda, the civil service, and "total efficiency." In Ali Farazmand, ed., *Handbook of bureaucracy.* New York: Marcel Dekker, Chapter 14. In press.

DiMaggio, Paul J. 1988. Interest and agency in institutional theory. In Lynne G. Zucker, ed., *Institutional patterns and organizations.* Cambridge, Mass.: Ballinger, pp. 3–22.

DiMaggio, Paul J., and Walter W. Powell. 1983. The iron cage revisited: Institutional isomorphism and collective rationality in organizational fields. *American Sociological Quarterly* 48: 147–160.

DiPalma, Guiseppe. 1990. *To craft democracies: An essay on democratic transitions.* Berkeley: University of California Press.

Dix, Robert H. 1987. *The politics of Colombia*. New York: Praeger.

Dogan, Mattei, ed. 1975. *The mandarins of Western Europe: The political role of top civil servants*. New York: John Wiley & Sons.

Dorsey, John T. 1962. An information-energy model. In Ferrel Heady and Sybil L. Stokes, eds., *Papers in comparative public administration*. Ann Arbor: Institute of Public Administration, University of Michigan, pp. 37–57.

Downs, Anthony. 1957. *An economic theory of democracy*. New York: Harper and Row.

Dwivedi, O. P., ed. 1987. *Perspective on technology and development*. New Delhi: Gitanjali.

Dwivedi, O. P., and Keith M. Henderson, eds. 1990. *Public administration in world perspective*. Ames: Iowa State University Press.

Dye, Thomas, and Harmon Zeigler. 1993. *The irony of democracy*. Pacific Grove, Calif.: Brooks/Cole.

Edmond, J. B. 1978. *The magnificent charter: The origin and role of the Morrill Land-Grant colleges and universities*. Hicksville, N.Y.: Exposition Press.

Eisinger, Peter K. 1988. *The rise of the entrepreneurial state*. Madison: University of Wisconsin Press.

Esman, Milton J. 1971. Foreign aid: Not by bread alone. *Public Administration Review* 31(1): 92–100.

———. 1991. *Management dimensions of development: Perspectives and strategies*. West Hartford, Conn.: Kumarian Press.

Facts on File. 1992. November 26. New York.

Farazmand, Ali. 1989a. *The state, bureaucracy, and revolution in modern Iran: Agrarian reform and regime politics*. New York: Praeger.

———. 1989b. Crisis in the U.S. administrative state. *Administration and Society* 21(2): 173–199.

———. 1991a. State tradition and public administration in Iran in ancient and contemporary perspectives. In Ali Farazmand, ed., *Handbook of comparative and development public administration*. New York: Marcel Dekker, Chapter 19.

———. 1991b. Bureaucracy and revolution: The case of Iran. In Ali Farazmand, ed., *Handbook of comparative and development public administration*. New York: Marcel Dekker, Chapter 55.

———. 1994a. Introduction: The multi-facet nature of organizations. In Ali Farazmand, ed., *Modern organizations: Administrative theory in contemporary society*. Westport, Conn.: Praeger. In press.

———. 1994b. Organization theory: An overview and appraisal. In Ali Farazmand, ed., *Modern organizations: Administrative theory in contemporary society*. Westport, Conn.: Praeger, Chapter 1. In press.

———. 1994c. Introduction. In Ali Farazmand, ed., *Handbook of bureaucracy*. New York: Marcel Dekker. In press.

———. 1994d. *Administrative reform in developing countries*. JAI & The Policy Studies Organization. In press.

———. 1994e. *International handbook of public enterprise management*. Westport, Conn.: Greenwood Press. In press.

———. 1994f. Symposium: Civilization and administration: Contributions of ancient civilizations to modern governance. Special issue of the *International Journal of Public Administration*. In press.

Fosler, R. Scott. 1992. State economic policy: The emerging paradigm. *Economic Development Quarterly* 6: 3–13.

French, Hilary F. 1991. You are what you breathe. In Lester R. Brown, ed., *The world watch reader*. New York: W. W. Norton, pp. 97–111.

————. 1992. Strengthening global environmental governance. In Lester R. Brown, ed., *State of the world*. New York: Norton, pp. 155–173.

Fried, Robert. 1976. *Performance in American bureaucracy*. Boston: Little, Brown and Co.

Friedland, Robert, and A. F. Robertson, eds. 1990. *Beyond the marketplace*. New York: De Gruyter.

Frye, Richard. 1963. *The heritage of Persia*. New York: World Publishing Company.

————. 1975. *The golden age of Persia*. New York: Harper and Row.

Gable, Richard W. 1976. *Development administration: Background, terms, concepts, theories and a new approach*. Washington, D.C.: American Society for Public Administration, SICA Series (June) 7.

Galán, Luis Carlos. 1991. *Ni un paso atrás, siempre adelante!* Bogotá: Fundación Luis Carlos Galán.

Galaskiewitz, Joseph, and Ronald S. Burt. 1991. Interorganization contagion in corporate philanthropy. *Administrative Science Quarterly* 36: 88–105.

Galbraith, John Kenneth. 1974. The U.S. economy is not a free economy. *Forbes* 113(10): 99.

Game, Kingsley W. 1979. Controlling air pollution: Why some states try harder. *Policy Studies Journal* 7: 728–738.

García González, Jorge. 1993. El proceso de modernización del Estado en Colombia. *Política Colombiana*, revista de la Controlería General de la República, 11(3): 53–63.

Garcia-Zamor, Jean-Claude. 1968. A typology of creole bureaucracies. *International Review of Administrative Science* 38(1): 49–60.

————. 1973. Micro-bureaucracies and development administration. *International Review of Administrative Science* 39(4): 417–423.

————. 1985. *Public participation in development planning and management: Cases from Africa and Asia*. Boulder, Colo.: Westview Press.

————. 1990. Risks and conflicts in centralized state intervention in development organizations. In Manuel J. Pelaez, ed., *Studies in economics*. Barcelona, Spain: University of Malaga Press, pp. 219–215.

————. 1991. Problems of public policy implementation in developing countries. In Ali Farazmand, ed., *Handbook of comparative and development public administration*. New York: Marcel Dekker, pp. 435–444.

————. 1992. Neoteric theories for development administration in the New World Order. Paper presented at the 1992 Annual Conference of the American Society for Public Administration, Chicago, April 11–15.

Gaviria Trujillo, Cesar. 1992. Saldremos adelante muy pronto. *El Tiempo*, 21 de Julio, 8A.

Gibbs, David. 1991. Private interests and foreign intervention: Toward a business conflict model. Paper presented at the 1991 Annual Conference of the American Political Science Association, Washington, D.C., August.

Giloth, Robert P. 1988. Community economic development. *Economic Development Quarterly* 2: 343–350.

Global Climate Change and Public Policy—A Special Symposium. 1991. *Policy Studies Journal* 19(2): 43–162.

Golembiewski, Robert. 1977. A critique of "democratic administration" and its supporting ideation. *American Political Science Review* 17(4): 1488–1507.

Goodsell, Charles T. 1981. The new comparative administration: A proposal. *International Journal of Public Administration* 3(2): 143–155.

————. 1983. *The case for bureaucracy*. New York: Free Press.

————. 1990. Emerging issues in public administration. In Naomi Lynn and Aaron Wildavsky, eds., *Public administration: The state of the discipline*. Chattam, N.J.: Chattam House, pp. 495–509.

Gore, Al. 1992. *Earth in the balance: Ecology and the human spirit.* Boston: Houghton Mifflin Company.

Governance. 1992. vol. 5, 4(October).

Gow, James I. 1992. Diffusion of administrative innovations in Canadian public administrations. *Administration and Society* 23: 430–454.

Green, Roy, ed. 1991. *Enterprise zones.* Newbury Park, Calif.: Sage.

Greenwood, Royston, and C. R. Hinings. 1987. Organizational transformations: Editorial introduction. *Journal of Management Studies* 24: 561–564.

Habermass, Jurgen. 1975. *Legitimacy crisis.* Translated by Thomas McCarthy. Boston: Beacon.

Hage, Jerald, and Kurt Finsterbusch. 1987. *Organizational change as a development strategy: Models and tactics for improving third world organizations.* Boulder, Colo: Lynne Rienner Publishers.

Hamilton, Edward. 1989. *America's global interests: A new agenda.* New York: Norton.

Hamilton, Lee. 1988. Remarks on activity of the Foreign Affairs Committee Task Force on Foreign Assistance. Washington, D.C.: U.S. Congress, September 14.

Hanlon, J. 1984. *Mozambique: The revolution under fire.* London: Zed.

————. 1991. *Mozambique: Who calls the shots?* Bloomington and Indianapolis: Indiana University Press.

Hardin, Garrett. 1977. The tragedy of the commons. In Garrett Hardin and John Baden, eds., *Managing the commons.* San Francisco: W. H. Freeman, pp. 17–30.

Harmon, Michael, and Richard Mayer. 1986. *Organization theory for public administration.* Boston: Little, Brown and Co.

Hass, Peter M. 1990. Obtaining international environmental protection through epistemic consensus. *Millennium* 19(3): 347–364.

Hawley, Amos. 1968. Human ecology. In David L. Sills, ed., *International encyclopedia of the social sciences.* New York: Macmillan, pp. 328–337.

Hayter, Theresa. 1971. *Aid as imperialism.* London: Penguin Books.

Heady, Ferrel. 1991. *Public administration: A comparative perspective.* New York: Marcel Dekker.

Hedlund, Gunner. 1986. The hypermodern MNC—A heterarchy. *Human Resource Management* (Spring): 9–35.

Heilbroner, Robert. 1991. *An inquiry into the human prospect.* New York: Norton.

Hellinger, Stephen, Douglas Hellinger, and Fred M. O'Regan. 1988. *Aid for just development: Report on the future of foreign assistance.* Boulder, Colo.: Lynne Rienner.

Hembra, Richard L. 1990. Observations on the Environmental Protection Agency's budget request for Fiscal Year 1991. Statement before the Committee on Environment and Public Works, U.S. Senate, March 7.

Henderson, Keith. 1969. Comparative public administration: The identity crisis. *Journal of Comparative Administration* 1: 65–84.

Henderson, Keith M., and O. P. Dwivedi. 1992. Administered development: The fifth decade—1990s. *Indian Journal of Public Administration* 38: 1–16.

Henning, Daniel, and William R. Mangun. 1989. *Managing the environmental crisis: Incorporating competing values in natural resource administration.* Durham, N.C.: Duke University Press.

Hermand, Edward, and Frank Broadhead. 1984. *Demonstration elections.* Boston: South End Press.

Hinings, C. R., and Royston Greenwood. 1989. *The dynamics of strategic change.* New York: Basil Blackwell.

Honadle, George. 1982. Development administration in the eighties: New agendas or old perspectives? *Public Administration Review* 42(2): 174–179.

Huntington, Samuel. 1991. *The third wave: Democratization in the late twentieth century.* Norman: University of Oklahoma Press.

Iaccoca, Lee. 1984. *An autobiography.* New York: Bantam.

Jabbra, Joseph G., and O. P. Dwivedi. 1989. *Public service accountability: A comparative perspective.* West Hartford, Conn.: Kumarian.

Jackson, Robert G. A. 1969. *A study of the capacity of the United Nations development system.* 2 vols. Geneva: United Nations.

Jacob, Gerald. 1990. *Site unseen: The politics of siting a nuclear waste repository.* Pittsburgh: University of Pittsburgh Press.

Jones, Garth N. 1970. Failure of technical assistance in public administration abroad. *Journal of Comparative Administration* 2(1): 3–51.

Jones, Charles O. 1975. *Clean air: The policies and politics of pollution control.* Pittsburgh: University of Pittsburgh Press.

———. 1984. *An introduction to the study of public policy*, 3d ed. Monterey, Calif.: Brooks/Cole.

Jreisat, Jamil E. 1975. Synthesis and relevance in comparative public administration. *Public Administration Review* 35: 663–671.

Jun, Jong S. 1976. Renewing the study of comparative administration: Some reflections on the current possibilities. *Public Administration Review* 36: 641–647.

Kaufman, Herbert. 1970. *The forest ranger: A study in administrative behavior.* Baltimore: Johns Hopkins University Press.

Kemme, David M. 1991. *Economic transition in Eastern Europe and the Soviet Union.* New York: Institute for East-West Security Studies.

Kennedy, Paul. 1989. *The rise and fall of the great powers: Economic change and military conflict.* New York: Vintage Books.

Keohane, Robert, and Joseph Nye. 1977. *Power and interdependence.* Boston: Little, Brown.

Khator, Renu. 1991. *Environment, development and politics in India.* Lanham, Md.: University Press of America.

———. 1992a. Administering the environment in an interdependent world. Paper presented at the 1992 Annual Meeting of the American Society for Public Administration, Chicago, April.

———. 1992b. Bureaucracy, environmentalism, and industrial policy: A case study of Hong Kong. In H. K. Asmerom, R. Hoppe, and R. B. Jain, eds., *Bureaucracy and development.* Amsterdam: VU University Press, pp. 237–252.

Killick, Tony, and Simon Commander. 1988. State divestiture as a policy instrument in developing countries. *World Development* 16: 1465–1479.

Kissinger, Henry A. 1992. The new Russian question. *Newsweek*, February 10: 34–35.

Kitschell, Herbert. 1992. Political regime change: Structure and process-driven explanations? *American Political Science Review* 86(4): 1028–1034.

Klare, Michael. 1988. North-South vs. East-West: Shifting focus of U.S. military power. *Middle East Report*, March/April.

———. 1990. Policing the Gulf and the world. *The Nation*, October 15.

Kornai, Janos. 1986. The Hungarian reform process. *Journal of Economic Literature* 24: 1687–1737.

Korten, David C. 1980. Community organization and rural development: A learning process approach. *Public Administration Review* 40(5): 480–511.

Krumholz, Norman. 1991. Equity and local economic development. *Economic Development Quarterly* 5: 291–300.

Landazábal Reyes, General Fernando. 1990. *La salida del túnel.* Bogotá: Planeta Colombiana Editorial.

Laughlin, Richard C. 1991. Environmental disturbances and organizational transitions and transformations. *Organization Studies* 12(2): 209–232.

Leblebici, Huseyin. 1985. Transactions and organizational forms: A re-analysis. *Organization Studies* 6(2): 97–115.

Lenin, V. I. 1971. *State and revolution*. New York: International Publisher.

Lester, James P. 1980. Partisanship and environmental control: The mediating influence of state organizational structure. *Environment and Behavior* 12: 101–131.

Letwin, Oliver. 1988. *Privatizing the world: A study of international privatization in theory and practice*. London: Cassell.

Loehr, William, and John P. Powelson. 1983. *Threat to development: Pitfalls of the NIEO*. Boulder, Colo.: Westview Press.

Lowenthal, Abraham, ed. 1991. *Exporting democracy: The United States and Latin America*. Baltimore: Johns Hopkins University Press.

Luebert, Gregory. 1991. *Liberalism, fascism, or social democracy: Social classes and the political origins of regimes in interwar Europe*. New York: Oxford University Press.

Macpherson, C. B. 1987. *The rise and fall of economic justice*. New York: Oxford University Press.

Marktwirtschaft. Various issues, 1991/92.

Martin, Edward. 1969. *Development assistance: Efforts and policies of the members of the development assistance committee*. Paris: OECD, December.

Marulanda, Iván. 1990. *Testimonio al borde del abismo*. Bogotá: Producción Editorial, Folio Ltda.

Mathews, Jessica Tuchman, ed. 1991. *Preserving the global environment*. New York: Norton.

Matthews, R. C. O. 1986. The economics of institutions and the sources of growth. *Economic Journal* 96: 903–918.

Matthews, Tom. 1991. Decade of democracy. *Newsweek*, December 30: 32–42.

McClintock, Cynthia. 1987. *Agricultural policy and food security in Peru and Ecuador: Agrarian reform in reverse: The food crisis in the third world*. Boulder, Colo., and London: Westview Press.

McCurdy, Howard E. 1977. *Public administration*. Menlo Park, Calif.: Benjamin/Cummings.

Meadows, D. H., D. L. Meadows, and J. Randers. 1992. *Beyond the limits*. Post Mills, Vt.: Chelsea Green.

Meyer, John W., and Brian Rowan. 1991. Institutionalized organizations: Formal structures as myth and ceremony. In Walter W. Powell and Paul J. DiMaggio, eds., *The new institutionalism in organization analysis*. Chicago: University of Chicago Press, pp. 41–62.

Miami Herald. April 11, 1991, p. 16A; November 4, 1991, p. 11A; November 10, 1991, p. 6C; December 1, 1991, p. 1–3L; December 11, 1991, p. 20A; January 5, 1992, p. 23A; January 16, 1992, p. 23A; January 29, 1992, p. 11A; January 31, 1992, p. 17A; February 6, 1992, p. 19A; February 12, 1992, p. 1A.

Middle East Report. 1992. *The democracy agenda for the Arab world*. January/February.

Miller, Danny, and Peter H. Friesen. 1984. *Organizations: A quantum view*. New York: Prentice-Hall.

Milofski, Carl, ed. 1988. *Community organizations*. New York: Oxford University Press.

Misión para la Moralización y Eficiencia en Administración Pública. 1992. Nuevo tinglado contra la corrupción. *El Tiempo*, 31 de Agosto, 3A.

Molotch, Harvey. 1976. The city as a growth machine. *American Journal of Sociology* 82: 309–332.

Montgomery, John D. 1971. Transferability of what? The relevance of foreign aid to the domestic poverty program. *Journal of Comparative Administration* 2(4): 455–470.

Montgomery, John D., and William J. Siffin, eds. 1966. *Approaches to development: Politics, administration and change*. New York: McGraw-Hill.

Nachmias, David, and David H. Rosenbloom. 1978. *Bureaucratic culture: Citizens and administrators in Israel*. London: Croom Helm.

Newsweek. 1991. November 25: 47.

New York Times. 1982. January 13.

North, Douglass C. 1990. *Institutions, institutional change and economic performance*. New York: Cambridge.

————. 1991. Institutions. *Journal of Economic Perspectives* 5: 97–112.

Notisur. Latin America Data Base, Latin American Institute, University of New Mexico, Albuquerque.

O'Conner, J. 1973. *The fiscal crisis of the state*. New York: St. Martin's Press.

O'Donnell, G., P. Schmitter, and L. Whitehead, eds. 1986. *Transitions from authoritarian rule*. 4 vols. Baltimore: Johns Hopkins University Press.

O'Leary, Rosemary. 1991. Environmental administration, the courts, and public policy, 1980–89. *International Journal of Public Administration* 14(3): 303–314.

————. 1992. Regulatory takings taking its toll on local governments. *PA Times*, July: S1.

Offe, C. 1985. *Contradictions of the welfare state*. Cambridge: MIT Press.

Ostrom, Vincent, Jr. 1973. *The intellectual crisis of public administration in America*. Alabama: University of Alabama Press.

Paehlke, Robert, and D. Torgerson, eds. 1990. *Managing Leviathan: environmental politics and the administrative state*. Kenmore, N.Y.: Broadview Press.

Panandiker, V. A. Pai, and S. S. Kshirsagar. 1978. *Bureaucracy and development administration*. New Delhi: Centre for Policy Research.

Papke, James. 1988. *The Indiana enterprise zone experiment*. Indianapolis: Indiana Department of Commerce.

Pardo, Rodrigo, and Juan G. Tokatlian. 1988. *Política exterior Colombiana: De la subordinación a la autonomía?* Bogotá: Tercer Mundo Editores.

Parenti, Michael. 1978. *Power and the powerless*. New York: St. Martin's Press.

————. 1988. *Democracy for the few*. New York: St. Martin's Press.

————. 1989. *The sword and the dollar: Imperialism, revolution, and the arms race*. New York: St. Martin's Press.

Pearson, Lester B. 1969. *Partners in development: Report of the commission on international development*. New York: Praeger.

Perlman, Ellen. 1992. City-suburb income disparity growing. *City and State* 9(6): 21.

Peters, Guy. 1991. Government reform and reorganization in an era of retrenchment and conviction politics. In Ali Farazmand, ed., *Handbook of comparative and development public administration*. New York: Marcel Dekker, Chapter 28.

————. 1994. Government reorganization: A theoretical analysis. In Ali Farazmand, ed., *Modern organizations*. Westport, Conn.: Praeger, Chapter 4. In press.

Peterson, Rudolph. 1970. *U.S. foreign assistance in the 1970s: A new approach. Report to the President from the Task Force on International Development*. Washington, D.C.: U.S. Government Printing Office.

Pettigrew, Andrew M. 1985. *The awakening giant: Continuity and change in Imperial Chemical Industry*. Oxford: Basil Blackwell.

Pizarro, Eduardo. 1990. *Insurgencia crónica, movimiento guerrillero y proceso de paz en Colombia*. Conference Paper No. 45, Research Conference on Violence and Democracy in Colombia and Peru, held at Columbia University, November 30 to December 1, 1990.

Polanyi, Karl. 1944. *The great transformation*. Boston: Beacon Press.

Postel, Sandra. 1992. Denial in the decisive decade. In Lester R. Brown, ed., *State of the world.*
New York: Norton, pp. 3–8.

Presidencia de la República de Colombia. 1992. *Directiva Presidencial* No. 03, 20 Agosto.

Rabe, Barry G. 1986. *Fragmentation and integration in state environmental management.*
Washington, D.C.: Conservation Foundation.

Ramakrishna, Kilaparti. 1990. North-South issues, common heritage of mankind and global
climate change. *Millennium* 19(3): 429–446.

Randall, Stephen J. 1992. *Colombia and the United States: Hegemony and interdependence.*
Athens, Ga., and London: University of Georgia Press.

Riggs, Fred W. 1964. *Administration in developing countries: The theory of prismatic society.*
Boston: Houghton Mifflin.

———. 1970. *Frontiers of development administration.* Durham, N.C.: Duke University Press.

———. 1973. *The consulting firm, the U.S. AID Agency and the Chinese veterans program.*
Syracuse: Inter-University Case Program.

———. 1976. The group and the movement: Notes on comparative and development administration. *Public Administration Review* 36: 648–654.

———. 1988. The survival of presidentialism in America: Para-Constitutional practices.
International Political Science Review 9(4): 247–278.

———. 1993a. Fragility of the third world's regimes. *International Social Science Review* 136:
199–243.

———. 1993b. Presidentialism: An empirical theory. In Mattei Dogan and Ali Kazancigil, eds.,
Comparing nations: The pendulum between theory and substance. Oxford: Basil
Blackwell. In press.

———. 1993c. Bureaucracy and the constitution. *Public Administration Review.* In press.

———. 1993d. Public administration: The intellectual crisis and its resolution. *International
Journal of Public Administration.* In press.

———. 1994a. Bureaucracy: A profound puzzle for presidentialism. In Ali Farazmand, ed.,
Handbook of Bureaucracy. New York: Marcel Dekker. In press.

———. 1994b. Public administration: A futuristic vision. *International Journal of Public
Administration.* In press.

Roa Suarez, Hernando. 1992. *Los grupos de presión: Una aproximación.* Bogotá: Centro de
Publicaciones, Escuela Superior de Administración Pública.

Robertson, R. 1987. Globalization theory and civilizational analysis. *Comparative Civilizations
Review* 17: 20–30.

Rodriguez, Cecilia. 1992. King Pablo of Colombia. *Newsweek*, August 24: 4.

Rodriguez, Edmundo. 1985. *Despues del populismo: Hacia el cambio estructural?* Bogotá:
Empresa Editorial Universal Nacional.

Rosenau, James N. 1990. *Turbulence in world politics.* Princeton: Princeton University
Press.

Rosenbloom, David. 1989. *Public administration: Understanding management, politics, and
law in the public sector,* 2d ed. New York: Random House.

Rostow, W. W. 1988. Beware of historians bearing false analogies. *Foreign Affairs* (Spring):
863–868.

Rourke, Francis. 1991. American bureaucracy in a changing political setting. *Journal of Public
Administration: Research and Theory* 1(2): 111–129.

Rueschemeyer, D., E. H. Stephens, and J. D. Stephens. 1992. *Capitalist development and
democracy.* Chicago: University of Chicago Press.

Ruffing-Hilliard, Karen. 1991. Merit reform in Latin America. In Ali Farazmand, ed., *Handbook of comparative and development public administration.* New York: Marcel Dekker, pp. 301–312.

Savage, Peter. 1976. Optimism and pessimism in comparative administration. *Public Administration Review* 36: 415–423.

Savas, E. S. 1982. *Privatizing the public sector*. Chattam, N.J.: Chattam House.

Schaffer, Bernard. 1973. *The administrative factor*. London: Frank Cass.

Schraeder, Peter J. 1992. *Intervention into the 1990s: U.S. foreign policy in the third world*, 2d ed. Boulder, Colo.: Lynne Rienner.

Schutz, Barry, and Robert Slater, eds. 1990. *Revolution and political change in the third world*. Boulder, Colo.: Lynne Rienner.

Sedghi, Hamideh. 1992. The Persian Gulf War: The new international order or disorder? *New Political Science* 21–22: 41–60.

Segal, Aaron. 1990. Small and poor countries in a world of big science and technology. *Science, Technology & Development* 8(3): 222–233.

Seidman, Harold. 1980. *Politics, position, and power: The dynamics of federal organization*. New York: Oxford University Press.

Senge, Peter M. 1990. Catalyzing systems thinking within organizations. In Fred Massarik, ed., *Advances in organization development*. Norwood, N.J.: Ablex, pp. 197–246.

Shaiken, Harley. 1986. *Work transformed: Automation and labor in the computer age*. Lexington, Mass.: Lexington Books.

Shea, Cynthia Pollock. 1991. Mending the Earth's shield. In Lester R. Brown, ed., *The world watch reader*. New York: W. W. Norton, pp. 60–74.

Sigelman, Lee. 1976. In search of comparative administration. *Public Administration Review* 36: 621–625.

Smith, Michael P. 1988. *City, state and market*. New York: Basil Blackwell.

Springer, J. Fred. 1976. Empirical theory and development administration: Prologues and promise. *Public Administration Review* 36: 636–641.

Steers, Richard. 1991. *Organizational behavior*, 4th ed. New York: Harper Collins.

Subramaniam, V., ed. 1990. *Public administration in the third world*. Westport, Conn.: Greenwood.

Swerdlow, Irving, ed. 1963. *Development administration concepts and problems*. Syracuse: Syracuse University Press.

Teng, Ssu-Yu. 1943. Chinese influence on the Western examination system. *Harvard Journal of Asiatic Studies* 7: 267–312.

Thayer, Fred. 1981. *An end to hierarchy and competition*, 2d ed. New York: Watts.

Trudeau, Eric. 1992. The world order checklist. *New York Times*, February 19, p. 2.

Union of International Associations. 1986. *Encyclopedia of world problems and human potential*. Munich: K. G. Saur.

———. Annual. *Yearbook of international organizations*. Organization description and index. Munich: K. G. Saur.

United Nations. 1974. *Declaration of the establishment of a new international economic order*. New York: U.N. Resolution 3201 (S–V1), May 1.

———. 1983. *Enhancing capabilities for administrative reform in developing countries*. New York: ST/ESA/SER.E/31.

United Nations Food and Agriculture Organization. 1980, 1984. *Production yearbook*. Rome: UN-FAO.

United Nations Development Programme. 1988a. Development co-operation report 1988 for Mozambique. New York: UNDP.

———. 1988b. Technical assistance policies and requirements in Mozambique: A UNDP/NATCAP report (mimeographed). New York: UNDP.

———. 1989a. (June). Report of the mid-term review of the third country programme (1987–1991). Maputo: UNDP.

————. 1989b. United Nations Development Programme/Management Development Programme preliminary guidelines. New York: UNDP.

————. 1991. *Human development report 1991*. New York: Oxford University Press.

United Nations-DESD. 1992. *Size and cost of the civil service: Reform programmes in Africa*. New York: DESD/ESM.92/1, INT–90–R78.

Van Riper, Paul A. 1958. *History of the United States Civil Service*. Evanston, Ill.: Row, Peterson.

Veblen, Thorstein. n.d. *The theory of the business enterprise*. New York: New American Library.

Vernon, Raymond. 1988. *The promise of privatization: A challenge for US policy*. New York: Council on Foreign Relations.

Vidal Perdomo, J. 1982. La reforma administrativa de 1968 en Colombia. *International Review of Administrative Sciences* 48(1): 77–84.

Vogel, David. 1986. *National styles of regulation: Environmental policy in Great Britain and the United States*. Ithaca, N.Y.: Cornell University Press.

Waldo, Dwight. 1968. Scope of the theory of public administration. In James C. Charlesworth, ed., *Annals*. Monograph #8. Philadelphia: American Academy of Political and Social Science.

————. 1990. Bureaucracy and democracy: Reconciling the irreconcilable? In F. Lane, ed., *Current issues in public administration*. New York: St. Martin's Press, pp. 455–568.

Walker, David B. 1991. Reunification, its implementation, and German federalism. *Assistance Management Journal* 6: 1–24.

Wallerstein, Immanuel. 1987. World systems analysis. In A. Giddens and J. H. Turner, eds., *Social theory today*. Stanford, Calif.: Stanford University Press, pp. 309–324.

Warren, D. 1984. Managing in crisis: Nine principles for successful transition. In John R. Kimberly and Robert E. Quinn, eds., *Managing organizational transitions*. Homewood, Ill.: Irwin, pp. 86–106.

Weiss, Janet A. 1988. Substance versus symbol in administrative reform. In Carl Milofski, ed., *Community organizations*. New York: Oxford, pp. 100–118.

White, Leonard D. 1954. *The Jacksonians*. New York: Macmillan.

Wholey, Joseph, and Katherine E. Newcomer. 1989. *Improving government performance*. San Francisco: Jossey-Bass.

Whyte, William. 1957. *The organization man*. New York: Anchor.

William, J. O. 1993. Inside Chinese bureaucracy: Civil service reform in the Ministry of Light Industry. *International Journal of Public Administration* 6(7): 1035–1052.

Wilson, David. 1994. Bureaucracy in international organizations: Building capacity and credibility in a newly-interdependent world. In Ali Farazmand, ed., *Handbook of bureaucracy*. New York: Marcel Dekker, Chapter 19. In press.

Wilson, James Q. 1989. *Bureaucracy: What government agencies do and why they do it*. New York: Basic Books.

Wise, Charles. 1994. The public service configuration problem: Designing public organizations in a pluralistic public service. In Ali Farazmand, ed., *Modern organizations: Administration in contemporary society*. Westport, Conn.: Praeger, Chapter 3. In press.

Wolf, Michael A. 1990. Enterprise zones. *Economic Development Quarterly* 4: 3–14.

Wolman, Harold, and Larry C. Ledebur. 1984. Concepts of public-private cooperation. In Cheryl A. Farr, ed., *Shaping the local economy*. Washington, D.C.: International City Management Association, pp. 25–34.

Woods, Alan. 1989. *Development and the national interest: U.S. economic assistance into the 21st century*. Washington, D.C.: Agency for International Development.

World Bank. 1989. *Mozambique: Public expenditure review (Report no. 7615–MOZ)*. 2 vols. Washington, D.C.: Africa Region, Country Operations Division, Southern Africa Department, September 5.

———. 1991a. The municipal development program for Sub-Sahara Africa—A partnership for building local government capacity (program document for the Eastern and Southern Africa Module). Washington, D.C.: African Technical Department and the Economic Development Institute, World Bank, July.

———. 1991b. *World development report 1991: The challenge of development*. New York: Oxford University Press.

———. n.d. Local government administration and finances in Mozambique: Preliminary review. Washington, D.C.: Africa Region (filed without author, but attributed to Charles Downs).

———. n.d. Mozambique: Proposed US$900 million equivalent/IDA third rehabilitation credit/request to negotiate. Washington, D.C.

World Resource Institute. 1989. *World resources 1988–89*. New York: Basic Books.

Yepes Parra, Antonio. 1991. La Salud y la Seguridad Social en la Constitución de 1991. *Salud y Gerencia*, Boletín de la Unidad de Desarrollo de Sistemas de Salud, Universidad Javeriana, Bogotá, Oct.–Dic, 8:1, 4, 9, 10.

Yin, Robert K. 1978. Organizational innovation. In Michael Radnor, Irwin Feller, and Everrett Rogers, eds., *The diffusion of innovations: An assessment*. Evanston, Ill.: Northwestern University, Chapter 9.

Zeigler, Harmon. 1964. *Interest groups in American society*. Englewood Cliffs, N.J.: Prentice-Hall.

Zucker, Lynne G. 1977. The role of institutionalization in cultural persistence. *American Sociological Review* 42: 726–743.

———. 1988. Institutional theories of organization. In Lynne G. Zucker, ed., *Institutional patterns and organizations*. Cambridge: Ballinger, pp. xiii–xix.

INDEX

ABOUT THE CONTRIBUTORS

GERALD E. CAIDEN is Professor of Public Administration at the University of Southern California. He has published over twenty-five books and monographs and over 170 journal articles. In addition, he has acted as editorial consultant to several leading journals in the field of public administration. He has been a consultant, researcher, and administrator for a wide variety of public organizations, including the World Bank and the United Nations. He is known best for his research in administrative reform and organizational diagnosis.

ALI FARAZMAND is Associate Professor and Director of the MPA Program at Northern Kentucky University. His recent books include *The State, Bureaucracy, and Revolution in Modern Iran*, *Handbook of Comparative and Development Public Administration*, and *Modern Organizations*. He has written several articles in scholarly journals and is on the editorial board of the *International Journal of Public Administration*.

JEAN-CLAUDE GARCIA-ZAMOR is Professor of Public Administration at Florida International University. He has served as a senior specialist at the Organization of American States and as the controller of the Inter-American Development Bank. He is the author of three books, the editor of two books, and the coeditor of two others. In addition, his articles have appeared in several professional journals in the United States, Puerto Rico, Brazil, Belgium, Great Britain, the Netherlands, and India.

LAWRENCE S. GRAHAM is Professor of Government at the University of Texas at Austin. Among his eleven books and monographs are *The Political Economy of Brazil: Public Policies in an Era of Transition* and *The State and Policy Outcomes in Latin America*. In addition he has written over thirty-five articles in various national and international journals. His current research interests include the restructuring of politics and economics in Portugal, Brazil, and Mozambique. He has also served as consultant to the United Nations Development Programme.

FERREL HEADY is Professor Emeritus of Public Administration and Political Science at the University of New Mexico in Albuquerque, where he has also served as Academic Vice President and President. His publications include *Public Administration: A Comparative Perspective* (in its fourth edition). He is a past president of the American Society for Public Administration, a member of the National Academy of Public Administration, and a recipient of the Fred Riggs Award from the Section on International and Comparative Administration of ASPA. In 1992 he was a Fulbright Senior Lecturer in Colombia.

RENU KHATOR is Associate Professor of Government and International Affairs at the University of South Florida. She has written two books, *Forests: The People and the Government* and *Environment, Development, and Politics in India*. In addition she has published numerous articles in national and international journals. Her research interests include environmental policy and environmental administration in developing countries, Asian politics, and comparative public administration. She is a member of the International Task-force of the American Society for Public Administration.

MARGARET F. REID is Assistant Professor and MPA Director at the University of Arkansas, Fayetteville. She teaches courses in public administration, organizational theory and behavior, and public and private sector relationships. Her research focuses on the effects of massive transformations on the political economy of urban areas, administrative governance arrangements, and extant interorganizational linkages.

FRED W. RIGGS is Professor Emeritus in the Political Science Department at the University of Hawaii. He has published extensively in the fields of comparative public administration, social science conceptual and terminological analysis, and more recently on problems of presidentialism, with a special focus on the survival, exceptionally, of the U.S. Constitution. A festschrift in his honor, *Politics and Administration in Changing Societies*, was published in 1992.